M000218577

Letters from Sweden

MERCER UNIVERSITY PRESS

Endowed by

TOM WATSON BROWN
and
THE WATSON-BROWN FOUNDATION, INC.

Letters from Sweden

A TRUE LOVE STORY

David N. Schaeffer

MERCER UNIVERSITY PRESS
MACON, GEORGIA

MUP/ P674

© 2023 by Mercer University Press
Published by Mercer University Press
1501 Mercer University Drive
Macon, Georgia 31207
All rights reserved

27 26 25 24 23   5 4 3 2 1

Books published by Mercer University Press are printed on acid-free paper
that meets the requirements of the American National Standard for
Information Sciences—Permanence of Paper for Printed Library Materials.

Printed and bound in the United States.

This book is set in Adobe Caslon.

Cover/jacket design by Burt&Burt.

ISBN   978-0-88146-899-1
Cataloging-in-Publication Data is available from the Library of Congress

CONTENTS

This book is dedicated to the power of unconditional love, unwavering trust, and good old-fashioned handwritten letter writing.

Introduction

The "Greatest Generation" was filled with war heroes and love stories, during and shortly after World War II. Love of God, country, and family were the priorities of young men and women facing and surviving military service at that time. But many of their love stories were told in letters written from overseas and later hidden in dusty boxes in attics or locked away in storage chests.

But treasures are occasionally found, and their stories are uncovered.

This is the true story of Bill, an aspiring seminarian serving his country at a crucial time in World War II, attempting to find and sustain love during and after the war, and struggling to define and plan his future ministry. It is also the story of a cautious and pragmatic young woman, Mary, who, at age twenty-two, nevertheless quickly fell in love with this decorated World War II veteran. They got engaged on the same day he left for an eighteen-month post-grad religious and academic study program in Sweden in January 1947.

Almost seventy-five years later, a mottled-brown leather portfolio with more than three hundred letters Bill wrote to Mary from Sweden in 1947 and early 1948 was discovered among her things shortly after she died. He sent these letters, written on extremely thin, almost translucent paper, by air mail across the Atlantic, where they sometimes arrived in only three days. A few were typewritten, but most were handwritten in pen or pencil and were barely readable. Several pages have tattered, deteriorated edges, obliterating sentences that can never be recovered. Although she also wrote hundreds of letters to him, only four of her letters, handwritten on colorful stationery in exquisitely perfect cursive, were preserved.

The rest have disappeared.

The letters tell the story and provide a window into their whirlwind courtship, engagement, and hopes for a future together. Bill wrote the final letter on the day before he boarded a heavily laden cargo ship to return to America through the icy North Atlantic, leaving his planned reunion and potential future with his fiancée undescribed and unanswered.

Along the way, the letters, quoted extensively, describe this man's Scandinavian adventures, the varied postwar conditions in Sweden, Norway, Finland, Germany, and Belgium, and his religious journey.

The rest, as they say, is pure fiction. Well, not exactly. The remainder of the story is based on research from other sources, specifically brief autobiographies, newspaper articles, obituaries, church archives, and a separate cache of letters Bill, an assistant chaplain and medic, wrote home during his military service, including while the Nazis relentlessly shelled Allied forces in Belgium and Germany during the Battle of the Bulge.

This is the true postwar love story of Bill and Mary, challenged by an overseas separation of over a year immediately after they became engaged.

PROLOGUE

INITIAL LETTERS

Chapter 1

New York
(January 17, 1947)

A twenty-eight-year-old World War II veteran stood on the crowded deck of the MS *Gripsholm* of the Swedish-American Line as it left New York Harbor. It was the start of his fifth Atlantic crossing. As he later wrote that night, "It was slightly hazy as we left the pier, but the skyline of New York stuck out in all its magnificence. Lady Liberty waved goodbye as we sailed by. The sea was calm, and the air was brisk—perfect weather. I hope we will see plenty more like it."

His name was Bill, and he was simultaneously the happiest and unhappiest person in the world. How could he not be the happiest man? His sweet Mary had just accepted his proposal after an intense two-day visit, less than seven weeks after their first kiss. He could not believe he had asked her to marry him so quickly. He was even more amazed that she agreed to be his wife. He had not met her parents, let alone gotten her father's blessing. He felt bad about skipping that conventional step for an engagement. But his heart had completely overcome his head, and love and the exigency of his travel schedule had trumped tradition.

As he watched New York's jagged skyline disappear over the horizon and the cool, salty mist from the ocean sprinkled across his face, Bill felt lost. He had said goodbye to his sweetheart at midnight on the night of their engagement and left on a train to New York. His mind remained occupied with his tear-filled view of Mary waving at him from the train station platform. Three days later, he had boarded the ocean liner on the voyage to Sweden for an eighteen-month post-seminary study program. His excitement about exploring Lutheran churches and theology in Sweden to help him determine if he wanted to be a theologian or a parish minister was countered by his uncertainty about the staying power of the love he and Mary had just declared.

The seas got rougher as the ship headed north along the New England coast. In the increasingly chilly air, Bill buttoned up his old green army jacket and readjusted his scarf to cover his chin. As the ship churned through the waves, Bill's thoughts turned to full-scale concern, not about the weather or the rough seas, but regarding how he could convince Mary to wait for him to return from Sweden.

"Eighteen months is a long time," he thought to himself, "especially across three thousand miles of ocean. What if she doesn't wait for me?"

Mary was only twenty-two years old, six years younger than he was. She had completed her master's degree in public health at UNC-Chapel Hill and was now working in Greenville, South Carolina. She was so well educated, pretty, and smart that he feared she might have other suitors vying for her affection. She had no ring on her finger to ward off potential beaus, and there had been no time for any official engagement announcement in the local paper. Everything was unofficial. He trusted her to be faithful, but to make sure she knew he was totally committed, he vowed to himself that he would write her every single day.

By the time he boarded the *Gripsholm*, he had already written her three letters.

He wrote his first letter on stationery found in his YMCA room at the William Sloan House at 356 West 34th Street, New York, shortly after he arrived there by train on Wednesday afternoon, the day after their engagement. As he hunched over the small wooden desk and reflected on his chaotic engagement and departure, he had tried to explain his emotions in writing.

> My sweet Mary, I've had an awful empty feeling in my heart since the train pulled away from Greenville. Regardless of the happy days we have together in the future, there will never be two more perfect days than Monday and Tuesday. You must have been eavesdropping on all my dreams for the last ten years to make them all come true at once. You know, sweetheart, I had begun to get a bit cynical about women and disgusted with the way little things would annoy me about them. Now I realize that the trouble was that I just hadn't found the right girl. You were the answer all

along—and I didn't have sense enough to know it. I almost get scared when I think how close we came to missing each other. I'm not one to believe in pre-destination, but I'm sure God guides us in ways we never realize. I know that you are a gift from God….Don't you change a bit, little rascal. I love every inch and pound of you….You are perfect as you are. All my love, Bill.

He dropped the letter off at the concierge desk that Wednesday afternoon, hoping Mary would get it in Greenville within three days.

On Thursday morning, Bill discovered a color photo Mary had snuck into his bags, buried under his neatly folded trousers. "You rascal," he said to himself with pride. He could not stop staring at the photo, admiring the woman he loved. He had sent her a photo of himself for Christmas, but he kicked himself for not giving her another gift before he left. He immediately addressed another letter, this time to "Butch." Where Mary got that nickname is a mystery.

Hi Butch! I've got your pert little puss smiling in front of me this morning. I see that you are wearing the same pretty yellow blouse which you wore Monday night—which makes your picture so much more precious than it was before. I have to pinch myself a thousand times a day to be sure that I'm really your man and not just dreaming….I understand the *Gripsholm* docked yesterday after one of the roughest crossings in her history. I trust that means we will have a quiet sailing heading east. It can't be as bad as the trip last January regardless. So long for now. I'll probably write tonight and a couple times tomorrow. Here's a hug and kiss from…Your Bill.

The rough trip the prior January referred to Bill's voyage home from Europe just before he was discharged from the army in January 1946. So much had happened in the last year since he had returned from the war. Graduation from seminary. Courting the girl of his dreams. Getting engaged. Heading back overseas for another adventure of a lifetime and the opportunity to grow in his faith and find God's purpose for his life.

Bill's timing for his Swedish sojourn was unfortunate. But right now, he had only one thing on his mind—his future with Mary. He kept thanking God that he had mustered the courage to ask Mary to be his wife before he left and that she had trusted him enough to accept his rushed proposal.

That night from New York, Bill also wrote his father and mother to tell them that "they have a daughter-in-law in the making." He had not had time to alert them to the successful engagement, but he wanted them to know about his wonderful news without further delay.

He hoped they would not think he was completely crazy.

After an exhausting Thursday in New York making final arrangements for his trip overseas, Bill could not go to bed without writing yet another letter to Mary, his third letter to her in twenty-four hours: "My darling, I'm plumb tired out tonight after tramping around the sidewalks of New York all day. Anybody that spends a lifetime in this place is just plain nuts. How people can stand the torture of the hurry, crowding, and pushing in the streets and subway day after day is beyond me."

He also related a telephone call he had with his Washington, D.C., friend, Pauline Bresnahan, with whom he had confided his proposal plans. As part of his seminary education, Bill had interned in Washington and boarded at the residence of Mrs. John Bresnahan, a widow. Her daughter Pauline, who never married, had taken an interest in Bill's social life and insisted on playing matchmaker.

> I had hardly said hello when Pauline asked me how things turned out in S.C. When I told her that she could scratch me off the "available" list, she said I had a nerve asking you to wait while I ran off to Sweden. I think she was right, but I don't regret it in the least. Without a doubt, I showed more sense than any other time in my life. It's after midnight, and I have to be up early in the morning, so I'll sign off for a few hours…. Love, Bill.

The next morning, he dropped his second and third letters off at the post office on his way to the pier.

As he watched the sunset over the distant whitecaps from the rear deck of the *Gripsholm*, knowing there was no turning back, he wondered if Mary was already missing him as much as he was missing her.

Chapter 2

North Atlantic
(January 17–27, 1947)

The *Gripsholm* was not a luxury liner, but it was still the fanciest ship on which Bill had ever sailed. Meals were Swedish style, with pickled herring, cheese, salami, hard breads, and crackers served on fine china and white tablecloths. String quartets played during and after dinners. To Bill's surprise, because his ticket had "Reverend" in front of his name, he received special treatment and a private cabin with a small porthole. He was not in first class, but Bill thought the accommodations were much better than he deserved. He bounced on the bed, feeling like royalty. Truth be told, he was a bit disappointed to have a single room as he looked forward to having an instant buddy for the voyage.

The sole occupancy, however, did not prevent Bill from getting to know some of the interesting characters on the ship. He quickly met a US State Department official working in Stockholm who promised to help him with any needs once he arrived in Sweden. A middle-aged Finnish American pastor told him all about the recent surge of Lutheranism in Finland and asked Bill to look him up if he ever made it to Helsinki. He also struck up a conversation with a Polish Jew who had escaped Poland "two jumps ahead of the Gestapo," having to leave his wife and two children behind. The man had wandered through Russia and Japan and ended up in the United States eight months later. Now, he was on a social mission to help refugees and displaced persons of Sweden, Poland, Belgium, and Germany. Sadly, Bill also learned that the man's family had ended up in three concentration camps before being wiped out in one of Hitler's mass executions in 1944. In his next letter to Mary, Bill commented that he would have thought the man would be "vicious and bitter, but he still seems to have a generous spirit."

In one of his many letters to Mary during the voyage, written on *Gripsholm* stationery, with three blue crowns on the top just left of "SVENSKA AMERICA LINIEN," Bill also described being envious of one set of passengers:

> There is one young couple who stroll around arm in arm and look at each other as if this is a honeymoon trip. Makes me jealous! It would be wonderful if you were here close by my side. It would be perfect—but there will come a day before too long when we can be together…. Mary, you are taking an awful chance saying you'll marry me when you're never heard me preach. Just think what a time it would be if you don't like the way I preach. I guess you will have to sit and take it.

By January 20, 1947, in the North Atlantic, the weather turned bitterly cold. Ice began forming on the decks, ice floes scraped the side of the ship, and the heavy seas with long swells gave Bill spells of nausea and headaches. Even though he was woozy and seasick, he continued to write his daily letters to Mary.

> I wasn't by myself last week this time, Sweet Mary. The memory keeps me warm and happy though there is a long stretch of water between us now. It would be wonderful to have you close in my arms. I might even steal a kiss from your sweet lips. Do you get a sort of weak and humble feeling at the way love can come to two people? I do! I'll never stop being thankful for your love and trust.

He only wished there was some way to get his letters to Mary and for her to get letters to him during the voyage. He shared an imaginative solution.

> I certainly miss your letters. We should have gone into cahoots with one of the seagulls that are still following the ship so it could have done messenger service for us. I could whisper a lot of "sweet nothings" into your ear right now….Today a year ago I docked in New York, a happy day you can be sure. I hardly thought I'd be heading the other way within a year.

And in spite of all the interesting experiences that lie ahead, I know I'll be even happier to see Lady Liberty again. Because this time I'll have you to welcome me....I love you more each day, Mary. Bill.

On the tenth and last day of the voyage, Bill finished his batch of letters to Mary and was excited about finally being able to mail them. He wondered if there would be any letter from Mary waiting for him once on shore: "My sweet girl, it's wonderful to be able to write again and know that it will start on its way without a long wait. You will get the daily log that I've been writing ever since we left New York, but it is too weighty to send air mail. At least it will show you that you have been on my mind the whole trip—of course you know that anyway."

He could not help but brag that he was writing her from first-class quarters on the ship, at the invitation of the Finnish American pastor.

Right now, I'm being ritzy—strictly first class.... We were chatting in the fancy lounge, and I decided it would be a proper atmosphere to write the sweetest girl in the world. There is quite a contrast between the upper classes and tourist class. Down there we are rough, working-class people—here they dress for dinner. If the ship were full, it would be mighty crowded and smelly below, but it hasn't been bad this trip. I feel more at home with the common herd anyway. The worst thing about the whole business was having no mail. There was no letter from you in New York—I suppose it was too close a squeeze to have wished for one. I'll rush to the mail booth when I get to Gothenburg, you can bet.... The time has passed—but there has been plenty of time to think of you and the wonderful things that happened in two short days. Mary, loving you has been and always will be the greatest thing in my life. Everything that is good and beautiful seems to have been wrapped up in you. I tremble every time I think how close we came to missing each other. The months that are ahead will seem mighty long, but we will have long years to make up for it if God wills it that way. I love you, Mary. I feel it more surely every day that passes. Your Bill.

The next day, Bill woke up to the sounds of the boat approaching its moorings in Gothenburg, Sweden. The boat's bellowing horn let everyone aboard know that land was near. The noise of the crew's scurrying and shouting orders prevented anyone from rolling over and going back to sleep.

Bill dressed warmly, then quickly climbed the narrow stairs to the deck in time to watch the crew complete the docking process. Gothenburg was Sweden's major city and seaport. Beyond the concrete lading area and a large arrival building, Bill could see two prominent downtown church steeples. They reminded him about why he was coming to Sweden in the first place. Hope, faith, and love were the cornerstones of his life. He knew his journey to find them was coming together, but he hoped he had not left the greatest of these three cornerstones behind in Greenville.

Knowing he would have plenty of time before passengers were allowed to disembark, Bill returned to his stateroom as soon as the ocean liner was secured at port. He packed his things and got ready to leave, carefully tucking Mary's photo into his bags after gazing at it for a few more minutes. He found a *Gripsholm* postcard in the desk in his room and scribbled a note to let Mary know he had made it to Sweden, marking on the photo of the ship where he thought his porthole was located. "This is the baby that gave me some bad days—doesn't look so naughty, does she? I was somewhere near the X, but it is hard to figure it out exactly. All in all, I guess it wasn't too rough a trip," he wrote.

However, after ten days aboard the *Gripsholm*, there was only one thing on Bill's mind. Would there be a letter from Mary waiting for him?

He paced until the crew allowed passengers down the gangway, then rushed to get through customs and headed straight for the port's mail room. He bought a red Alfred Nobel stamp to apply to the *Gripsholm* postcard and dropped it in the mail slot. Mary would get that note first. The larger package with his series of full letters would take much longer. After a short wait in line, Bill gave his name and showed his passport to the man behind the small, barred window, then held his breath as he watched the man slowly flip through a pile of letters on a counter inside.

"Come on," Bill thought to himself. "It has to be there!"

The man finally pulled three letters out of the pile and returned to the window, checking the addressee on each letter to see if it matched Bill's passport.

"Ya...ya...ya," he said, handing the letters and the passport back to Bill.

Bill immediately recognized Mary's handwriting on the first two envelopes and his mother's cursive on the third letter. He held Mary's letters up to his nose. He hoped he could smell Mary's perfume, if only faintly. However, his sniff failed to detect anything other than a slightly clammy air cargo smell. Mary was not the type of woman to send scented letters, unlike several of his prior girlfriends.

Unable to wait any longer, Bill ripped open Mary's first envelope with his right thumb and, after carefully unfolding the three-page letter on light blue stationery inside, read it at least four times, savoring each word. He could not help but notice that Mary's cursive handwriting was flawless, no different from everything else about her. He read her second letter twice before quickly scanning the letter from his mother. On a nearby bench seat, he immediately responded with his final letter on the *Gripsholm* stationery, also in cursive, but more like a scribble than a textbook style. He hoped she would be able to read it.

Mary, my love, you can be sure that the best part of arriving in Sweden was getting your letter at the dock. I had been so lonesome for you that I would have been in bad shape in a few more days. I've almost worn it out already reading it so much, but I have to make up for those long two weeks without a word. It made me mighty happy, my own sweet Mary. One of the thousand things that makes me love you so much is the way you seemed to put all your trust and confidence in me. Before, you always were a little reserved. I suppose that was natural since you were still undecided as to your real feelings. But that made it all the sweeter when you came wholeheartedly into my arms. And I've never felt what a tremendous responsibility it is to be in love. Now we have to think for two people and feel for both of us.

As he closed his letter, he assured her that their engagement was acceptable to his family.

> A letter from Mother was waiting for me, too. She was as happy as yours that we decided as we did. She said she had to soothe Dad down a couple days because he expected me to telegraph him if you said "yes." A body would think parents might be a bit interested in what their young'uns do, wouldn't one? We will have a lot to live up to if we are going to deserve the blessing of our families, aren't we, Mary?...All my love, Bill.

The light blue letter Bill was reading over and over was written by Mary on Friday morning, January 15, 1947, three days after their engagement.[1] Probably she had not received his initial letters from New York as there is no mention of them in her letter. Instead, she had decided to write him independently.

> My dearest Bill, my dream came true! I'm quite beside myself. All the wonderful things I thought are even more wonderful now. Now I know what perfect contentment means. As you have probably gathered, I am not one who says much about how I feel. Maybe that will grow with me as time goes by and I become accustomed to the wonderful new experiences that your coming into my life has brought and will bring. There hasn't been any doubt in my mind as to how I felt when you left, nor did I think that it would have changed when you came back. That feeling has changed only in one respect—in that it has grown—intensively grown. Why I couldn't find the words to express this when you were here, I don't know— unless I was just too overwhelmed—but I do love you so much. Don't ever doubt that. I'm looking forward to our life and future together. It should be a good one and a serviceable one…. Gee—everyone wants to meet you. Everywhere I go— "Why don't you bring Bill around?" So—we'll have some visiting to do when you get back. It's high time I showed up at

---

[1] One of the four letters from Mary that were preserved.

the office—so I'd better scoot. Give your folks my love—but keep the most of it for yourself. Yours always—Mary.

"Serviceable?" Bill whispered to himself with a smirk. "What does she mean by that?"

Bill chuckled at the thought. He certainly hoped that their life together would be more than "serviceable." He already knew that his Mary was just as practical as she was pretty, and now he knew she was carefully understated in her choice of words.

"Serviceable" was probably a positive thing in her pragmatic mind. He hoped so.

When he returned to America, Bill promised to himself that he would make sure to exceed the "serviceable" level, perhaps even raising their married life together to the "wonderful, romantic, and passionate" tier. He hoped Mary would still love him and would even elevate her expectations of married life once they were together again.

Chapter 3

Lidings
(January 28, 1947)

With two letters from Mary in hand, the first thing Bill did once ashore in Sweden was to find a store where he could buy air mail paper to send even more letters. Because his packet of letters on the *Gripsholm* stationery was too heavy for air mail, he had wasted no time bundling up all eight two-sided pages for slow mail back to Mary by boat. It would take at least ten days to get to her, but the sooner he sent them, the earlier she would get them. With the thinner, almost translucent air mail paper he bought in Sweden, he knew Mary could get his next letters in less than a week.

When shopping, he noticed that all the Swedish women were dressed in bulky clothes, heavy woolen hose, and clunky ankle-high shoes. That night he wrote Mary, telling her that "American women would not be caught out on the street in such garb." Perhaps Bill was not yet aware of the direct impact Scandinavia's freezing winter temperatures had on local clothing choices.

His next stop was to get the ration coupons required to buy meat, bread, and butter. The war was over, but, even in Sweden, which had tried to stay clear of the conflict, supply chain problems persisted. As a veteran who had served in multiple locations in the war, Bill knew all about trying to keep supply chains open, but he thought most of them would be re-established by now, especially in a country that had stayed neutral.

Bill was assigned to a boarding house in Lidings, a town on the outskirts of Stockholm. The proprietor, a woman, greeted him warmly, but he did not realize he was receiving special treatment until dinner. While the other guests were served what Bill described as a "watery stew," the proprietor kept bringing him anchovies and liver, then baked potatoes, carrots, and hamburger wrapped in cabbage leaves. Bill felt like royalty without having done anything to deserve such special attention.

Apparently, the Swedes were grateful and excited about American students, especially war veterans, studying in their country. As Bill quickly learned, the Swedes had gleaned their image of the United States from Hollywood movies depicting America's glamorous society. So, wherever Bill went, the Swedish "high society" pulled out their best china settings, the most precious food, and the finest alcohol. Truth be told, he would have been happy with meatloaf and milk. He had not grown up eating fancy cuisine.

That first night in Sweden, Bill penned another letter to Mary on his freshly purchased air-mail paper, this time responding to Mary's second letter. That letter was not preserved, but based on Bill's response, it included reference to her mother's plan for a hope chest.

> Sweetheart, I won't mail a letter every day, but I'll try to run a sort of serial that I can send a couple times a week. It makes me feel better to scribble a line to you, even though I am thinking about you much more…. This morning before I mailed the letter to you, I just gave your letters a brief reading. I've been getting them out frequently since and basking in your love. It's a grand and glorious experience, isn't it, my little wife-to-be? When you mention your mother's plans for a hope chest, I have to pinch myself to see if it is all real. Your picture has the place of honor on a little table by my bed where I can see you the last thing before I go to bed and the first thing in the morning. I'm like you about reliving the all too brief hours we've had together.

PART I

BILL AND MARY'S EARLY YEARS

Chapter 4

Bill's Early Days
(1918–1926)

While reliving his brief courtship and sudden engagement in his lonely apartment in Lidings, Bill's mind churned almost out of control, thinking about the serendipity that led to him and Mary coming together. Everything in his life had led to this moment—his childhood, his upbringing, his education, and his war experiences. And, of course, his many failed prior relationships.

He wondered if God had ordained it from the start.

From the moment he was born, there was little doubt that Bill would someday become a minister, at least if his father and uncle had their way. His grandfather, father, and uncle were all Lutheran ministers. As the only male child in his family, the expectations of his elders were strong. It was never a question of *if* Bill would become a minister, but *when*.

Bill was born in Chattanooga, Tennessee, in 1918, where his father served Ascension Lutheran Church, his first congregation. Bill's birth was at home without a doctor present, as his father told him that he was "born into his hands." Some might say he was already an impatient child, ready to take on the world!

Six weeks after Bill's birth, his family moved to Atlanta, Georgia, so his father could help his brother, Bill's Uncle William, who was doing double duty as pastor of Redeemer Lutheran Church, the largest Lutheran parish in downtown Atlanta, and camp pastor at Fort Gordon during World War I. Bill's father took over the Fort Gordon position and began regularly serving as a supply pastor at Redeemer, freeing up Uncle William to help with the Lutheran support of the war effort regionally. Recruiting (and supporting) chaplains to minister to the tens of thousands of soldiers in World War I was a fulltime job.

That arrangement lasted about a year before Bill's family moved again, this time to King's Mountain, North Carolina, so his father could become pastor of St. Matthew's Lutheran Church there. That was the first home Bill remembered. His first memory was landing on his head after riding his little red tricycle over the edge of a stone wall surrounding the grass terrace in front of the house. The next time he tried it, he landed upright, a broad smile on his face.

While Bill's family lived in King's Mountain, his father bought sixteen acres of land on a hillside a few miles west of Hendersonville, North Carolina. The property would become the family's summer retreat and vacation spot called "Dogwood Dell." With the help of a builder and two carpenters from his congregation in King's Mountain, his father built a small, two-story white cabin on the property in just five days. Bill barely remembered sitting on a blanket next to his mother as they watched his father and the builders, stripped down to their sweaty undershirts, erect the framing for the cabin, then add roofing, siding, and windows. Bill wanted to help, but his mother kept him safely away from the nails and saws. Bill had to satisfy himself with banging away at some wooden pegs with a toy hammer, then riding proudly on his father's shoulders to see the progress at the end of the day.

When Bill was five, his family moved again when his father became pastor of St. Matthews Lutheran Church in Charleston, the largest Lutheran congregation in the Southeast. Bill remembered the church had a steeple that was higher than any other building in Charleston. He loved to climb high inside the tower to watch the carillon play. He always wanted to reach the top of anything he could climb.

Practically born into the ministry, Bill was taught to love and serve the Lord from his earliest days.

His father was a perfect role model. In their January 4, 1925, annual report, the St. Matthews church council "thank[ed] God for the pastor He has sent us, a true teacher and leader, ever ready to show us the way and always willing to assist us with the work that we have to do." Indeed, his father, in addition to being an inspiring preacher, was always ready to roll up his sleeves and pitch in on any project at the church. No task was too small, and no detail left unaddressed. "If you want it done right, do it yourself" was one of his mantras.

He boldly asked his congregation for the financial resources to make St. Matthews the best it could be. He proclaimed in a 1926 appeal,

> It is time to extend ourselves to the limit. We have come to the point where those who are loyal and true and devoted in their Christian living and serving must stand humbly and yet unequivocally for certain specific and definite standards for our congregation and its finest development and greatest usefulness. And this will necessitate increased devotion and a fuller consecration of life, talents, and possessions…. This stand must be for the fuller recognition of our congregation's place in the work of our church for the Kingdom of God and for the occupation of this place. Are our members ready to join the pastor in such a stand? We are in a new day! The time has come for the church to be adequately supported for its largest service. May God lead us in the paths of the sunshine of His grace that our lives might thrive in holy living and devoted service and secure the riches of His love.

Even as a youngster, Bill couldn't help but notice his father's example of charismatic devotion to God's service and the work of the church.

Chapter 5

Charleston, South Carolina, and Hickory, North Carolina
(1923–1934)

In 1923, Bill started elementary school in Charleston. A year later, when Bill was six years old, his younger sister, Betty, was born, completing the family. Bill remembered being driven by a neighbor to kindergarten, then, in first grade, walking to school with his older sister Clare. Bill did well in school, quickly moving ahead to third grade by 1926.

While in historic Charleston, Bill had several church members he called "aunts," who made sure he was exposed to everything the vibrant Charleston had to offer, including new gadgets called radios, player pianos spouting ragtime tunes, and holiday fireworks. The church gave his father a shiny new four-door Model T Ford, which the family used on numerous trips up the mountains to Dogwood Dell in the summers. It was an exciting time to be a child. Bill soaked it all in.

He also began to love music, perhaps when he heard the church's newly electrified main organ and a five-stop chancel organ installed in 1925, along with a new marble altar and baptistry. Improving the church's music program and choir was one of his father's top priorities at St. Matthews. Bill hoped he would someday learn to play the piano and sing well.

But the idyllic days in Charleston were fleeting. In 1926, Bill's father was offered the presidency of Lenoir-Rhyne College in Hickory, North Carolina, so the family moved to their fifth home in eight years. Bill would have to make new friends all over again. Fortunately, this time, he would stay put through high school.

The years in Hickory were challenging. One day a fire engulfed the main building at the college. Bill watched with wide-eyed fascination as the huge structure crowned by a central dome collapsed to the ground, orange embers flying high into the sky. Despite heroic efforts, firefighters were unable to save the structure. Bill's father raised hundreds of thousands of dollars to rebuild the school, with new administrative buildings, classrooms, library, dining halls, and dormitories. Three years later, the campus was far bigger and better than before the fire. Once again, just like watching his father build the cabin at "Dogwood Dell," Bill spent hours and hours watching the buildings go up, from the foundations to their highest points.

One of Bill's fond memories was the college's old Packard touring car that had been converted to a small bus to take basketball teams to other schools. In summer 1930, when Bill was almost twelve, his father arranged to borrow the Packard for a trip out West. That summer, his family and six other students and friends traveled to Yellowstone Park, Salt Lake, the Pacific Coast, the Grand Canyon, and the Petrified Forest. Bill remembered the Pacific Ocean was almost too cold to wade in. Of course, he checked it out, gasping for air and quickly returning to shore after jumping headlong into the water.

That trip was just the beginning. In summer 1932, Bill's father was invited to the Rotary's international convention in Vienna. Bill's mother insisted that the whole family go to Europe, paying for the extended trip with money she inherited from her father. So, at the wide-eyed age of fourteen, Bill made his first of what would be many Atlantic crossings, on a boat called the *George Washington*. His family stopped in Paris and Innsbruck on the way to Vienna. After the convention, which included a banquet at the Schoenbron Palace, they explored Berlin and "Luther country."

Always good Lutherans!

Bill, never bashful about speaking in front of classmates, proudly presented a detailed report, complete with colorful maps, about the trip when he returned to school that fall. It was rare for anyone from a small town like Hickory to travel to Europe at that time, so his teachers and classmates listened closely to his descriptions, mostly of palaces and churches. Not many rural Carolinians could claim to have seen most of the United States, let alone much of Europe by age fourteen. With so many experiences, many of which qualified for Boy Scout merit badges, Bill was well on his way to becoming an Eagle Scout by the time he reached high school.

At a hundred pounds and barely five feet tall, Bill was the littlest kid in his class at high school. He was too small to play most contact sports, but he participated, no matter the size of the challenge. He managed to make the tennis squad, winning a couple of interschool matches. He always competed, but he was never a star athlete.

He made up for it in other ways, serving as the assistant editor of the school newspaper, the *Hickory Log*, and he was voted "Most Studious" and "Most Capable" senior by his peers. He later humbly declared that his school superlatives were "good evidence that his classmates were not very smart."

Bill's final years in Hickory were more difficult as the Depression took its toll. He earned extra money by pulling weeds at the college for ten cents an hour. He worked in the college kitchen during a summer-school program. During that job, Bill, the only male, was assigned to kill the chickens for the meals. He will never forget the day he had to kill 125 chickens by himself, using a wire loop placed around their necks, followed by a sharp yank.

Just before Bill graduated from high school, his father presented a proposal to deemphasize sports and focus on a church-centered curriculum at Lenoir-Rhyne. The board of trustees, under pressure from sports-loving alumnae, did not accept his plan. Soon he was out of a job, resigning rather than leading a school whose board had decided to emphasize football over religious studies.

That summer, Bill's family moved to Dogwood Dell, but spent much of the hot season in Eastern Tennessee with his mother's extended family members. Most of them lived on tobacco farms, with plenty of cows, hogs, and chickens around. Bill enjoyed hunting for fresh eggs much more than killing the chickens. He also learned to milk cows, to "worm" the tobacco and "sucker" the stalks with Uncle Junius, and to bundle hay. He loved swimming in the dammed-up creek in front of Aunt Tulin's house and savoring the bitter but tasty horehound candy and licorice from Uncle Bruce's country store. On one of the visits to Tennessee, Bill also saw his first hog killing. Despite the gory, close-up kill, Bill always loved ham and bacon.

At age sixteen, Bill was ready for college. Bill's older sister Clare had already completed her first year at Lenoir-Rhyne. Unbeknownst to Bill, his father had arranged for him to go to Emory University in Atlanta. However, the expensive Emory plan was abandoned once his dad resigned from Lenoir-Rhyne.

In August 1934, Bill's father took Bill and Clare for a walk at Dogwood Dell and told them that they would both be going to Newberry College in South Carolina in the fall. Bill and Clare knew little about Newberry, but they were not given a choice. It was a good Lutheran school and the only option presented.

Bill accepted the decision, but he vowed to himself that he would thereafter chart his own way. Little did Bill know at the time that Newberry College would serve as an indirect path to his future happiness.

Perhaps it was all part of God's plan.

Chapter 6

Mary's Early Days in South Carolina
(1924–1940)

While Bill was graduating from high school and heading off to college at age sixteen, Mary was almost ten years old and living on a farm in central South Carolina with her family. As Bill woke up dreaming of Mary in the first few days in his Swedish "exile," he still could not believe he had managed to overcome their age difference. But, despite their short courtship, he already knew Mary was an older soul than her chronological age.

Mary had lived practically her entire life in rural South Carolina. Born in 1924 at McLeod's Infirmary in Florence, South Carolina, she was the second child of her parents, both of whom were educators. Her brother, Marion, was ten years older and left for college the year Mary began elementary school. For most of her childhood she was on her own, with her parents frequently being her teacher or headmaster.

As a "teacher's kid," she had to mind her manners. Her parents taught her to be independent, sensible, and responsible—the latter reinforced by an occasional switch behind the knees.

Mary's first memory as a child was being pulled in a red wagon by her brother at their home in Scranton, South Carolina. Her next memory was from the rural community of Lone Star, where her father had become headmaster of the town's school. Mary remembered having to cross a railroad track on the way to and from the school, sometimes having to wait for the massive, smoking locomotive to pass, its horn blowing so loudly that she could hear nothing else even after the train disappeared in the distance. The railroad track became the subject of a persistent nightmare in which she and her father, instead of crossing the tracks, took off the tracks as the speeding, horn-blasting train chased them. She would awaken in a sweat just before the impending catastrophe. Perhaps because of that train track, she learned to be cautious at an early age, almost always taking the safest path in life.

It was an exciting day when Mary's family got their first car, a touring sedan called a Star, complete with isinglass window curtains which were put up when it rained. She and her parents would drive to the "big city," St. Matthews, South Carolina, where she and other neighborhood children delighted in running around on the broad train depot platform.

When Mary was five, her family moved to Monetta, South Carolina, where her mother resumed her teaching career at a school with one building housing all eleven grades. Back then, there was no twelfth grade, and most children, if they continued their education, started college at age seventeen. To Mary's chagrin, the following year, her mother became her teacher for second grade. The school had a dirt court for its girls' basketball team. After that team won several state tournaments, Mary dreamed of someday becoming a star basketball player.

That was one dream that never came true. Mary had little aptitude for sports.

During that time, Mary heard that anyone who saved a hundred Claussen bread wrappers could earn a pair of roller skates. Excited at the prospect, Mary steadfastly collected the wrappers from her family, church members, and neighbors. Soon, she had a brand-new set of metal-wheeled skates. But the only paved place to skate was on the small front porch or the busy highway in front of her house. Her father quickly pulled her off the road any time a car or truck approached. Mary never became entirely comfortable skating under those conditions. However, collecting things and being thrifty was a lifelong lesson…and entirely safe.

Other than peanut boils and fish fries, there was not much to do in Monetta. Her family's main social outlet was traveling to Batesburg, South Carolina, to the nearest Lutheran church, where they faithfully worshipped every Sunday and attended church-related social events. Mary enjoyed participating in the Light Brigade children's youth group, where she could play and learn Bible stories with other youngsters. She loved to sing "Jesus Loves Me" and developed a strong faith in God from an early age.

When the Depression hit, South Carolina's education department was unable to pay its teachers, including Mary's parents. Instead, they were issued "claims," a sort of IOU, which some, but not all, merchants accepted. With little or no actual money coming in, Mary's family eked by with a large garden, from which canned vegetables were put up for the winter. They also raised chickens for sale and their own use. Any extra vegetables were sold or exchanged for foods they could not produce themselves. Subsistence living and bartering for goods or services were the only options in those times.

Mary's father took a huge risk about a year later, borrowing money from Uncle Sam to buy an eighty-five-acre farm in Saluda County, just west of Columbia. The only equipment her father had at the time was a garden push plow. However, with the help of a Black couple they called Uncle Hince and Aunt Julia, who had a plow and a mule and quickly became tenant sharecroppers, they raised corn, wheat, oats, cotton, and sweet potatoes, along with their usual large vegetable garden. The grains provided flour and grits for family use. Cotton and any excess crops and vegetables were sold to make ends meet. They also had a few cows, hogs, and chickens, which provided milk, meat, eggs, and some additional income.

Mary loved growing up on a farm, running around bare footed in the hot summer sun, adding a tan to her slightly olive skin and bowl-cut, short dark hair. She never learned to milk a cow, but she mastered the art of churning butter and making buttermilk and clabber. Uncle Hince and Aunt Julia became members of Mary's extended family, and, when Mary was a youngster, she learned to respect folks regardless of the color of their skin.

The Saluda County farm was Mary's home starting in fifth grade. Her brother had left for college, so Mary was the only child at home. When Mary was lonely, her mother taught her to whistle and sing "Oh Susannah," "I've Been Working on the Railroad," "My Clementine," and other songs to pass the time. The chickens probably got tired of Mary singing, "Oh my darling, oh my darling, oh my darling Clementine...," over and over, or whistling until the sun went down. As a teenager, Mary continued to sing and whistle long before Rodgers & Hammerstein made whistling happy tunes popular in a musical about a teacher and a very bald king somewhere in Southeast Asia.

At her high school in Johnston, Mary loved math and sciences. Given the occupations and expectations of her educator parents, Mary had no choice but to excel in school. However, due to the distance between the school and the farm, she was unable to participate in many extracurricular activities. Besides, there were many chores to complete before dinner every day.

She had little time for boys.

In 1941, when it came time for Mary to go to college at age sixteen, there was only one place to go. Newberry College, a Lutheran school, where both of her parents, four uncles, and an aunt had gone, and where her brother, Marion, had graduated six or seven years earlier.

Where else would she go? Her extended family were all good Lutherans, and Newberry was the closest Lutheran college, less than thirty miles from the farm.

At that time, Mary could not know the role that Newberry would play in her future happiness. She certainly did not know that her future fiancé had already graduated from Newberry and that their college years would not overlap.

But she had faith that her life was safely in God's hands.

Chapter 7

Bill's College Days:
Newberry and Laurens, South Carolina
(1934–1939)

In 1934, seven years before Mary graduated from high school, Bill enrolled at Newberry College. He was just sixteen.

As a freshman "rat," he was assigned a tiny room on the third floor of Carnegie Hall. The first students Bill remembered meeting at Newberry were two fellows sitting on his dormitory steps when he arrived. One was a junior named Johnny, a pre-ministerial student who was also an end on the football team. The other was a senior named Marion, nicknamed "Buck," who was student body president. The two upperclassmen took Bill, wide-eyed and appearing lost and overwhelmed, under their wings. The three of them became close friends.

Though Bill did not know it at the time, Bill's sister Clare would be wooed by Johnny, and they married in 1939. Johnny later became a Lutheran minister, serving multiple congregations in Virginia and South Carolina. Bill also had no idea that "Buck" had a little sister named Mary, living on a farm somewhere in South Carolina.

Bill and Clare joined the Newberry College Singers, even though Bill had never sung in a choir. With a youthful, high voice, Bill was assigned to the tenor section, where he learned to read music and harmonize on the fly. It helped that his mother had paid for Bill and Clare to take piano lessons, giving them ears for music.

Younger than most of the girls at Newberry, Bill mainly socialized with groups of students. Clare was his "date" for many dances or other events, at least until Johnny swept her off her feet.

Things came easily for Bill at college. He never felt he was academically challenged at Newberry, whether in English, math, history, science, Bible, French, or Greek. He always made the honor roll, almost without trying. Despite his diminutive stature, Bill quickly became well-known throughout the campus through his multiple extracurricular activities. Elected president of his sophomore and junior classes, he also performed as a cheerleader. He worked his way up from sports editor, assistant editor, and ultimately became editor-in-chief of the *Indian*, Newberry's weekly newspaper. He competed in intercollegiate tennis tournaments and in oratory contests and debates, winning several of them. He also toiled away in the mess hall, waiting on tables for three years, while also making extra money representing a local shoe shop off-campus.

Never a dull moment in Bill's busy life...and certainly not much time to study.

In his junior year, Bill shocked everyone by deciding to become a teacher. He hadn't consulted his father or Uncle William, both of whom expected him to go immediately to seminary. But Bill wanted to determine his own destiny and, despite his religious upbringing, was not sure he had a strong enough faith to follow in his father's footsteps. It was one thing to believe in God's grace and another thing to preach it to others. He was not ready for that challenge, at least not at age nineteen, and maybe never. With his change in plans, to get a teacher's certificate, Bill had to double up on education courses in his last three semesters.

Bill graduated from Newberry cum laude in 1938, earning the class superlative as "Most Intellectual Boy," a moniker he frequently said was never again said about him!

Bill lined up a teaching position at a high school in Laurens, South Carolina, for the first year out of college. His job included teaching history and directing mixed, girls', and boys' choruses. It was a comfortable life, but not too satisfying. The same routine day after day did not appeal to him. After a year, Bill realized he was not suited for teaching. Dealing with and disciplining high school students, especially athletes, who took his chorus courses as a laugh, was not his cup of tea. Serious students were rare. Bill had never been too serious a student himself, but he never disrespected his teachers. Ultimately, he did not feel he was accomplishing anything significant in his teaching role.

33

So, Independent Plan A was out. Expected Plan A was back on the table. Bill decided to go to seminary the next fall.

However, instead of going to the Lutheran Southern Seminary in Columbia, where his father and Uncle William had gone, he chose Gettysburg Seminary in Pennsylvania. Bill had enjoyed visiting that divinity school on one of the Newberry College Singers' tours, and he had heard that Gettysburg had the best young faculty of any Lutheran seminary on the East Coast. Going north of the Mason-Dixon Line was a risk if he eventually wanted to get pastoral calls in the South, but Bill was intent on charting his own path.

Before going to Gettysburg, Bill decided to see more of America. With little or no planning, he embarked on a whirlwind hitchhiking trip to the West Coast, carrying only a light blanket and a tote bag. He slept outside in the elements everywhere except for a night at a YMCA in Chicago, one night in a Seattle flophouse, and two nights at a cheap hotel in San Francisco. Wearing his "N" letter sweater, he got dozens of friendly rides. Sometimes, the people who picked him up even let him drive.

One ride Bill hitched late in his trip was with a professional wrestler heading from Las Vegas to Phoenix and on to El Paso. Bill thought the wrestler got "torn to pieces" in the Phoenix bout. But the guy said he had deliberately taken a fall to build up the popularity of the Indian champion in Phoenix. Still thinking that the wrestler was beat up, Bill offered to drive to El Paso, but the wrestler declined. A few hours later, Bill abruptly woke up from a nap just as the car was going off the road, the wrestler having fallen asleep while driving. Bill grabbed the steering wheel just in time to avoid disaster.

Hitchhiking out of El Paso the next morning, Bill made it the first one hundred miles quickly, but then his luck ran out. No one would pick him up. In the afternoon, he heard a rumor that a hitchhiker had killed a driver on the same road just the day before. With a hitchhiking ride unavailable, Bill hopped aboard a train at a water tower and spent the night with fifteen to twenty other hobos on the moving train, heading east.

Bill's entire trip took only seventeen days, ending in Jackson, Mississippi, where his father had taken a job with the Lutheran Board of

American Missions. He arrived just in time for Clare and Johnny's wedding. Bill's younger sister, Betty, played the piano for the wedding, and Bill, a newly clean-shaven hobo with many talents, ushered, sang a solo, and was Johnny's best man.

Newberry had already brought Clare and Johnny together. Betty would soon be going to Newberry College herself. As would Buck's sister, Mary.

It was a small, small world.

Or maybe God was making it so.

Chapter 8

Bill's Seminary Years:
Gettysburg, Pennsylvania, and Washington, D.C.
(1939–1941)

Bill entered Gettysburg Seminary in September 1939. He and his roommate were given a room in the well-worn and dusty Old Dorm, which had been there during the Gettysburg battle in the Civil War. Having slept many nights outside or on floors when hitchhiking across the country, Bill never worried about the quality of his accommodations. He could get a good night's sleep in a barn, under a tree, in a moving boxcar, or the oldest dorm room in Pennsylvania.

In his first year of seminary, Bill was assigned to a small church in York, working with the youth and helping with Sunday worship services. During his second year, Bill's duties shifted to Zion Lutheran Church in Harrisburg, one of the largest in the area. He fondly remembered assisting in Holy Communion on Easter Sunday for thirteen hundred communicants and singing a solo when the seminary choir gave a concert at the church. By then, his tenor voice had gained a reasonable level of resonance, giving Bill the confidence to perform as a featured singer.

Studying the Old and New Testaments and constantly being part of church leadership, Bill found himself regaining his faith, which had wavered in college, and rekindling his confidence about one day becoming ordained. He loved worshipping with a full musical liturgy and leading the congregation for the sacrament of communion with bread and wine. "The body and blood shed for you." It was both an intimate and collective spiritual experience unlike any other.

Bill paid his way for his second year at the seminary by working in the kitchen, running the commercial dishwasher, and setting the tables for all three meals. Always a happy toiler, he earned his own way, including a few extra dollars for personal spending.

After hitchhiking home to Jackson, Mississippi, for Christmas 1940, Bill received an unexpected notice that he was to report for induction into the army. The United States was staying out of the impending war in Europe, but droves of young men were being drafted in case America would be dragged into the conflict. Because he was in seminary, Bill could have avoided the draft entirely. However, his love of country and a willingness to serve despite the rising threat of war in Europe had led him to waive his exemption to the draft when the government began enrolling young men in fall 1939. Despite the waiver, when he reported to the induction office in Jackson, he was told he would not be called up until he completed his second year of seminary in June 1941.

In spring 1941, Bill returned to the draft office for medical tests in anticipation of being called up in early summer. Once again, his enrollment was delayed, this time because of his poor eyesight. He had worn glasses since age five, leading to a 4-H rating.

With no induction in sight, Bill was able to take advantage of a Gettysburg Seminary–sponsored internship program at St. Paul's Lutheran Church in Washington, D.C.; it was the main downtown Lutheran church in the nation's capital. For the internship, he spent one hundred dollars on his first car, a well-worn '34 Chevy sedan he promptly named "Jasper." Bill was given responsibility for the youth activities, helped with Sunday school and worship services, and preached every Sunday night for vespers. It was in Washington, D.C., that he met Mrs. Bresnahan and her daughter Pauline, members of St. Paul's Church. St. Paul's pastor dropped Bill off at their home without notice right before the pastor left for a month's vacation—presumably to avoid Mrs. Bresnahan declining the opportunity to host an intern. Mrs. Bresnahan, a feisty widow who had recently broken her arm, had not committed to take in an intern. So, Bill was an unexpected guest, unknowingly thrown into the lion's den.

Given the awkward introduction, Bill knew he had to quickly earn his keep. The day Bill arrived, Mrs. Bresnahan and Pauline had a bushel of peaches that needed to be processed. Bill immediately asked,

"How can I help?" He then sat down and began peeling and cutting up the peaches, a chore most men in those days would have avoided. For hours, Bill kept at it, his hands and fingers soaked in sticky peach juice, all the while chatting away and joking about everything happening in the world. Mrs. Bresnahan and Pauline were themselves chatty conversationalists and had sarcastic senses of humor, breaking into laughter every few minutes. By the end of the evening, Bill had earned their acceptance. Simultaneously, he wondered what he was getting into.

Bill found Mrs. Bresnahan to be a "sassy hoot." Soon he was calling her "Mrs. B" or by her nickname, "Glamourpuss." Pauline, who was eight or ten years older than Bill, quickly assumed a social adviser role for him. Bill quickly learned that he could be himself with them, with no subject out of bounds, and no parental judgment. His feisty give-and-take dynamic with Pauline led to a lifetime platonic friendship.

As Bill later relived his love-life journey on his first night in Sweden, Bill thanked his lucky stars that Pauline's matchmaking skills had been fruitless throughout his seminary years and military service, as if they had been successful, he would never have managed to stay single long enough to meet and court Mary. His journey to find a wife had taken many twists and turns during his military service, not unlike many other servicemen finding themselves in a war overseas.

PART II

THE WAR

Chapter 9

Wartime
(1941–1944)

December 7, 1941, the night Pearl Harbor was attacked, Bill was preaching at a Vespers service at St. Paul's in Washington D.C. Mary, still only sixteen, had started college at Newberry just three months earlier. After Pearl Harbor, many of the male students at Newberry left to serve in the military. Newberry was assigned to house a naval unit providing basic training. However, Mary was more interested in studying than dating a bunch of would-be sailors who would soon be off to battle in the Pacific.

Shortly after the Pearl Harbor disaster, Bill received a new notice from the draft office. He had been re-classified to 1-A, despite no further medical exam. Apparently, after Japan attacked the United States, bad eyesight no longer mattered. Now, the US army needed every able-bodied soldier, even those bespectacled ones in seminaries.

Bill thought he would get called up within days, but Easter and most of the summer passed without any notice for induction. Finally, he wrote to check his status, and, not surprisingly, by return mail, received his notice. Duly reporting to duty, he was inducted on August 22, 1942, assigned as a chaplain's assistant, and started basic training at Camp Shelby in Mississippi.

Meanwhile, Mary was happy at Newberry. She enjoyed math and sciences, got good grades, and was on track to graduate in three and a half years. Like Bill and Clare six years earlier, she particularly enjoyed singing with the Newberry College Singers and joining the college's theater group, frequently whistling her way to rehearsals. It was nice to be able to interact regularly with others besides her parents. Away from her ever-present parents, she steadily blossomed as a confident, pretty, but still demure young lady. While at college, Mary allowed her dark hair to grow out from the girlish bowl cut to a more fashionable shoulder-length style. She never went back to a short style and always wanted to look her best. She chose conservative but colorful clothes, almost always in happy colors of blue, red, and yellow.

One of Mary's roommates at Newberry was a girl from Jackson, Mississippi, named Betty. They, and another roommate named Margaret became best friends. Betty occasionally talked about her older brother who had been going to seminary "somewhere up north," before being inducted into the army. But Mary paid little attention. She focused on her education and worked hard not to be distracted from her goals.

Bill kept in touch with Pauline Bresnahan and her mother while in the army. Pauline must have bet him that he would never be inducted, as his first letter from Camp Shelby started with, "You lose, Pauline! I am now a member of Uncle Sam's army. I was sworn in yesterday afternoon about four o'clock."

Indeed, Bill, like all his fellow rookies, spent countless hours on the drill field, marching, maneuvering, erecting pup tents, and "sweating like pigs" in the hot Mississippi sun and humidity. At first Bill enjoyed the physical exertion, but after a few weeks, the relentless drills grew tiresome. He wondered why an assistant to the chaplain had to be in such good shape.

One day, his Camp Shelby group was required to stand at attention on Hattiesburg's main street for two hours in the hot morning sun. Then he was told the morning session was just practice for the afternoon. At 3 p.m., his unit resumed standing at attention for two more hours, perspiring profusely in the humid heat, again with no explanation. Finally, for no apparent reason, an order to present arms was given. Moments later, a motorcade of black limousines turned a corner and sped by Bill's unit, the colorful flags on the vehicles billowing in the wind. That night, Bill wrote Pauline. "No less than FDR and a bunch of big shots drove through. President Roosevelt must have heard that I was in Shelby!"

The presidential motorcade reminded Bill that he had been forced to leave his aging car, "Jasper," in Jackson with his father. Jasper had suffered two flat tires on the long drive to Mississippi, and with Bill now in the army, it was time to say goodbye. In a letter to Pauline from Camp Shelby, Bill confirmed the car had been sold. His father had found a fellow willing to pay $100 for the old heap, the same amount Bill paid for it several years earlier. Bill told his father, "Get it quick before he realizes how foolish he is."

In his letters from Camp Shelby to Pauline and Mrs. B., Bill also confessed that he had written letters or sent cards to a few girls Pauline had introduced him to, including one named "Beautiful." But they had not responded. "All my gals are letting me down," he lamented. Perhaps his opinion of his own bespectacled looks may have contributed to his downhearted mood. His photo had been taken by the army photographer. He wrote Pauline, saying, "I must say the proofs weren't so hot—they looked just like me."

His loneliness for female companionship became a theme. In a November 4, 1942, letter to "Dear 3602," the street number of the Bresnahan residence, Bill described having to do twelve hours of guard duty from 6 p.m. to 6 a.m., which would "knock me out of some of my beauty sleep." He sarcastically added, "Aren't those pleasant hours to be out jaywalking? It could be alright if I had a moon and a blonde, but Uncle Sam doesn't furnish such accessories yet."

In one of her letters, Pauline had mentioned the availability of a diamond if he needed one. Bill quickly responded, "Now, what earthly good would a diamond do me? You know it takes a girl first—that's the mostest thing I ain't got."

Clearly, the army duty was not only interfering with Bill's love life, but also rapidly undoing years of proper grammar and education!

One of the highlights of Bill's first year in the army was the Christmas Eve service at Camp Shelby. Still in the era of segregation, Camp Shelby had White rookies come to the reception center for two weeks, then Black rookies for the next two weeks, carefully housing them in separate quarters. In the absence of the lead chaplain that Christmas, Bill and another chaplain's assistant surprised everyone by holding a huge service of lessons and carols for one thousand Black rookies on the parade grounds. Bill set up the organ on a rough platform, starting the service by singing several carols that were familiar to all present.

Christmas scriptures were read, and Bill gave a short homily for the occasion. Then, without prompting, and to Bill's surprise, the Black rookies took over the service. Eight or ten came up front and led the gospel singing. Then two quartets took turns singing their favorite selections in perfect harmony, followed by a Black preacher stepping forward and beginning to pray in a deep bass voice. At first, the preacher's voice was almost a whisper. Then, as he slowly began to raise his voice, a little hum began to run through the crowd, getting more musical and growing louder as the preacher's prayer for peace and safety reached its climax. Soon, the entire parade ground crowd was spontaneously swaying and rocking to the music, their arms raised toward heaven.

Chills ran down Bill's back.

It was the most memorable, inspiring Christmas Eve service Bill had ever experienced. He could not understand or support racial discrimination and separation, which was ubiquitous in the South, especially in churches. He hoped to do what he could to change that, believing that all people, no matter the color of their skin, are children of God. At least on that one night, he had made a wonderful Christmas Eve worship service possible for the Black recruits.

And it was a beautiful experience for him as well.

In April 1943, after Bill took some sort of intelligence test, he was called before several interview boards, which were recruiting soldiers to study psychology in a special STAR program. Bill repeatedly told them he did not care to go back to school unless it was back to seminary, but soon learned that in the army, "you no longer have the privilege of saying yea or nay." Shortly thereafter, he was reassigned to the Army Special Training Program at the University of Alabama in Tuscaloosa, which focused on psychological warfare. However, after a few weeks of marching, physical training, and orientation to the psychology program, the ASTP unit was abruptly closed. Bill was sent to Virginia Polytechnical Institution to study civil engineering and military logistics instead.

Off to Blacksburg, Virginia, he went. The physics, math, and differential calculus classes at VPI were a bit harder than the math and sciences he had studied at Newberry. He managed with the help of a very smart roommate. For two semesters, Bill worked through the civil engineering curriculum, learning how to build pontoon bridges strong enough to support tanks and heavy equipment, with considerable physical training on the side. He found time to be active in the local Lutheran church in Blacksburg, sang in the army chorus, and found some girls to date—one named Marge in neighboring Lynchburg, who continued to write letters to him throughout his stint in the army. VPI and his life in Blacksburg were easy—essentially like being back in college.

Bill also at least twice filled in as preacher at a Lutheran church in Radford, Virginia. The local Radford paper, in an article titled "Soldier Will Be Guest Preacher at Christ Lutheran," noted that Bill preached at the local church several months ago and was "highly acclaimed." When he sent the article to Pauline, Bill wrote that, although the services in Radford went off alright, "the stuff you read in the paper, you can take with a shaker of salt."

Bill's heart in 1943 seemed to be focused on a girl named "Spin," a girl he was introduced to by Pauline in D.C. during his internship. "Spin" was a nickname, perhaps short for Espinosa. Who knows? Bill and Spin had initially enjoyed some fun but casual dates, mostly with other friends along. Bill hoped they would become an exclusive couple. After Bill joined the army, Spin regularly wrote him, letting him know what was going on in Washington as he was going through various army stations and keeping him informed about the engagements and weddings of several of their friends. In a letter to Pauline on his birthday in August 1943, Bill expressed frustration about planning a furlough trip back to Washington to see Spin, only to find that she had drawn the evening work shift the entire time he would be there. To make it worse, he learned that Spin's ex-boyfriend was back in town after a year in South America. The ex-boyfriend was heading overseas, but Bill also knew that Spin was moving to Norfolk, Virginia, where there would be navy guys all over the place. In his exasperation, Bill found a sarcastic poem, which he shared with Pauline:

I'm done with all Dames.
They cheat, and they lie.
They prey on us males
To the day that we die.

They tease and torment us.
They drive us to sin.
Hey—who is that Blonde that's just coming in?

Blondes, however, were not Bill's favorites. While at VPI, Bill dated two fair-headed women, one a senior at Randolph Macon College who was "very charming gal, a preacher's daughter, quite attractive, and interested in music and religion," and another in Blacksburg. But, after describing them to Pauline, he concluded, "I don't know why they all have to be blondes!"

In late spring 1944, with the United States' role in World War II rapidly escalating, everything changed. All the civil engineering students were sent to Camp Claiborne in Louisiana for infantry training. Suddenly, army life got serious. Instead of hitting the books, Bill was in full-fledged military training, with live ammo and exploding grenades, wallowing in the dirt, and crawling through the mud under barbed wire.

On April 3, 1944, Bill wrote Pauline and Mrs. B. to tell them, "Yours truly is now a rough, tough, root-toot-tooting infantryman. Surprised? I am!" He was now a member of the 84th Infantry Division, commonly known as the Abe Lincoln or Railsplitter Division. He thought it "quite an outfit for a good southern rebel!" Bill looked forward to "the intensive 25-day training with hiking and firing—carbines, grenades, M-1, and everything." Tired of engineering classes, he was ready for action.

Bill qualified for sharpshooter with the Garand semi-automatic, gas-operated rifle, but he was average on the sniper course. He surprised himself by having no qualms about throwing live grenades. He described other fellows "shaking like a leaf," but the live ammo and grenades did not bother him. After essentially being an academic most of his army stint to date, Bill was proud to be a part of the real infantry, training to go into combat in what he was told might be "the roughest, goriest part of war." He was anxious to find out what his war job ultimately would be if he finally got deployed. Whether it was an infantry man or an chaplain's assistant, or both, he felt ready for the challenge, perhaps somewhat naively.

The elusive Spin was also becoming a challenge. She wrote him several times after arriving in Norfolk, leading him to visit her there in early June 1944. After that visit, he declared to Pauline that Spin is "the same sweet gal." But Bill and Spin had spent the whole weekend with her roommate, Anna. Bill had almost no time alone with his favorite girl.

Later that same month, Bill got a three-day pass and went home to Jackson, Mississippi, for a few days to see his parents and his sister Betty. Betty brought her two college roommates, as they had just finished their early summer semester at Newberry. It was the first time Bill's family had been all together in eighteen months.

Bill thought Betty's roommates, Mary, a pretty brunette, and Margaret, a cute blonde, were nice girls. Mary was Buck's little sister, so Bill knew she came from a good Lutheran family. But she was still a teenager. Still, there was a spark of attraction. When he told Pauline about the visit, he merely said, "Betty had two girl friends from Newberry with her, so they added to the fun." Nothing more.

It was not the time to start a relationship, especially with his war deployment just around the corner. He could be sent overseas and into combat at any time.

Chapter 10

Bill's War Service:
Germany, Battle of the Bulge
(Fall 1944)

Bill's deployment came quickly. In September 1944, Bill sailed for Europe with the 84th Infantry Division, his third crossing of the Atlantic. In one of his last letters to Pauline and Mrs. Bresnahan before leaving, Bill thanked them for sending pieces of cake from a wedding they had attended, but declared, "Strangely enough, I am still single and have no prospects for any change of status." He also thanked them for trying to set him up with a girl named Marian from Youngstown, Ohio, but lamented that he was having a hard enough time trying to keep in the running with the girls he was already dating. In truth, as he headed into battle, Bill had not found the right woman and had no solid possibilities, despite Pauline's help.

Bill's division landed in Liverpool, spending a few days in London and three weeks near Winchester in Southern England before crossing the channel to Omaha Beach in Normandy. In London, Bill saw firsthand the effects of the relentless German bombing attacks from earlier in the war. In a letter to Pauline, written on stationery imprinted with the seal from the House of Commons, Bill described the damage: "Even after two years comparatively free of bombing, you can see how the people of London suffered. It is wonderful how they can still treat the soldiers like kings and go on in spite of the havoc of war." But Bill was still to see such havoc in real time. He prayed every day for himself and his fellow soldiers to remain safe and unharmed in the days ahead.

After landing on Omaha Beach, Bill's division moved forward through the bomb-shelled French countryside to the Holland-Germany border. There, they joined General Montgomery's 9th Army, made up of American and British troops. Bill was assigned as the chaplain's assistant for the battalion aid station for the 335th Regiment of the 84th Infantry. The hierarchical chain of command among armies, battalions, infantry, and regiments seemed endless. Bill only knew that he was the sole rifle-carrying member of the battalion aid station group, which was made up mostly of medics.

Up to this point, Bill's military service had been preparatory, safe, and nonthreatening. Now things were getting real, and Bill's excitement was building. He still had no clue about what war entailed other than his brief infantry training and the tales of glorious heroics that filtered back to the United States as prior units had taken back most of France. He would soon find out that, along with glory, came a lot of gruesome injuries, suffering, and death.

Once close to the front at the German border towns of Geilenkirchen and Gulpen, Bill was quickly drawn into the combat zone, helping set up a battalion aid station less than a thousand yards from the front. Geilenkirchen, which had been almost demolished in the prior Allied push, was an important target as the Germans, in their Ardennes Offensive, tried to retake territory lost in the prior months.

For Bill, it was baptism by fire. Under constant shelling, he and his unit of medics struggled to handle the volume of wounded soldiers, triaging their injuries, patching them up as well as possible, and preparing them for amputations of legs or arms, or both, before putting them on transports to the rear for major medical treatment. Every few hours, Bill and his fellow servicemen had to retreat to the cellars of the aid station building as Nazi artillery threatened to demolish everything above ground.

After having slaughtered dozens of chickens and witnessed a hog killed and butchered as a youngster, Bill was used to blood. But now the gaping wounds and blood were from fellow soldiers, some of them friends. Helping the medics attend to their physical needs was the easier part of Bill's job. The tougher assignment was to help them spiritually. As assistant to the chaplain, Bill knew that many of them would not survive their wounds or would be permanently injured. He initially was overwhelmed by the task, but he had little or no time to dwell on his own welfare. He did not even have time to bathe, shave, or keep up normal hygiene, wearing the same soiled clothes for days at a time. He did his best to make the wounded as comfortable as possible, praying with them for their healing while trying to keep a positive attitude amidst the brutality of the war. No one had trained him for this role. He could only draw on years of watching his father pray with congregants suffering from some illness or family problems, then apply that empathy and prayerful consolation to the battlefield victims. Bill wondered if he was making a difference or easing the soldiers' spiritual pain. How could he convince them that God cared for them when the artillery barrages continued to wreak havoc, indiscriminately mutilating so many young men? He did his best but worried that he was inadequately equipped to alleviate their suffering.

As he was not yet an ordained minister, he could not offer the wounded the sacrament of communion without the blessing and administration of the bread and wine being led by the chaplain. In any case, the Eucharistic concept of human sacrifice and Christ's body and blood shed for the forgiveness of sin and the forces of evil was hard to square with the discriminant and relentless German assaults on not only soldiers but also innocent civilians. Bill was too busy helping and praying for the wounded to solve the question of how God could allow such atrocities to occur or how the Nazis could be forgiven, if ever. No one was "turning the other cheek" under these circumstances.

During a lull in the bombardment, on December 6, 1944, Bill described some of the military action in Geilenkirchen in a lengthy letter to Pauline and Mrs. Bresnahan from "somewhere in Germany." For security purposes, he couldn't disclose his location. He wrote,

> All's quiet on our front for a little while—we are in a rest area to catch our breath after a spell of action on the front lines. It seems wonderful to have a shower and put on clean clothes for the first time in weeks. We don't even have that constant serenade of shells and bombs and bullets.... Several days ago, a couple of aid men borrowed the old jeep to bring in some casualties. That was the last we heard of them or the jeep. I hope they were captured by the Germans and not blown to bits by a German 88.... You might be interested in a few comments on what's happened to me. I can begin by adding

my "amen" to Sherman's statement about "war being hell." You can't even imagine what an infantry rifleman goes through. Thank God I don't have to take what they do. It's rough enough being back a thousand yards or so with the battalion aid station. When there is a job to be done, I'll do it willingly, but I want to keep my hide unbroken if it is at all possible. I don't know what we would do without these stout German cellars for underground protection. For a few days, we were shelled so continuously that we only stuck our noses above ground when something had to be done. One day a shell caved in a basement room which I had left a few minutes earlier and buried four fellows under a mass of brick and steel. Miraculously, all escaped with minor cuts and bruises. Another time, I was on the back cellar steps when a Jerry plane dropped a bomb a few yards away. I thought the whole works was coming in on me, but I escaped with nothing more than a sore rear from bouncing down the brick steps. A fellow on the front steps was unlucky enough to bounce down on his head. He was evacuated and given the purple heart.

Bill knew that he was just one bomb away from a similar fate, but so far, he had been lucky. He thanked God he had not gone with the aid men who borrowed the old jeep to rescue some injured soldiers.

After almost a month, the shelling of Geilenkirchen subsided. It seemed no one knew where the German army was heading. In the Battle of the Bulge, the enemy was moving and attacking at different locations in a final effort to recapture territory taken by the allies. As a result, Bill's unit was relieved from duty there and got orders to head south to Marche, Belgium, on the west side of the Ardennes Forest area.

With limited facilities and little spare time, Bill had not shaved for the entire time in Geilenkirchen, growing a scruffy, full beard for the first time. After the bombing stopped, his service company captain saw his beard and asked, "My God, what happened to you?" Bill promptly ditched the beard. He felt better clean-shaven.

He dreamed about returning to America, where his only worry would be how and when he would graduate from seminary and find a wife. During the war, he was writing letters or sending postcards to several women he had met along the way, including Betty's roommates, hoping that somehow and somewhere he would find the right girl.

But for now, he just had to stay alive.

Chapter 11

Mary's Postgraduate Path: Shallotte, North Carolina, and Greenville, South Carolina
(1944–1945)

While Bill was dodging bombs in Europe, Mary graduated from Newberry and applied to the University of North Carolina at Chapel Hill
for a master's degree in public health. However, UNC deferred her acceptance for a year, informing her that she was still too young and had
insufficient real-life work experience. To get that experience, Mary
took a teaching job in Shallotte, North Carolina, a small town just
across the state line north of Myrtle Beach.

At age nineteen, Mary was younger than many of her students,
some of whom had left school to have babies and were returning to earn
a diploma. Though still a teenager, Mary had seen her parents teach
students of all ages and aptitudes for decades, so she found she was up
to the task. Teaching science and health classes came easy to her. Gaining confidence steadily, it took little time for her to recognize that the
teenage mothers who had returned to further their education were her
best students. Perhaps UNC was right to let Mary experience real work
life before taking on the stringent public health program.

While in Shallotte, Mary kept in touch with Betty, her best friend
from Newberry, so she knew Betty's brother Bill was now somewhere
near Germany. She was pleasantly surprised to receive several postcards
from Bill from Europe. But she had heard servicemen wrote letters to
any girls they knew, in the hope of receiving as many letters from the
States as possible while in the war zone. It appears that Mary did not
keep those cards. If she responded to them, her responses were not

preserved.

By April 1945, Betty was planning for her own wedding in August to a recently ordained Lutheran minister from South Carolina. Mary thought Betty's fiancé was nice enough, but she wondered if Betty had chosen the right guy. She suspected Betty, though fiercely independent, was simply honoring her father's wishes or following in Clare's footsteps in marrying a Lutheran minister.

In June 1945, Mary began her master's program at UNC. While supervised by an experienced health educator, she soaked up the basics about communicable diseases, community health, and testing. She especially enjoyed learning about treatments for tuberculosis, which was spreading across the South, as well as most recent initiatives in the public health field. Though she felt she was barely keeping up with all the reading assignments, research, and writing, she diligently finished all requirements and received her master's degree in only nine months.

As part of her program, her class went to Washington, D.C., and the National Institutes of Health to learn more about nationwide best practices. She also attended an American Public Health Association conference in New Orleans, where she obtained many up-to-date manuals and resource materials for local public health departments. Mary spent many late hours poring over the manuals under a small lamp, studying every paragraph and word and marking the key points with her freshly sharpened No. 2 pencil.

Having never traveled far from home before, Mary loved the opportunity to see new places and gain new experiences. Excited about the career she had chosen, she could not wait to get started.

With a job already lined up in Greenville, South Carolina, she did not have the time or inclination to worry about finding a guy with whom to share her life. She was an independent woman making it through the world in difficult times, just fine on her own.

At least for now.

Chapter 12

Bill's War Service:
Marche, Belgium; Push into Germany,
(1944–1945)

In a letter to Pauline Bresnahan dated January 9, 1944 (the correct year was 1945), Bill described the Belgian town of Marche. "It is a beautiful, old, picturesque town set in rolling hills that remind you of western Virginia. The big, gothic church is in the middle with a tall tower with a pear-shaped top. Narrow, winding streets were interesting to wander on."

Bill had spent Christmas 1944 at the large Bourguignon family home in which his battalion's new service aid station was set up near the center of town. The Bourguignon family's beautiful, stone and brick house had been built in 1673 and was filled with exquisitely crafted furniture and woodwork, oil paintings, crystal chandeliers, and Louis VI and VII secretaries. Bill loved the candle-scented and furniture-oiled smell of the place. It reeked of old aristocracy. Monsieur and Madame Bourguignon, a grandfather, and their five children were one of the most prominent families in Marche. Their home was large enough to accommodate the necessary medical gear and makeshift treatment rooms, as well as housing the service aid station medics. Bill hoped it would be a pleasant and safe place to spend the next few months of his military service.

However, the first night after the aid station was set up, German tanks began to shell the town. Explosives in the street and yard broke out all the windows on the side of the Bourguignon home, sending shards of glass everywhere. All occupants retreated to the home's cavernous basement. By morning, it was obvious that Germans had surrounded the city. The fighting was fierce. Immediately overwhelmed with wounded soldiers, Bill's unit struggled to triage and patch them up before evacuating the survivors through the one open road out of town. With the shelling continuing, the aid station was moved down to the basement of the massive home. Bill's bed was a blanket and pillow in one of the basement hallways. Even though he was exhausted, it was impossible to get any meaningful sleep while the bombing continued.

Fortunately, the shelling temporarily subsided for Christmas. Two packages of goodies from Pauline Bresnahan arrived just in time for Bill to share them with his fellow soldiers and the Bourguignons. Bill gave a little wooden horse to the youngest daughter, Theresa, whom Bill called "Peewee." She was "the liveliest little nine-year-old that you ever saw," he wrote. He gave a small pin to the fifteen-year-old girl, Colette.

Bill was equally thrilled to receive a parcel from Spin, filled with "many pretty packages." He and the Bourguignon children had fun trying to guess what was in each package. Perhaps all was not lost with his favorite gal.

Bill and the chaplain tried to visit several nearby army companies for Christmas services, but they were blocked by checkpoints and only able to reach a few. At midnight that Christmas, local Belgians and dozens of American soldiers lined the basement at the Bourguignon home, quietly singing Christmas carols and praying for peace in the damp, dimly lit cellar. The sandalwood smell from the candles reminded Bill of midnight Christmas Eve services at his father's churches, where freshly lit candles adorned the Christmas trees.

What a contrast to the joyous, spine-chilling spirituals at Camp Shelby with the Black soldiers just one year earlier!

The battle around Marche and the larger Battle of the Bulge went on for several more very rough weeks after Christmas. Bill and the medics had more than their share of wounded warriors to treat, many of which did not survive their injuries. Bill, gaining experience, helped in every way he could. He consoled the wounded and prayed over the dead. He began to feel God's presence as he more confidently brought peace and hope to soldiers who had lost a leg or an arm, or both, or who were just plain "shell-shocked." It remained no easy task. In war, evil is all around and only the most faithful souls can find solace in the Lord's healing presence. Bill hoped he was making at least some significant spiritual difference to his maimed fellow Railsplitters.

Fortunately, after incurring heavy casualties, the Allied troops were able to stem the last major thrust of Hitler's army, primarily because the Nazi battalions ran out of supplies and fuel to keep up the counter-offensive. Once the tide had turned and the Germans withdrew, Bill's unit had a few weeks to rest as it moved northward towards the German border to join the Allied push to the Rhine River.

During the break, Bill had a chance to catch up on his mail. With the war in Europe seemingly nearing an end, Pauline and Mrs. B were still trying to set Bill up. They gave him the name of a young lady from South Dakota named Norma, who reportedly was quite bright and was on track for becoming a college administrator. Plus, she was a good Lutheran. Sight unseen, Bill was asked to write her from Europe. He did so, reluctantly at first, asking Pauline to forward the letter to Norma, as he had lost her address. He added, "You needn't apologize for helping me find a wife. I'm working on the proposition. However, you don't bother too much about such things over here. I am certainly thankful that I don't have a wife at home now. It's too easy to turn up missing in this war business. However, I'm managing pretty well so far."

The Bresnahans, however, were relentless in their efforts to set Bill up with the perfect woman. In January 1945, after mentioning several of Bill's friends who were now engaged, Glamourpuss and Pauline insisted that Bill disclose his list of favorite prospects.

Bill responded in a letter dated January 23, 1945.

And speaking of my love life—!! Spin is still #1. You may be interested to know that I wrote Marian a long letter after I received a nice Christmas note from her. Robbing the cradle, eh! A little gal from Blacksburg has been writing pretty regularly. "Bright eyes" from Mississippi says she still loves me. I found Norma's address and will write her another letter one of these days. You can see that I'm not putting all my eggs in one basket—much as I would like to.

Three days later, after Bill received a new letter from Spin, he wrote the Bresnahans again, this time with a heavy heart. "Spin writes that that a Navy Lieutenant is beating my time—the tone doesn't sound as if she was kidding. C'est la guerre!" Perhaps the Christmas package from her was her parting gesture.

Not long thereafter, Spin wrote him a "Dear Bill" letter, informing him she was engaged to the navy guy. Bill was stunned by the speed with which his favorite girl had abandoned him. He wrote Pauline, "Spin and I are through!! Sad, but not exactly a surprise."

So much for #1 on Bill's list! The war was bad enough, but now it was taking its toll in more than one way. In his letters to Pauline Bresnahan, Bill put up a facade to conceal his disappointment, but down deep, he was hurting, wondering if he would ever meet the right girl.

In early February 1945, Bill's division lined up near the town of Linnich on the border of Germany, waiting to cross over into Germany. As soon as the battalions pushed forward, a massive artillery barrage began. The world felt like it was shaking to its core. With explosions right and left, Bill's unit crossed the Ruhr River on engineered pontoon bridges and pushed slowly forward under heavy shelling. The original bridges had been destroyed in prior battles. If Bill had expected to be thrown into one of the goriest parts of the war, his expectations were coming true. Driving a jeep pulling a trailer loaded with medical supplies, Bill kept his eyes on the road directly ahead to avoid focusing on the chaos around him.

As his unit finally reached the town of Baal among continued shelling, a brick-and-stone house with a small courtyard was selected for the battalion aid station. While Bill was still unloading medical gear from the trailer, German tanks stepped up their bombardment. Amid the constant barrage, one of the bombs hit at the entrance to the courtyard and sprayed shrapnel in all directions.

"Medic!" Bill yelled instantly after a sizeable piece of metal caught him in the back of his left knee and calf. In disbelief, he looked at the blood pooling across the back of his pant leg. He dropped to the ground, pressing down on his bleeding wound with both hands. The pain was excruciating, compounded by a deep, disabling ringing in his ears. Once on the ground, Bill thought he was going to pass out. Medics ran toward him, but everything seemed to be moving in slow motion, adding to his confusion.

Then things sped up quickly. Two medics he knew well were attending to him, one trying to keep him conscious and the other stemming the bleeding below.

"Stay with us, Bill. Focus hard. Don't let yourself go unconscious," the first medic said forcefully. Bill had heard the medics giving the same instructions to hundreds of other wounded soldiers at Geilenkirchen and Marche. He looked the medic straight in the eyes and held on, fighting to stay alert. Suddenly, as he looked at the medic and his breathing calmed, he realized he could no longer feel any pain. Perhaps he was going into shock. Or maybe the pain medication injected into his leg by the second medic was taking effect.

Within seconds, Bill had gone from a healthy, working infantryman assisting other battle victims to one of the wounded casualties, much like the hundreds he had seen over the last two months. The medics temporarily stopped the bleeding, putting him in an ambulance with the shrapnel still embedded in his leg. Division medics in the rear would do more work on the wound and then place him on a hospital train for evacuation to Paris. After that, Bill was not sure where he would be sent. He only knew that he was lucky to be alive. Had the shrapnel hit him two feet higher, he probably would have been dead. He still wondered whether he would lose his left leg. He had seen soldiers with similar injuries require amputations once infections set in.

Two nights later, Bill was flown to South England, then transported to a hospital in Wales. For almost a week, he was given shots of morphine every four hours to deal with the throbbing pain in his leg. It was fully five days before surgeons removed the shrapnel. Fortunately, no amputation was needed.

Now, Bill was the war hero with a purple heart to be awarded— but he didn't feel like a hero. He would have given everything to be back at the aid station helping, consoling, and praying for others, even under the constant shelling. Instead, he was praying earnestly to God for his own healing and salvation.

Despite his wound and ongoing pain, Bill still had a sense of humor. In a letter from Paris on February 26, 1945, before being flown to the United Kingdom, he wrote, "Dear Mrs. B and Pauline, I collected one souvenir too many a couple days ago. I got a piece of shrapnel in my left calf. It's not serious, but I suppose I'll be in the hospital for a little while. I would prefer taking in the sights of Paris on two good legs though." He also mentioned the "good-looking nurses."

There would be no Paris sightseeing on this occasion. He had dreamed of one day visiting Paris and strolling along the Seine with a pretty girl who loved him. But now he had no girlfriend and couldn't stroll down the infirmary's hall let alone along a riverbank in the most romantic city in the world.

As he was being evacuated to safety, one wonders whether Bill's leg or his heart had taken the bigger hit. It had been a tough month. Spin had spurned him and was no longer a prospect, let alone his #1 hope. He had struggled to help others cope with their injuries and dwindling faith. Now he was disabled. He prayed that his leg would eventually mend, but the verdict was still out on his heart.

Thank God he was still alive.

Chapter 13

Bill's Rehab, England and Scotland
(March–April 1945)

"Dear Pauline and Mrs. B, the old leg is coming along fine. The stitches are out. The bandage is gone. I'll soon be hobbling around. The only things holding me back now are the tender nerves and stiff muscles. They should come around alright with exercise."

It was March 16, 1945, just over three weeks after Bill was hit by the shrapnel in Baal, Germany. He was still at a hospital "somewhere in England." Bill was told that once his leg healed, he would get a week or two off to rest in Scotland before being redeployed to the front. With the allies pushing well into Germany, he hoped the Germans would surrender by then.

Bill's biggest setback during his recuperation was getting no incoming mail. Even Pauline's letters were not coming through. Being cut off from the world back home eliminated one of the few joys Bill had amid the casualties and chaos around him. Bill lived for the letters and word from home. For him, being isolated was almost worse than the injury itself.

He found solace at an Anglican church for Easter Sunday, his first opportunity to go to church in several months. Though the service was decidedly "high church," Bill enjoyed worshipping with a regular liturgy supported by an excellent organist and choir. The beautifully decorated sanctuary, complete with bright yellow daffodils and other spring flowers, complemented the Easter message of new life.

Since he had been absent from church for too long, after shaking the hand of the pastor and greeting some members, he returned to the sanctuary. His head in his hands, he sat in a pew midway on the right side of the church and quietly prayed for a full recovery for himself and his fellow wounded warriors, then implored God to bring an end to the war.

Despite his leg being fully healed, Bill did not leave the hospital until April 16. As promised, he was given leave to spend a week in Scotland before returning to the battleground. In his next letter to Pauline, he said, "I fell in love with the country—and a couple more weeks and I might have fallen in love with one of its women. They really have some bonnie lassies in these parts." Indeed, in his April 25 letter to Pauline, the last one before he was redeployed to Germany, he complained, "Of course, I would meet the nicest girl on the last night of my leave."

Good timing was never Bill's strong suit when it came to his relationships with members of the opposite sex. He was beginning to think he was jinxed.

Heading back to the front, Bill did not know anything about his redeployment or how long it would be, except that within ten days he would be rejoining the 84th Infantry somewhere in Germany. By then he still hoped the war would be over, as the news reports indicated that the allies were overwhelming the remaining German troops and were bearing down on Berlin.

Sure enough, on Bill's "dirty, slow" train to Belgium from Le Havre, France, VE Day was announced. Victory in Europe! Hitler had killed himself and his forces were surrendering. The war was over—at least on this side of the world.

The towns and villages on both sides of the tracks almost instantly became gaily decorated with French and American flags and colorful bunting, and the local citizens waved and cheered as the train passed. Bill and his fellow infantrymen on the train were excited, but their celebration was muted because they knew their role in the occupation of Germany was just beginning. And the war was still going on in the Pacific. Unfortunately, Bill's unit was still solidly on active duty.

As the train chugged into Belgium, he wished he could go home to America or maybe back to Scotland to spend more time with Greta, the "nicest girl" he had just met in Edinburgh.

Chapter 14

The Occupation
Heidelberg, Germany
(June 1945)

In June 1945, Bill reunited with his infantry division in Hamelin, Germany, "the spot where the Pied Piper got in a few hot licks if you remember your childhood stories," as Bill described it to Pauline Bresnahan. On the way into town, Bill had seen beautiful tree-covered hills, green fields, and picturesque villages with a "deep red hue from weathered bricks and tile roofs." However, he remarked, "Towns, cities, and rail centers of any size might as well be marked off the map because they have certainly been pulverized."

In Hamelin, he was thrilled to find more than a hundred pieces of mail and various magazines waiting for him. Eighteen of the letters, dating back to February, were from the Bresnahans and a few were from women they promoted to him, including two from the woman named Norma from South Dakota. Bill wrote Pauline, acknowledging that Norma was an interesting writer he hoped to meet one day.

There were a dozen or more letters from church-related contacts and members who had heard about him being wounded. The seriousness of Bill's injury and his purple heart status had been exaggerated back at home. Bill still did not feel like a hero; to the contrary, he felt a bit guilty for having such a good time in Scotland before returning to his unit.

Meanwhile, Bill's battalion's future was in limbo. It could remain in Germany as part of the occupation, or it could go to the Pacific, like other divisions that had fought through Europe. The strongest rumors had the 84th Infantry eventually heading across the Pacific to the "CBI"—the China-Burma-India theater.

One sad letter he received was from his mother, who informed him that his sister Betty's August wedding to the Lutheran minister had been called off. In his next letter to Pauline and Mrs. B, Bill told them what happened:

> Betty is really heartbroken—her fiancé has called off the engagement. The only reason that he gives is that she is so smart and talented that he feels inferior to her. Isn't that some excuse? The engagement had been formally announced and Betty had resigned her job effective the last of May. I think she will go home and spend the summer. I would like to give him a swift boot in the ass.

Perhaps God had other plans for Betty besides being a Lutheran pastor's wife.

By mid-June 1945, Bill's unit had been moved to Heidelberg, Germany, a beautiful city along the Rhine, which was spared the Allied bombing in the war. Heidelberg's famous university and castle high above the Rhine remained physically untouched by the war. Fortunately, Heidelberg was not an industrial town or transportation hub, so, militarily, it had no strategic or tactical value. The Allies passed it over, bombing instead the nearby industrial city of Mannheim. In the occupation, Heidelberg became a major garrison base for the US Army.

Despite a general rule that American soldiers were not supposed to live with civilians during the occupation, Bill and another nine or ten infantrymen from his unit were billeted in the home of the Schmidt family, a couple in their fifties and their twenty-two-year-old daughter named Lore, who had a twenty-month-old son. Lore's missing husband, a German army officer, was rumored to be a prisoner somewhere in the United Kingdom. The family had been anti-Nazi before and during the war. As a result, the father had lost his business, and Lore had been expelled from the city's prestigious university. Bill felt sorry for them, but he knew that he could do little to help.

As for the local women, the army had a strict non-fraternization policy. But the policy was terribly hard to enforce. With ample numbers of attractive single German women around, many of them war widows, American soldiers newly freed from intense battle conditions were unlikely to follow the rules. Many members of Bill's unit found ways to fraternize, for better or worse. One night the military police even nabbed a dozen or more members of the "brass" from the 84th Infantry's general's office violating the policy.

As a chaplain's assistant, Bill knew he had to resist such urges.

But he was attracted to the young Frau Schmidt. He described her to the Bresnahans as "a very intelligent girl, eager for the fun she has missed during wartime, and one of the hardest workers I've ever seen for a young girl." He helped her around the yard, picking currants, raspberries, and gooseberries for the table. Lore also began teaching German to Bill and one other soldier for an hour every evening. One afternoon, the three of them took a boat ride up the Rhine, with Lore pointing out landmarks, ruined castles, and wonderful scenery on the surrounding hills. As the descending sun neared the top of hills, highlighting Lore's tresses, Bill could not help but admire the beautiful young woman before him.

Of course, there were other, less prohibited distractions in town, including service company parties on Friday nights. At one, Bill described meeting a group of WACs—"one grayhead, a blowsy blonde, one drunk, and two brunettes." But none were at all attractive to Bill. Bill still enjoyed being out with his friends, but he always left early, before the parties became brawls. He preferred spending quiet evenings at the Schmidt home.

On July 10, 1945, Bill wrote Pauline and Mrs. B to let them know his division was scheduled to stay in Europe the rest of the year. Bill applauded that decision because "plenty can happen in the Pacific in the next six months, and we may not have to meet the Japs at all."

More good news concerned Clare's husband, Johnny. He had been deployed to Europe prior to Bill and had seen even more combat, barely avoiding serious injury when his jeep was hit by German artillery. But he was now safely headed home, on his way to a happy reunion with Clare and their two girls, Brenta and Trudy. While Bill was biding time in Heidelberg, Johnny and Clare spent Johnny's furlough time at Dogwood Dell. Bill's mother, father, and Betty joined them.

Only Bill was still missing.

Bill's pleasant life in Heidelberg was too good to last. The 7th

Army's headquarters was reassigned to Heidelberg, so everyone else had to move out. Bill's unit was moved to St. Leon, a small farm village further down the Rhine. Outside his new bedroom window was an outhouse, a water pump, a couple of grunting pigs, and the unpleasant stink from the nearby manure pile. There was no shower or bathtub. Fortunately, Bill was still close enough to the Rhine to bathe the old-fashioned way.

But Bill's biggest problem with the move was the heightened restriction on travel and fraternization. Heidelberg and Lore, just up the river, were strictly off limits. The brass was clamping down on "such foolishness." In a moment of pure candor, Bill wrote Pauline and Mrs. B, informing them that "maybe it is just as well that I left Heidelberg, as Lore and I were beginning to like each other more than was wise."

Still, in early August 1945, during a few days of furlough, Bill and two other soldiers, both also named Bill, drove to Heidelberg. They spent several hours with Lore, "eating plums and chewing the fat," before visiting other friends. The next night, Bill managed to sneak Lore into a party hosted by regimental medics at the fancy club, La Flamingo, slipping by the MPs in town. It was "by far the nicest party" that Bill had been to in the army.

Under other circumstances, Bill and Lore might have developed a relationship. The cruel irony was that she was already married, a mother...and the wife of a German officer. He also knew well the army's nonfraternization policy during the occupation.

She was off-limits on many levels.

With his romantic options narrowing, Bill told Pauline that he had heard from Norma again. Norma had gotten a job as the dean of women at Augustana College in Illinois. He was impressed that she was taking on such a challenging position at such a young age. In his letters to her, he wished her success and again indicated he hoped to meet her someday. Corresponding with a woman he had never met was not too satisfying, but he appreciated the package of "Tollgate" cookies she sent him after exchanging a few letters.

In August 1945, Bill took his chaplain's jeep to a local church in St. Leon to practice on the organ for a service the next day. When he exited the church, he was shocked to find that the jeep was gone. The lieutenant colonel of the battalion, who happened to see the jeep un-guarded outside the church, had ordered it to be picked up. Jeeps were not permitted to be left unmanned, and Bill had not brought a guard with him. Bill told Pauline and Mrs. B that he narrowly avoided a court martial—but he was placed on probation.

"No one accused me of being a good soldier!" he wrote.

V-J Day was announced that week, so Bill and his buddies got a week-long furlough with passes to the French Riviera. The war was now completely over, and rumors were flying about everyone in the 84th Infantry going home in the next six weeks. Bill could not pass up a free week on the French Riviera.

The seaside town of Nice, France, was "perfect!" For Bill, it was like stepping into a whole new world. In contrast to the old German and Belgium cities and buildings darkened by the war, Nice was full of white buildings, brilliant sunshine, and sparkling waters. Plus, he had upscale quarters with no grunting pigs, nasty aroma, or outhouses.

One of Bill's friends from back home worked in Nice and met him at the train station. His friend's staff, made up of a couple of guys and several attractive French and Italian girls, invited Bill to join them during the evenings, going out for clubbing and dancing. Bill also managed to schedule a tour of much of the Riviera, from Nice to Monte Carlo, and spent the rest of the week sunbathing, biking, and swimming in the warm waters of the Mediterranean Sea. He knew that after the war, if he ever came back to the Riviera, he would not be able to afford any of these luxuries.

According to Bill, "Uncle Sam really did things up brown on the Riviera."

Chapter 15

Bill's Demotion:
Germany
(September 23, 1947)

On September 23, 1945, after a few weeks back in Germany following his sojourn on the French Riviera, Bill wrote the Bresnahans to let them know he had a new army job.

He explained,

> You see, last Tuesday night I decided I needed a change of scenery and went into Heidelberg to see Lore. It was strictly unauthorized of course. Unfortunately, I met a jeep coming in the other direction and the lieutenant in it recognized me.... All the officers were trying to find out why the chaplain's assistant was going in that direction at that time of the evening. There was quite a stink.

Despite being caught red-handed, Bill told the Pauline and Mrs. B that he had "no regrets." He "knew the chances he was taking and was willing to take the consequences." He "expected to be busted any day."

Bill was fired as assistant to the chaplain and assigned to the bottom rung of the motor pool. Mysteriously, he faced no further punishment, and no court martial proceedings materialized despite that he was already on probation from the unguarded jeep incident. Frankly, as he wrestled with changing greasy parts and enormous tires on two-and-a-half-ton military vehicles, Bill hoped they would send him home, even if it meant a dishonorable discharge. Instead, an order was issued assigning him to the University of Glasgow in Scotland to study more theology until his army duty was up in four to six more months. Bill never knew how that transfer came about. Perhaps the army brass felt he needed to re-focus on religious matters, rather than more secular temptations.

One thing was clear. He would not be making any more secret excursions to see Lore Schmidt. He had made his last visit to Heidelberg.

Maybe God was looking out for him once again.

Chapter 16

Bill's Punishment:
Glasgow and Edinburgh, Scotland
(Fall 1945)

Bill's "exile" at Glasgow University in fall 1945 following his demotion was a huge contrast to his restricted life in occupied Germany. While technically he was still in the army, there was no one to supervise or order him around. He was attending only thirteen hours of classes a week, for no credit. With no grades at stake, he did not spend much time studying.

With free time on the weekends, Bill explored Glasgow, Stirling Castle, Robert Burns country estate in Ayrshire, and Inverness up north. He visited Edinburgh at least every other weekend. The main draw there was not the magnificent castle on the hill or the many sight-seeing attractions, but the girl named Greta, the "nicest" girl he told Pauline Bresnahan he had met on his last day in Scotland before being redeployed in April.

A petite, pretty, and outgoing girl, Greta wanted to know all about America and other places beyond the confines of Scotland. As she listened with rapt attention, Bill told her about growing up in the South, his trips out west to see the national parks, and his love of the North Carolina mountains and Dogwood Dell. Greta soaked it all in, laughing at Bill's shenanigans and wild stories, all the while gazing at him with her sparkling eyes. Bill found himself being drawn to her. And she was clearly attracted to him. It was a wonderfully carefree four months, with a curious and engaging Scottish lass to keep Bill company.

However, he knew he could not pursue a long-term or romantic relationship. The war was over. He wanted to get back home as soon as possible. He would probably be eligible for an honorable discharge early in 1946, meaning he could possibly return to the States in January or February. He was tired of being in the army, even in the unsupervised atmosphere in Scotland. And there was one more thing holding him back. He had a hard time dealing with the indisputable fact that Greta's parents were communists, prominently displaying a picture of Joseph Stalin in their living room.

Still, Bill would miss Greta's feisty conversations, affection, and perkiness. In a letter to Pauline shortly after leaving Scotland, he confessed that he had reluctantly made one last trip to Edinburgh to say goodbye to his "wee Scottish sweetheart."

He left Scotland behind, a bit downhearted, but ready to get back to America.

Bill had orders to rejoin his division in Germany by December 10 so he could sail with them back to America. True to form, he took his time getting there, stopping in Paris, exploring the Louvre, and taking in the Folies-Bergère's. He still had no girlfriend to stroll along the banks of the Seine.

From Paris, he told Pauline that, once home, he may visit his relatives in Eastern Tennessee to unwind for a few weeks or months. He added, "And, of course, I will have to be looking around for that wife. As soon as anything definite comes through, I'll let you know."

To be sure, he would be starting all over, hopefully finding a pretty brunette with no absentee husband and certainly no Joseph Stalin portrait in her living room.

PART III

THE COURTSHIP

Chapter 17

Bill's New Beginning: Gettysburg, Pennsylvania, and Burlington, North Carolina
(1946)

Bill was discharged from the army on January 26, 1946, a few weeks after a very rough voyage across the brutally cold and icy North Atlantic, his fourth crossing of the ocean. His prayers for calm seas had gone unanswered, but he felt God was with him through the massive swales and constant seasickness, bringing him safely home to New York harbor and the Statue of Liberty.

Despite initially thinking he might take the spring semester off for rest and relaxation in Eastern Tennessee, after a brief stay with his parents, Bill almost immediately went back to Gettysburg Seminary to finish up his third year. He found himself a stranger there. A whole generation of students had gone through while he was in the army, and most of his favorite professors had moved on. Being the only one fresh out of the army, Bill had little in common with the other seminarians.

The war had changed everything. He felt alone.

At the persistent urging of the Bresnahans, Bill arranged to meet Norma over Easter break. They had been writing each other for more than a year, so Bill decided to see if she was as interesting in person as she was impressive in her letters. They agreed to meet in Chicago.

Bill could not help feeling a bit sheepish, traveling halfway across the country to see a girl he had never met and who did not live in the South. Norma had written dozens of perfectly beautiful, sensible letters to him while he was in the army. He had greatly appreciated receiving them, along with a batch of tasty cookies from her on one occasion. But she was a mystery woman. When he finally stepped off the train, she was waiting for him on the platform. They shared an awkward hand-shake and light hug and went to lunch at a nearby café. Within a few hours, Bill knew she was not the girl for him. While Norma was nice, extremely intelligent, a good conversationalist, and a very solid Lutheran, there was simply no magnetism, no butterflies, no romantic attraction from Bill's end. He was not sure how she felt about him. But either way, they did not click. He spent a couple of pleasant days, seeing some sights in the Windy City before saying goodbye to her. On the long train ride back to Pennsylvania, he knew his marital prospects had taken yet another hit.

With few social activities to distract him, Bill concentrated on his seminary studies the rest of that semester, essentially biding his time for love to reenter his life.

In May 1946, on a whim, Bill traveled to Burlington, North Carolina, to visit his younger sister. Betty had taken a job there as a parish worker after her wedding plans had been called off. Because Betty had to work part of the time Bill was there, she invited Mary, her old room-mate, to come over from UNC-Chapel Hill, where Mary was finishing her master's degree. Though Betty's motives are unclear, she and God may have been working together to help Bill meet the right girl. Betty, still reeling from the collapse of her own engagement, was always looking out for her older brother, who, despite his outgoing nature, seemed to be clueless when it came to women.

That weekend in Burlington, after his initial surprise at hearing Mary's voice, Bill could not help but notice how much she had grown up since he first met her back in 1944 at his parents' home in Jackson, Mississippi. He remembered her and her other roommate as fun-loving but shy young teenagers. Now she appeared to be a poised, confident, and mature woman. Bill was impressed by her academic and teaching accomplishments and her excitement about the public health field. Plus, she was exceedingly pretty with dark brunette hair, a healthy tan, and the cutest widow's peak he had ever seen.

What a difference two years had made.

During that visit, they talked, comfortably and naturally, about almost any issue under the sun, though Bill changed the subject when she asked about the war. He did not want to ruin the weekend with negative tales of bombardments and atrocities. He wanted to move on to more happy subjects. Besides, he found himself melting into Mary's warm brown eyes. Deep mahogany-colored, they had a certain brightness that revealed a positive outlook on life. He saw no sorrow, no pessimism there. Only a gentle, forward-looking spirit. She was a great listener who seemed to have empathy for his struggle to renew his way through life after three years in the army.

Bill had long since thrown away his "list," but Mary would have shot to the top by the time he left Burlington. However, he had no idea if she liked him. She was not the type of girl who openly swooned over any guy, let alone an older army veteran straight back from a horrendous war. While being friendly and hospitable, she had said nothing to encourage him from a romantic standpoint. Somehow, for Bill, her caution made her even more attractive. He only wished he could read her mind.

Truth be told, on that visit, Bill did not reveal his feelings either. Mary was not sure he was interested in any relationship with her or whether he was merely visiting his sister and being polite to her. She was both attracted to and mystified by her former roommate's older brother. She knew he was an Eagle Scout and preacher's kid, but he was much more down-to-earth and much less socially aggressive than she expected for a man of his experiences. He was kind, courteous, respectable, and, while not the most "tall, dark, and handsome" guy she had ever met, he was cute behind those rimless spectacles. She had never met anyone like him. Mary even found herself wondering what it would be like to be a pastor's wife. But she quickly checked herself. "Don't put the cart before the horse," she thought. "If it's meant to be, God will make it happen."

Back in Gettysburg, Bill promptly wrote a letter on seminary stationery:

> Dear Mary, hearing you at the bottom of the steps in Burlington was about the nicest surprise I've had in a long time. You were a sight to make any fellow feel better—so pretty and neat and happy. I'm certainly glad that Betty had you for a roomie because I probably would never have known you

otherwise. It was a pleasure to find someone so interested in her work as you are about yours. God bless you in your studies.

Then, after writing about his trip back to Pennsylvania, his feelings of being a stranger after returning to seminary following the war, and his uncertainty about what to do once he graduated, he closed the letter by mentioning Mary's brother. "I hope Buck is home by now. Please give him a good kick in the pants for me when you see him."

And his final thought: "I'll be waiting for a letter. Bill."

Meanwhile, Bill had to finish seminary and figure out how he wanted to spend his future in the ministry. Because Gettysburg did not have a summer program that year, Bill went to a summer term at Union Seminary in New York City. He took courses with Reinhold Niebuhr and Paul Scherer, two highly prominent theologians. He visited numerous churches in New York, hearing the great preachers of the day. If he was going to be a minister, Bill wanted to be the best preacher possible. He doubted that he would ever be a soaring firebrand, but he wanted to bring a hopeful message to God's people consistent with the scriptures, hopefully in a practical way that would help them cope with life's daily struggles.

With no clear vision of what to do after he would graduate at the end of the fall semester, Bill decided to use his GI bill benefits to support a further year of study abroad. Sweden was the only Lutheran country not fully disrupted in the war, and Germany was still not open to foreigners, so his options were limited. He enrolled in a new American Course at Stockholm University, which would include intensive studies in the Swedish language and ample opportunity to observe Lutheran churches in another country and culture. He was excited to experience life in Scandinavia, a major center for the Lutheran church. Maybe another year immersed in church leadership and religious study would help him crystalize his future in the ministry.

It never dawned on him that, by committing to the foreign study program, he could be running away from a wonderful future with someone who was already starting to fall in love with him.

Chapter 18

Mary's Vocation
Greenville, South Carolina
(June 1946)

In June 1946, Mary started her job with the health department in Greenville, South Carolina, as its first health educator. After a few months under the supervision of a veteran health educator from a nearby city, she essentially created her job on the fly.

She traveled across the county, working with teachers and community leaders, spreading information on the services offered by the health department, encouraging them to use those programs, and giving speeches to Rotary clubs and at various businesses. She accompanied public health nurses to "well-mother" and "well-baby" clinics, immunization units, and tuberculosis diagnosis centers. She developed specific projects to deal with health problems facing individual communities or businesses, sometimes with only reluctant support from their leaders. She visited high schools to teach students healthy habits.

Though it was challenging and exhausting, Mary loved it. And everyone she met loved her. She was always well-prepared, punctual, persuasive, and composed, even when dealing with much older businessmen and community leaders. It did not hurt that she was an undeniably attractive woman, modestly dressed, with practical solutions for community health problems.

Two long-term projects became her main responsibility. The first was a countywide seminar for teachers concerning simple health practices and hygiene practices in the classroom to minimize transmission of diseases among the school children. The second was a countywide chest X-ray campaign to identify workers with tuberculosis. The local power company agreed to provide electric power to support the multiple community X-ray units. The South Carolina Department of Health provided a mobile X-ray unit. Mary traveled extensively, encouraging businesses to participate in the program, but it was an uphill battle. Managers of the many textile mills in Greenville County were leery about requiring their workers to undergo the X-rays because, in those days, it was a shameful thing to have TB. Fortunately, through unending persistence and pluck, Mary was able to persuade the textile mills to participate. A sizeable number of TB cases were discovered, allowing those workers to be properly treated. Family members of those affected could attend sessions to help them take precautions to prevent tuberculosis spreading further. Mary also met with Black families and workers to help them interact with the public health department since many minorities had no access to adequate health care.

With all the work dominating her life, Mary had little time for socializing.

She often thought about Betty's brother. He seemed to be a nice guy, and she was flattered that he seemed interested in her career. But Mary hesitated to envision a future with a man six years older who had just gotten back from the war. Plus, so far, he had not indicated any romantic inclination. He had been a perfect gentleman in Burlington—almost too perfect.

And he had left without making any further plans to come back to see her. She wished he had. But with her expansive job responsibilities, she was too busy to dwell on it.

Except for almost every night, sitting alone in her apartment.

Chapter 19

The Football Game:
Clinton, South Carolina
(Thanksgiving 1946)

In September 1946, after a few weeks in Jackson, Mississippi, Bill returned to Gettysburg for his final semester, in anticipation of finishing his academic work in November. He briefly stopped to see Mary in Greenville during a train layover on the way up to Pennsylvania. She seemed happy to see him, but once again, in the short visit between trains, she did not express any feelings for him. However, she sent him a somewhat encouraging follow-up thank you letter that Bill took as a positive sign. He decided to surprise her by showing up at Thanksgiving and taking her to a homecoming football game.

Presbyterian College, generally referred to as PC, was the place to be on Thanksgiving Day, November 28, 1946. In Clinton, South Carolina, the Presbyterian Blue Hose and the Newberry Indians, rivals for decades, were playing for the bronze trophy at PC's football stadium on a cold and windy afternoon. A Newberry grad had originally owned the bronze trophy, but it had been stolen by some PC students before being retrieved by the owner and his friends before the game. Rather than devolve into one theft after another, the rival students agreed that the winner of the football game would keep the trophy until the following year. Thereafter, PC and Newberry played for the bronze trophy every Thanksgiving—that is, until PC moved up to NCAA Division I.

There was always a big crowd for this rivalry game. Alumni from all over the Carolinas regularly attended. Bill had attended only one Newberry game since his graduation and was hardly a football fan, despite having been a cheerleader for the Indians for two years in college.

However, on that night, he had only one thought on his mind—squiring Mary to the game. The PC-Newberry game was their first official date. They drove down from Greenville together and joined friends from Newberry.

The game was a nail-biter, with Presbyterian's Blue Hose ultimately prevailing, 14-13. But for Bill and Mary, the game could have been a zero-zero tie or a blowout for all they cared. They paid little attention to the football or their friends after the first quarter. It was if no one was there but them. After three quarters of snuggling together to stay warm, Bill knew the time had come to let her know how he felt about her.

During the fourth quarter, Bill took her hand and stole her away from the grandstands and crowd.

"Where are we going?" Mary asked.

"Somewhere where we can talk privately," Bill responded.

But there was no talking once they reached the secluded shadows near the stadium fence. Bill leaned in toward her, starting to close his eyes. She shied away—but for only a second. He took her chin in his hand and lifted her lips toward his. This time she let him guide her.

Their first kiss.

"I think I love you," he mumbled.

Mary trembled ever so slightly, hoping he did not notice.

"What is happening to me?" she thought—then realized she had said it out loud. Inside, she was excited and giddy. No one had ever kissed her so tenderly. On the outside, though, she remained cool and collected. She was still holding back, not convinced that starting a relationship with an older man she barely knew was practical. She kept her excitement to herself, lest she encourage him further.

For Bill, that first kiss was the start of a dream coming true. He noticed Mary's slight shudder when he kissed her. In truth, he was trembling a bit himself.

He thought about the dozen or more women he had dated or written to over the last five years, but none of them were "the one." The one girl he especially liked while he was in the army had gotten engaged to a navy lieutenant in his absence. Another favorite was already married before he met her. "Verboten!" A third was probably a communist.

Now, none of that mattered. Bill loved everything about Mary—her shyness, dark hair, and widow's peak. He loved the way she dressed, the way she smelled, the way she looked at him with her soft brown eyes. And, of course, after their kiss, he loved her sweet lips.

Something told him unequivocally that Mary was the only girl for him. He wished he knew whether he was the only guy for her. But he still did not know. Even after the kiss, her feelings were a mystery.

On the drive back to Greenville, Bill twice started to tell her he was falling for her. She did not respond. He suggested that they were meant for each other and that she should at least toy with the idea. She smiled but stayed quiet. One thing Bill knew for sure. Mary would never be an easy catch.

As he later wrote from Sweden, "Every once in a while, I think back to last summer and Thanksgiving when I wasn't sure what you thought of me and can't help but grin at myself. You were such a prim little lady!"

He needed more time with her, but he had to get back to Gettysburg for his graduation. He suddenly wished he had gone to seminary in Columbia, South Carolina, only a ninety-mile drive from Mary in Greenville, so he could see her every weekend. But at Gettysburg, he would be four states away. Mary told him she would be spending Christmas holidays with her parents in eastern South Carolina. And in six or seven weeks, he would be leaving for Sweden for up to eighteen months. He might never see her again.

His mind raced, analyzing his dilemma and asking himself question after question.

A couple of letters. One date. One kiss. How could he know if it was just short-lived passion or infatuation? He had failure after failure with girls so far. Even if Mary shared his feelings, how could they survive eighteen months apart after just getting to know each other? Was this budding relationship doomed because in less than a month, he was not going to be around? What was he thinking when he committed to study in Sweden?

On the train back north, Bill had a heavy heart. He was already in love, but he saw no way things could work out.

He was afraid he and Mary were like ships passing in the night.

Chapter 20

The Last Visit:
Greenville, South Carolina
(January 12–13, 1947)

In December 1946, Mary could not concentrate on work. She was having trouble focusing on anything except a certain gentleman. Despite struggling to share her feelings, she was surely experiencing them. That first kiss had been life changing.

Bill was not the most savoir guy she had ever met. He was not tall. His hair was already starting to thin on top. But behind his wire-rimmed glasses, which made him look quite intelligent, he was a good-looking man. He was obviously older than her and considerably more worldly, having traveled all over the United States and Europe and experienced the horrors of war. Even though Betty told her Bill had dated many girls and was a bit of a gadabout, she found him to be genuine, huggable, and bit shy. He was Lutheran and clearly shared her faith in God.

She trusted him.

She was not sure why.

But he was going overseas for another year in less than a month. If he loved her so much, why would he leave just when they were really connecting?

She remembered her mother's advice to her when she went off to college: "When you find the right one you will know it." After confiding in her mother on Christmas Eve about her feelings, vocalizing them out loud for the first time, Mary suddenly realized that Bill indeed was the right one. She had to let him know.

Mary wrote Bill on Christmas night, 1946, on unscented, tan

stationery.[2] Her letter, addressed to "My dear Bill," started slowly, teasing him about being a "growing" boy. At her parents' house for the holidays, they had all stayed up late and Mary had not been getting her nine hours of sleep per night. So, she told Bill that she would be "spoiled sure enough when I get back to Greenville." She told Bill about her trip to Columbia with Buck and Sue and about the many presents under the tree. Apparently, Bill had sent a photo to his parents in Mississippi with directions that they send it to Mary for Christmas. Mary thanked him, adding, "And speaking of Santa, the Mississippi Santa did too visit this house. The picture came Thursday before I left. I missed the other, but I was quite satisfied with the picture. 'Tis very good and I'm so glad I have one. Thank you so much."

She finally got personal.

> Bill, I know I've been letting you do it all—but only because I was afraid that I might say something I might later regret. But I don't think I need to worry too much anymore. The turmoil in my mind has ceased and I'm happy. Th'ot you might like to know that. You told me to "toy" with the idea. I have been, and it grows better each day. Bill—your last visit was the nicest surprise I've ever had. And to think you almost didn't come. Horrors! What a thought! Anyway—I'm glad you did read that letter over and did come. Here's hoping you had a most wonderful Christmas. My love to your family— And to you—Mary.

Bill's heart skipped a beat when he read the letter. He read it over and over. Her "turmoil" has "ceased." She's "happy." His was the "nicest" visit ever. "My love"—"and to you!"

"She loves me!" he exclaimed to himself.

Now he had no choice. He had only two weeks left before leaving for Sweden. He had to make one more trip to Greenville.

Traveling by train from Pennsylvania over the second weekend in January, Bill was left with only a two-day visit with Mary on Monday and Tuesday, January 12 and 13, 1947. Bill had one goal in mind. As

---

[2] This is the first of her four letters preserved.

he told Pauline Bresnahan in D.C. by phone at the train station, he hoped to propose to Mary by the end of his visit. He had no engagement ring and was uncertain what Mary's answer would be, but he was a man on a mission.

At the same time, Mary's heart leapt at the chance of seeing Bill and giving him some tender loving care during those two days before his big trip overseas. She was not expecting a proposal. They barely knew each other. One kiss and some letters. He had not even met her parents. But she was happy to give him something to think about. They went to a restaurant called Poinsett on Monday night, Mary pulling out a special yellow blouse for the occasion. She cooked for him on Tuesday. She showed him around Greenville, walking hand in hand in the cool, winter air, hugging him on the walks, and endlessly kissing and caressing on her apartment's squeaky sofa.

After two intensely romantic days together, Bill could not wait any longer. He popped the question on Tuesday evening under the Southern pines and a moonlit sky. There was no ring, no special event, no clever surprise. Just a confession on one knee of his unconditional love and commitment—straight from the heart.

Incredibly, Mary said, "Yes." Without any hesitation.

Bill instantly teared up, his long search for a wife over. "She said yes," he thought to himself. "I'm the luckiest man in the world."

Later that night, after many more kisses, Bill waved goodbye at the Greenville train station to head for New York and Sweden. As the train pulled out, Mary waved back with tears welling, wondering what in the world she had just done.

PART IV

SEPARATION IN STOCKHOLM

Chapter 21

Letters from Lidings
(Late January 1947)

By Wednesday, January 29, 1947, Bill had settled comfortably in Lidings, Sweden, a town on the outskirts of Stockholm, just two weeks after Mary accepted his proposal. He only wished Mary was there to share the experience.

Initially, Bill was impressed by the friendliness of the Swedish people. "It does you good to have people so interested in your welfare when they never have even seen you before." However, though the accommodations were nice, Bill soon learned that the boarding house was charging $57 per month for bed, breakfast and dinner, a price he could not afford. Worse yet, he discovered that an obnoxious atheist from the *Gripsholm*, who had claimed science was the only truth and ridiculed Bill's belief and faith in God, was planning to move into the same house. Bill wrote Mary that night, "I can't stand that guy."

The rest of the day had been better. Bill had visited the busy square in the center of Stockholm, with scattered vendors selling trinkets, scarves, and various food items on a chilly but bright day. He found the "immaculate and new" Lutheran bookstore. He contacted a Swedish tutor recommended by the university, who seemed to be a "prince of a fellow." He visited a gentleman named Lindstrom, whose name and address had been given to him by his Gettysburg Seminary contacts. Mr. Lindstrom had received a letter for Bill from his sister Betty. That night, Bill explained to Mary that he and Betty were "sorta like you and Marion—we've become good friends after we grew up. She was worrying about missing our wedding if she goes off as a missionary."

He closed his nightly letter to Mary that evening, "I love you, my brown-eyed beauty. May God bless you and keep you safe until we are together once more. Your Bill."

The next night, Bill started another letter, "Hi Brown-eyes!" before relating his daily activities, including his first Swedish lesson from the language coach, Mr. Jansson. "I don't think I did too badly, but I have a long way to go."

He spent much of that letter not about himself, but about Mary.

> Mary, I find myself talking only about myself very selfishly, but that does not mean I'm not interested and concerned in what you are doing. I particularly like your reports about the contact with the high school kids. I hope it will develop into something good. There is too little thought given at that age to anything serious and helpful, and there is plenty of room for all the encouragement they can receive. Keep at it, Miss H.E.

Indeed, as a health educator in Greenville, Mary was trying to instill healthy habits among the population, young and old, especially students.

In the next day's letter, in which Bill addressed Mary as "Min kara flicka," meaning "my sweet girl," he delved into women and dating. Apparently, he had lost one of his roommates, who suddenly had been invited to stay with Swedish relatives of some friends of his from Seattle.

> I wish I could get a break like that. "Mike" is typical of so many fellows I ran into in the army—pleasant and likeable, but chiefly interested in women. It's amazing the number of fellows who have no regard for sexual relations except for what pleasure they can get out of it—and they look at women with that angle in mind. He seems to be thinking, seriously, of marrying the Swedish girl he knew when he was interned here, however.

He then turned to how he and Mary should deal with "going out with other fellows or girls" during their time apart.

> I'm not the jealous type (within certain limitations) and certainly won't object if you date as you please. Any man in his

good mind would want to be with such a sweet girl. But I would rather that you went with other people and wouldn't make a habit of being with any particular guy. Right now, you are probably like me, and the question doesn't enter your mind, but we have a good many months to wait yet. I promise you that I will never see any girls enough for there to be any danger of more than friendship developing. I'm strictly a "one woman-man," and you're that one.

He then wrapped up a small Valentine's Day gift, which he planned to send to Mary, as a "trial package." He told her it cost less than a dollar, so she should not get her hopes up. He added that at least she would not have to pay duty on it.

Bill closed the letter, "I love you more every day. Bill."

On one of his first Sundays in Sweden, Bill attended Engelbrektskyrkan, the largest church in Stockholm, completed in 1914. The beautiful cathedral, with its red roof and green spire, towered above Stockholm's city center from the top of a rocky knoll. Seating over a thousand people, the church was filled with the rich music of the choir and organ, especially when the organist hit the low bass notes on his peddles. Bill sang along with the hymns though he did not understand the words.

That night, after expressing that he felt lost and out of place without understanding the Swedish language, Bill admitted he was already needing some tender loving care in the cold Swedish winter.

Mary, my darling, if you were here tonight, I would have to hug you mighty tight to keep warm. Of course, that would be the pleasantest bit of work I can imagine. Sweden has to go easy on the coal, and few of the houses or buildings are comfortably heated. Along the streets in the middle of town you see big piles of wood. So, I need a warm-blooded Southern gal to keep me in condition.

Wrapping up his letter just before climbing in bed, Bill wrote, "It's bedtime! One particular reason why this is the best time of the day is that I always spend the last few minutes before I fall asleep recalling our happy moments together and planning all the happy hours we'll have together when we are Mr. and Mrs. You are always in my thoughts and prayers."

That Monday, which Bill described as a "great day," he bought a new bike and got a new roommate. He told Mary all about them. "It looks almost too bright and shiny to use, but it rides pretty well. My old bones and muscles will take a while to get into shape, so perhaps it is just as well that the weather is not conducive to too much cycling. I'll be ready come summer." Bill's new roommate, Hal, was another fellow he had met on the *Gripsholm*. In that night's letter, he mused, "I run through roommates pretty fast, don't I? I think we will get along pretty well."

The other major activity that day was his second Swedish lesson with Mr. Jansson, followed by a pleasant evening with his family, a wife and three boys. His wife served tea, bread, and cheese. Bill wrote Mary that night, "Being a cheese lover, I'm doing alright in Sweden. You can put a note in your cookbook about that!"

But for Bill, the highlight of the day was simple. "This has been a great day—I got a letter from you. That makes my day perfect. It took a while to come. The first one you wrote in the apartment. It's good to know you have moved in where I know you will be happier." To make sure Mary knew that he expected frequent letters from her, Bill added, "I think I may have missed one letter of yours along the line some-where—or were you a bad girl and waited a whole week between January 21st and 28th? I'm afraid you had to wait a good while between the last card and the first letter from Sweden."

He then noted, "The bottom of the page comes mighty fast. A little poem in my lesson had a nice little goodnight word—'SOV ooH, min skatt' which means 'sleep sweetly, my treasure.' That's you alright, Bill."

Chapter 22

Letters from Stockholm
(February–March 1, 1947)

Prince Gustav Adolf of Sweden, the second in line for the throne, died in a plane crash at the Copenhagen airport on January 26, 1947. The popular prince had been an Olympic horse rider, an avid supporter of scouting, and a sports fanatic. On his way back to Stockholm from a hunting trip, his KLM Douglas D-3 aircraft stalled almost immediately after takeoff and plummeted nose-first to the ground, killing all twenty-two people on board. His funeral procession was held in Stockholm the following week. Bill knew almost nothing about Prince Gustav or Swedish royalty. Still, he stood among the local tear-filled crowd for a couple of hours, freezing to the bone, as he watched a solemn troop of cavalry in shiny black helmets lead the procession, followed by a horse-drawn caisson with the flag-covered casket, a dozen limos, and a final cavalry unit.

Later that day, a reporter for the biggest newspaper in Stockholm interviewed Bill and his new roommate, Hal Nelson, an American from Montana. A two-column story about the two American students, complete with photos, appeared in the next day's edition. The following night, Bill sent Mary the newspaper clipping, noting,

> It was an interesting experience to say the least. A body might think we were important characters.... How do you like the wild-eyed creature in the clipping? I was really surprised at the size of the picture and the length of the article. I'll bet you have a time getting it translated. I got out my dictionary and worked it out word by word—the interviewer wasn't too exact in her quotes.

He opened that letter reminiscing about Greenville. "Mary, my love, the old moon is shining through the fir trees tonight just like it peeks through the pines in SC. You know who it made me think of immediately. Of course, the new fallen snow on the ground and trees was a bit out of place."

The next day, Bill went to the city's post office, the warmest place in Stockholm. It was another great day when he saw a letter from Mary had arrived. He quickly wrote a response.

> There was a letter waiting for me, so there's a big grin on my puss. It's amazing what a boost to a guy's morale it is when the familiar handwriting turns up. I hope you had a wonderful time at home. There is nothing I would like better than to be there with you and meet your parents. It's a shame we couldn't have done it before I left. You must send me your father's initials and I will write them. I thought about it before but neglected to do it. It's swell of them to be so pleased about a fellow they have never met. You hit me hard when you talk about the apartment. Makes me dream too much! How it will be when I can come home to get a great big kiss and some of your cooking. I can't think of anything more wonderful than looking at you across the breakfast table for the rest of my life!

Mary also must have described her outreach to minorities in Greenville, as Bill revealed his thoughts about race relations.

> Your visit to the Negro Farm Group meeting hits one of the things I've been interested in. One of the reasons I hope to work in the South is to see if there is anything I can do to improve the colored-white situation in some small way. I've been interested in the problem for four or five years and hope that we can be more Christian about it in the future than we have been up until now.

Earlier that day, Bill and Hal had lunch with a gentleman Hal had met who had business and real estate connections. Hal felt that the boarding house in Lidings was too far out of town. By the end of the meal, Bill and Hal had a plan to move to a two-bedroom apartment in downtown Stockholm. Bill was a bit hesitant because the proprietors of the boarding house had been so kind, but he agreed to the plan since the apartment would be cheaper and more convenient for the school year.

That night, he wrote Mary to discuss packing up for another move.

Sweetheart, sometimes it seems like I'll just have to pack up and head back to S.C. and have a long evening with you. To-night is one of those times. It's quiet, I've had a busy day, and it would be wonderful to put your head on my shoulders and hold you close. Maybe you would play shy like you did at Thanksgiving and I'd tilt your chin up for a kiss. A guy can dream!! I love you, I love you, I love you, I love you, I love you.

On Saturday, February 8, Bill got up early that morning to go on a "frigid" bike ride downtown and when he returned to the boarding house, he found a letter from Mary that had been mailed on February 3, only five days earlier.

I could hardly believe my eyes. It made me mighty senti-mental—you really do things to make me feel a thousand times better than I've ever felt before. I certainly feel sorry for all the people that don't have such a wonderful girl to love them. I thank God every night for your love. Now I must head for that dinner. I am afraid that it is going to be a little more "society" than I'm used to, but it is good to see how the other half lives. I'll give you a full report tomorrow. Goodnight sweetheart!

The dinner Bill referenced was a large party at the spacious resi-dence of the prominent Wennenholm family. The next day, on Sunday afternoon, Bill used an extra page of the air mail paper to describe the evening's festivities.

Well, last night was interesting, but not exactly enjoyable. Hal and I were a bit out of place being the only ones present with-out tux, and we discovered that it was a teenage gathering. However, the Fru Wennenholm was very gracious, and the apartment was huge and elegant with heirloom furniture and crystal chandeliers. There were about 50 present—the majority, boys and girls, were much taller than I. I went into dinner with Elsa, the daughter of the house. I was lucky—she spoke good English and was as lively as any kid I've seen recently. It's too bad she has such a hooked nose to go with it.… We started dinner with little round sandwiches of all kinds of Swedish fish, cheese, vegetables, etc. You either drank vermouth or schnapps with them—I turned my insides on the schnapps. Then we had a buffet course of jellied fish, sauce, and potatoes. A light white wine accompanied same—which was more pleasant. Then we had ice cream (glace) with hot chocolate to pour over it. I was still a bit hungry when I got through, but it was too big a party for a big spread. Then we went into the five or six sitting rooms and parlors for coffee and cigarettes. After that, the dining room was cleared for dancing to the music of a good popular pianist and guitarist. From eleven o'clock on, Hal and I were just bored to death. It's amazing the difference a few years make when around 16–18. I felt like an old man chaperoning a high school party. So, we struggled along, stepping on the toes of the poor young things until 2:30 a.m.… All in all, I can't say it was too pleasant a night.

He closed the letter, writing, "The mailman is my best friend—your letters are the bright spot in the week. All my love, Bill."

"Hi little rascal!" led off Bill's next letter to Mary from Sweden. He quickly described the new apartment in Stockholm, complete with a hand-drawn diagram showing the placement of rooms and bath. The main draws for the downtown apartment in Bill's mind were that it was conveniently close to the university and was in a "new, modern building that actually felt warm." He hoped to move in by the end of the week.

A large group of Americans arrived the following day at Stockholm, just in time to get oriented before classes started. Bill hoped that this gang of Americans would help show that "all of Americans are not 'Hollywood' Yanks."

That week, Hal invited Bill to an evening at an art gallery with some girls recommended by Hal's aunt. Bill was a bit anxious about attending since he knew the aunt was wealthy and the "so-called sophisticated type." He had already been embarrassed about being sorely underdressed at the Wennenholm affair. But he found most of the folks at the gallery to be "unusually interesting and homey," especially the artist and his fiancée. He also attended a high-brow concert with the gentleman who had arranged for the new apartment. Bill wrote Mary, "I appreciate his friendship, but I'm afraid he and I don't run in the same circles financially. I seem to be meeting only the wealthy and social-minded people—that is strictly out of my class."

Turning his attraction to a modest lifestyle, Bill assured Mary that she fit perfectly into his vision.

> That's one thing that makes me happy about "us." We have about the same background and tastes. I'd like to have nice things, but I'm more interested in a place that is comfortable and built for living, not show. And that's why I like the way you dress—no fuss and feathers, but simple and attractive clothes. I haven't seen you in anything that didn't suit me to a "T." I know I'll be mighty proud to tell everybody that the beautiful brunette beside me is my wife. How can we arrange it that all our children will take after their mother's side of the family? Stay sweet! I love you heaps and heaps, Bill.

On February 12, Bill wrote Mary, telling her that nothing exciting happened that day, but he "can't let a day go by without telling you I love you."

The next night he wrote again.

> Mary, my sweet, it just doesn't seem possible that it is only a month tonight since we spent those precious moments in your apartment.... So much has happened in a month's time but there has been too much free time that the hours often seemed to drag. The weeks have only made me more certain of my love for you though. I hope that the days will pass rapidly for you, and I think I'll be much happier when the course begins next Monday. Regardless of how interesting and valuable the coming year will be, I know that there will be a great

regret that you can't be here, and we are separated so long. So, it does my old heart good to hear you talking about the "day" and of hope chests and linen tablecloths. Just the last few nights I've been mentally busy, thinking about our home and furniture and such stuff. It's silly in a way, isn't it? It's a lot of fun though. And I think we will both enjoy making plans even if we have to make them across 3000 miles of water.

He then described another fancy evening with Hal's friend, involving dinner at the swanky Rainbow Restaurant with a concert pianist playing Beethoven's *Piano Concerto No. 5*. He added, "The atmosphere was strictly high class. I still prefer the Poinsett, especially after being there with you…. God bless you, my sweetheart, All my love."

Bill "scribbled" another letter to Mary on February 14, after a busy Valentine's Day and the opening festivities at the University in Stockholm. "Honeychile! It's 1:00 a.m. and well past my bedtime, but you are much more important than a little sleep. The goblins would probably chase me in my dreams if I didn't scribble a few lines before I close my eyes."

Regarding the university's opening festivities, Bill wrote, "They really did things up brown," describing speeches by the consul general, the US cultural minister, and various other dignitaries, followed by drinks and a dance with live music.

The band was HOT—I don't know whether it was the American influence or whether they naturally play the jive style pieces most of the time. I enjoyed some of the slower dances—getting old I guess…. There were more pretty girls than I've seen the rest of the time I've been in Sweden—but they all lack that certain something you have, Mary. Or maybe there is a bond between us that changes our perspective. At any rate I know I missed you all evening. I love you, Mary.

The next night, Bill was thrilled about his move to downtown Stockholm. "Boy, I feel wonderful now—a good hot soak and bath makes a man feel great. You see I'm finding out how swell our new home is. Already it seems like a new world after our cold, dull days in

Lidings. I think we are going to be very happy here." He drew an even more detailed diagram of the new apartment and described the furnishings. Everything was great, except that he would not have hot water for two weeks due to a shortage in the coal and fuel supply. Despite all the "high class" events Bill had been experiencing, the lack of basic resources and materials in Sweden was a clear reminder that the post-war recovery still had a long way to go.

Bill's three-page letter that night concluded with his response to a letter he received from Mary that day.

> This morning I got the letter you wrote on Thursday. You are a cruel girl to talk about what a happy time we could have there "playing house"—but I loved it. I could see it so vividly that I could almost taste your cooking and could almost feel you in my arms. You needn't worry about my running off anywhere without you. I won't get a step away from your apron strings. Of course, I could take turns and tell you how perfect it would be to have you here with me tonight. I'm all alone too—Hal's out with the prettiest girl I've seen in Stockholm. So, I certainly could make you comfortable in our cozy new home. There will come a time though, Mary, and we must try not to be impatient. I know that I will value such happiness all the more dearly because of the years that I've been wandering around and the long miles of separation from the one I love so dearly…. Your Bill.

Bill started his next daily letter to Mary, "Somehow, I always seem to miss you most on Sundays." He had attended a lackluster church that morning, near the central station. This time, the congregation responded feebly to the liturgy, so Bill was disappointed with the service. Afterward, Bill traveled by train to the home of the Asp family in Tureberg, a small resort town about twenty minutes from Stockholm. He had met the Asps' daughter on the *Gripsholm*. He described the Asps as "an average middle-class family I would imagine," but he was still treated in grand style. Coffee and cakes, a walk down to a frozen lake, and pre-dinner drinks of vermouth, Four Roses bourbon, and soda water started the afternoon. Bill took the whisky doused with plenty of soda water. Apparently, even a middle-class family hosting an American put out a special smorgasbord, with "pickled herring first, then smoked salmon, crab mayonnaise, stewed eel, a sort of omelet with mushroom sauce over it, tiny little meatballs with fried onions (the last two hot), liver paste and pickles, and finally three types of cheese (Roquefort, Swiss, and Swedish)," all washed down with vermouth and schnapps—and beer as a chaser. And that was just the appetizers. The main course included "Swiss steak, big white asparagus, peas and carrots." Dessert was home-canned raspberries and sugar cake, accompanied by a glass of Madeira, coffee, and some homemade liqueur. Bill told Mary that "the liqueur looked like number 20 motor oil but tasted slightly different." He mentioned that his mama had accused him of "taking up drinking," but he explained to Mary that he had not "been able to figure any way to refuse the drinks without hurting the host's feelings."

That night, he closed his letter, "It's bedtime, so I'll give your picture a goodnight kiss and climb under the covers. I must say that your lips are a bit more enticing than cold glass. Always yours, Bill."

Bill's classes started at Stockholm University on February 17, 1947. He attended lectures on sociology, economics, industrial development, and Scandinavian literature, followed by breakout groups to learn the Swedish language. Having already been tutored for four weeks, he joined the higher-level group in Swedish. When his Swedish tutor, Mr. Jansson, offered to continue Bill's separate lessons, Bill quickly agreed. Having a strong grasp of the Swedish language was imperative if he wanted to truly experience Sweden over the next many months.

That night Bill wrote Mary, thankful that he had only two classes the next day. He told her he would use the extra time to write Mary's parents: "I hardly know what to say except that I love their daughter and will spend the rest of my life trying to be worthy of her." He still felt guilty about having proposed to Mary without first meeting her parents and getting her father's blessing. Writing them without meeting them was not a suitable substitute, but it was the only option available.

Meanwhile, Bill found that his cooking skills were sadly lacking, limited to making a good pot of coffee and some toasted cheese sand-wiches for lunch. In his letter that Tuesday night, he deferred future meal preparation to Mary. "I'll leave the kitchen to you, little one. I enjoy puttering around occasionally and even wiping a dish or two, but I would much rather eat your cooking. It will be great to be able to hear you around the house when I'm busy in my study and when there will be no more separation."

He ended the letter, "Every time I get one of your letters, Mary, I feel like a new man. You have been mighty sweet about writing, but of course you are a mighty sweet girl. God bless you always, your own Bill."

The next day, as promised, Bill confirmed he had finally sent a letter to Mary's parents, who lived in Cross, South Carolina.

I did take time out to write your mother and dad. It was a rather peculiar situation, you must admit. And what's more, I just remembered that I didn't even think about asking your parents if I could marry their daughter. I suppose we are just too modern and independent these days to think about such things. But I gather from your letters that we have their ap-proval. It's too bad that we didn't have time to visit in Cross before I left the States.

That night, with tired eyes and a lonely heart, he closed his letter to Mary, "My bed looks pretty good right now. Getting up at seven is a bit different from the hours we used to keep before school started. So long for tonight. I love you more every day—and miss you more, too, unfortunately."

Bill started his daily letter to Mary on February 21, with his ver-sion of a want ad. "Honeychile! Your man has had a busy day. What I need is a wife to come home to and a nice open fire to sit by. I might possibly be persuaded to take the wife without the fire. If you hear of anybody that's interested in the job, let me know."

His busy day had included his first experience with a Swedish steam bath at the invitation of one of the assistant professors. "First, we went into the steam room where we roasted until we were cherry red (temperature 150 degrees), and then we went to the washroom to get clean (it was just as hot there). After taking a shower, we went into the big pool for a swim. The water was cold and salty. It leaves you feeling like a million dollars." To top it off, they had gone to a restaurant where they enjoyed "reindeer hamburgers."

With that letter, Bill sent a photo clipped from the Stockholm newspaper. In it, Bill was posing with a female student from Mississippi. The photo, taken from his rear, showed the girl, a "Southern belle," facing the camera with the back of Bill's suit in the foreground, with no sign of his face. Bill was nonplussed. "The pictures of our coeds were in the paper tonight. The back and fanny to the left belongs to one Bill from Jackson, Mississippi. You would have recognized me immediately, I'm sure. The gal is Lela Douglas from Oxford, Mississippi."

The next night, after a Saturday night party with "cocktails galore," Bill introduced yet another nickname for Mary. "It's almost bedtime my little apple dumpling, but I guess I can keep my eyes open long enough to finish the page." He added, "It was a very pleasant evening. My friend Dag likes you very much. Naturally, I have to tell all my friends about you. I love you! Sweet dreams! Bill."

On the following night, Bill was in a "mellow mood," listening to some good music on the radio. He let Mary know yet another reason why he loved her.

> Sweet Mary, this is a quiet Sunday evening and I'm all alone—except for your ever-present spirit. I've got your picture perched right up on the table so I can look right into your dear face. I'm awfully glad you are a brunette. Blondes always seem sort of lifeless and artificial. I wish I could tickle my nose in your hair now and catch its sweet smell that I remember so well. Did I ever tell you that I like your little "widow's peak" too? It will easily take the rest of my life telling you about all the things that make me love you.

As he enjoyed the radio, Bill also had the economic status of pastors on his mind.

> I've always wanted to have a good collection of records, but I've never had the money to get a decent phonograph. Preachers don't usually have much extra cash for things like that.

And I pray that I will never get to the place where money will ever be a consideration in my work. I would hate to be in a position where I didn't know all my congregation well and always be where they could call on me when they wish.

After reassuring Mary that he was writing her every day, he reminded her to keep the letters coming.

There was no mail again today—it's a week now since I've had a letter from you. That doesn't make this old boy very happy. I look forward so much to every letter that comes in. I guess I'm just impatient when it comes to things like that. But it's because I love you so much. Every little thing that brings you closer to me is something to be cherished. God bless you, Mary, and keep you safe and well. Your Bill.

Bill wrote his shortest letter yet the following evening, despondent about still getting no mail from Mary. "Sweetheart, I'm not in the writing mood tonight. Somehow, it was a mixed-up day and I've never had time to slow down at all. And there was no letter again today either—I'm just a spoiled brat, I guess. Tomorrow I only have three classes, so I'll take time off and scribble to my heart's content. So long now."

The next day, his "spirits took a decided change for the better," when two letters from Mary arrived. She had forgotten to mail the first one and sent two letters together. Despite having described his own "mind blank" just two days before, when he forgot about a Swedish lesson with his tutor and went to see a movie instead, Bill asked Mary how she got so absentminded that she forgot to mail a letter. "We can't afford for poppa and momma both to be that way. What chance would our youngsters have with parents like that?" But Bill turned the ten-day gap between letters into a positive. "The silence was not completely bad though. I've seen the day when I'd be imagining all kinds of things when letters wouldn't come. It's different now! It gives you a great feeling to have complete trust in a person and never have any doubts for a second. That's just the kind of girl you are, Mary—absolutely 'true blue.'"

For Bill, it was a perfect evening. Two letters from his sweetheart, followed by a "magnificent performance of Bach's Mass in B Minor at the concert hall with 250–300 voices and a 60-piece symphony orchestra." Suddenly a music critic, Bill felt Bach was a "master in composing inspiring religious music with a variety of expression and depth of feeling."

Apparently, on the other side of the ocean, Mary had finally received Bill's first monthly gift. So, he told her that he had another "little doodad" for her, something called a "TRAFAGEL." Rather than tell her what that was, he said, "Now start guessing!"

He closed his letter, "Don't get into too much mischief! Remember I've got my magic eye watching you. All my love, Bill."

On Thursday, February 27, Bill was happy, simply because he got yet another letter from Mary. "My Mary," he wrote, "After treating me so mean for a week, the mail man is going all out into the other direction now. I got another letter today. It really came quickly—S.C. to Sweden in three days. I was really surprised to see it leaning up against your picture when I came home this afternoon. The cleaning lady was here today, so I guess she put it there."

Mary had not been feeling well. Bill responded, "That headache and upset tummy business doesn't sound good, honeychile. You will have to take good care of yourself. You know I'm too far off to hold your hand and rub your forehead—much as I would like to. It couldn't be your cooking, could it? (That was a nasty crack—but too good an opportunity to miss!). Anyway, I hope they don't return…. Don't get into too much mischief, Butch. And take care of yourself. I wouldn't want you to be sick when I'm so far away."

Bill then included a diatribe about how Swedish men treat their women.

> Women have a very different position in Sweden than in America. You realize it gradually, but it becomes all the more obvious then. All the little common courtesies that American girls expect—and deserve—are unknown. A fellow never holds the girl's coat or pulls out her chair; it's unheard of to send flowers for a dance; the fellow is just liable to walk out of the door first; usually a couple goes "Dutch" or takes turn about paying for the evening's amusement; it's quite alright to put the girl on a streetcar and let her find her way home

alone—I don't think American males or females would like such a system.

He finished off his rant with a flourish.

After all the talk I heard about the beautiful girls in Sweden, I've been a bit disappointed. I haven't seen more than two or three that I consider really attractive. Most of them look better in ski clothes and sporty things than fancy dresses. Maybe that's because they are apt to wear a fancy dress and finish off with heavy wool stockings and ski boots. At any rate, they would all look sad besides you, sweet Mary. I'm a bit prejudiced!

Bill's next letter started with yet another nickname for Mary, more descriptions of young ladies, and food, always food!

Bright eyes! I had an unexpectedly good time last night. It was strictly an American evening. There were four girls: Lee, a sophisticated blonde glamour girl who is over here with her wealthy grandparents; Ann, a Swedish girl who has lived in the States most of her life; Tobey something-or-other, who is spending a year here with her aunt; and Ingrid, a big, husky Swedish girl who is plain and nice. Then there was Hal; Pete, another American student; Ingrid's brother; and me. We all sat on the floor and peeled apples for the pie Lee had promised to make. The food consisted of hot dogs, potato salad, pickles, peanut butter (the first I'd seen in Sweden and a prime favorite of mine), and cheese crackers. The pie was delicious—and a surprise since Lee doesn't look like the cooking type. We topped the pie with ice cream. Then after we had rested from our exertions, we popped popcorn. It was just a little bit of the US.

Perhaps in response to Bill's tales of going out most every night or his raising the issue in a prior letter, Mary must have addressed the subject of dating while apart. Bill replied, "I'm exactly like you about the dating proposition. Several times Hal or some other of the fellows have wanted me to go out with them, but I haven't the least desire to take a girl out. It is fun to get together with a group like last night and spend an enjoyable evening, but I'm constantly amazed at the way being in love changes your outlook on things."

While his outlook on love had cleared up nicely, Bill's outlook about his ministerial future was still uncertain. He had several options. He could keep studying, followed by an academic career as a full-time theologian or professor. He could work for the Lutheran World Federation, organizing churches internationally. Or he could go straight into a parish ministry back home. His initial thoughts favored the latter, but he was not sure where he might settle down. "I would like very much to get a church in Virginia or one of the Carolinas. I don't know how it will work out. North and South Carolina don't look with favor on fellows who go north to school." He planned to write the presidents of the synod in spring 1948 to tell them he is "available Jones." He assured Mary that he knew key people in Virginia and the Carolinas, so he felt confident about finding a church. "I am not in the market for a 'plum' either, so that will help."

He closed that letter by responding to Mary's continued questions about furniture. Mary was counting on some items from her parents, but Bill cautioned her about "cutting her parents off without a chair to their name.... Anyway, I won't care what's in the house as long as you are there. That's what counts."

The next night, after trudging to a neighborhood church for Sunday services in a brutal snowstorm, Bill penned another letter. "I wonder what you have been doing today. Sometimes I relax and try to imagine what's happening way over there in Greenville. But it's a bit too far for my mental telepathy to work most of the time. I just have to play 'make-believe' so I can be with you. It's a far cry from holding you tight in my arms like I'd love to do though. I love you with all my heart, Mary. Yours always, Bill."

Chapter 23

Life for Mary:
Greenville, South Carolina
(Spring 1947)

On the other side of the ocean, Mary anxiously awaited each of Bill's letters. She received his two letters from New York within a week of his departure. But she had to wait almost three weeks for the postcard and series of letters he wrote on the *Gripsholm*. The card came first, but the larger pack of letters, too heavy for air mail, came by slow boat. Mary, nervously hoping for news every passing day, was relieved that Bill had arrived in Sweden safely. She knew each crossing of the Atlantic, especially in the winter, carried significant risks. While ocean travel had improved dramatically since the *Titanic* disaster, ships were still being lost. Bill was now over three thousand miles away, but at least he was safe.

As the weeks went by, Mary was just as thrilled to receive Bill's daily letters as he was to get word from her. She began reciprocating, writing Bill once every three or four days.

For the first two months, she had thrown herself into her work, leaving whatever little social life she had behind. Bill's constant communications made her long days working on her public health projects feel a bit shorter. Every letter gave her an extra boost of energy. Without a car, her job hours were long and tiring. She had begun looking for a car, but new ones were scarce so soon after the end of the war and her application had not yet resulted in any available vehicle.

She was a bit concerned when Bill raised the issue of dating others while they were already engaged. Though their engagement had not been publicly declared in the traditional sense, she had no thoughts of going out with any guys, at least not on their own. Greenville was filled with eligible bachelors, and, without a ring on her finger, she was a likely target for their affections. However, she had chosen Bill as her "one and only." She was not about to share herself with anyone else, even if she was lonely in his absence. Instead, as the weather warmed up, she occasionally took advantage of going to events with girlfriends and groups, such as alumni weekends at Newberry and trips to the beach.

Luckily, she was used to being alone, having lived much of her life essentially as an only child. Still, she yearned for Bill's touch. She missed his arms around her, his kisses, his broad smile, and his warm brown eyes. The Christmas photo was nice, but it was no substitute for the real thing. Her confidence in Bill's steadfastness was reinforced by his diligence in letter writing and constant reassurance of his love for her. She only wished he could hold her rather than write her. In the evenings, she read each of his letters over and over, carefully penciling in the date they were written when Bill had included only the day of the week. Every letter was placed in a small leather portfolio Mary kept in the drawer of her bedside table. If she felt lonely, she could pull a letter or two out, reading them slowly and melting away the miles between them.

At least in her mind.

She tried to share her love for him in her letters. She could not match Bill's romantic phrases, which she adored regardless of how hopelessly corny they were. Rather than try to replicate Bill's prose, Mary simply expressed her trust and her sense that, despite their separation, their love was still growing stronger each day.

With what little time she had outside work, Mary focused on planning for the future. On trips home to see her parents, she and her mother began designating various pieces of furniture she might take once Bill returned and married her. A hope chest. Various silverware and glassware. She was not sure what furniture Bill had in mind, if any. So, she was creating her own list and knew she had at least a year to make it happen. She might trust in Bill's love, but she certainly had no idea if he had any sense when it came to furnishing an apartment or picking out kitchen utensils and appliances.

She would have her own back-up plan.

Of course, Bill had left so quickly that there was no formal engagement announcement, party, or diamond ring on her finger. It was a bit awkward when, after telling her girlfriends and colleagues that she was engaged, they all asked where Bill was, when she was going to introduce him, and why she did not have a ring. It was almost as if they thought she had made up an imaginary, out-of-town fiancé. After all, what guy would propose one night and immediately depart for another country, indeed another continent, leaving the girl he loves behind for over a year?

Mary understood why her friends were skeptical. However, she decided to trust Bill no matter how long he was away. His faithful letters and declarations of love helped her maintain that trust as the weeks and months passed by.

Her parents had taught her patience. She exercised that virtue every day.

Chapter 24

Letters from Stockholm
(March 1947)

My darling, the moon is shining brightly tonight. It is a shame to let it go to waste. I have a little difficulty imagining vividly enough to feel you in my arms, but I certainly wish you were here. Of course, it's really too cold out anyway to make love in the moonlight—it probably is even in S.C. But we could take a brisk walk to make us appreciate a nice warm room. Such talk! Pretty soon I'll have myself homesick, or lovesick, or something. I must admit that sometimes I feel ready to hop the next boat home and rush right down to Greenville. Thank goodness the time passes more rapidly now that I'm busy at school.

That was Bill's complete letter on Monday, March 3, 1947, less than two months after he left Mary at the train station. He wondered how in the world he would make it through a whole year and a half away from the love of his life. The next night, he acknowledged, "I didn't get much written last night—started dreaming and never did get back to earth."

In the morning, Bill was "quite pepped up after just reading [Mary's] latest epistle." Mary had described leading a health department presentation to a teachers' group. Bill encouraged the new project, noting that teachers can have a tremendous influence on the community. He closed his letter with one of his favorite phrases: "Don't get into too much mischief, little rascal. Your Bill."

Little did he know that later that evening, he would be the "rascal" getting into a lot of mischief—on skis. In his next letter, Bill couldn't wait to tell Mary all about it.

Hi, my little apple-dumpling, there were two letters waiting for me when I came in just now. Needless to say, they were a big boost to my morale. I needed it! Last night I went skiing for the first time in my life. I didn't know about it until late yesterday afternoon.... I borrowed boots, skis and poles and we went out to some woods in a suburb of Stockholm.... You would have died laughing at my antics. It seemed as if I was spending half the time dragging myself out of the snow. I don't see how two little pieces of wood can go so many directions at the same time. Naturally, every time they went astray, I landed in the snow.

On the bright side, when not buried in snow, Bill had enjoyed a beautiful night, with a full moon illuminating the blankets of snow on the boughs of picturesque fir trees and across the mountain tops. But his description of his adventure was not yet done.

"Then we started cross-country! When we went uphill, I would go one step forward and three back at first. When we hit a well-traveled path, my feet would slide out from under me. When we went through un-broken snow, my skis would wobble and throw me. A gay time!" At the top of the uppermost hill, Bill "started out like a whiz before taking a header," but the rest of the trip downhill was "worth a hundred falls."

After skiing, the group went to an artist's house, for a "bath." Unabashed, Bill depicted the scene for Mary.

The five of us stripped and then headed out buck naked through the snowy yard to a little house about a hundred feet away. It was to be a Finnish bath, I learned. There was a roaring fire going into the airtight little building. We climbed on a bench so that we sat near the ceiling. They poured on the wood until we were sweating to beat the band. But that wasn't nuttin' yet. When the stove was cherry red, they threw water on it and made clouds of steam. Before that, I thought I was cooked to a turn, but when the steam hit me, I was sure I was home in Mississippi. When I breathed, it seemed I could feel my stomach burning. And all the while the Swedes were raving about how wonderful it all was. Well, after that torture, we went out and rolled in the snow. I had heard about such stuff—now I believe it. Then we went slopping through the house to the bathroom where we all dunked in a big tub of ice-cold water. And I must say that I felt like a new man after the brisk rub down! But I don't think I'll take that custom back to the States with me. Glad?

Despite having a Swedish test first thing the next morning, Bill did not get back to his apartment until 1:30 a.m. Academics always took a back seat to Bill's adventures.

Nevertheless, the next morning, Bill aced the test. Better still, upon returning to his apartment, he discovered two more letters from Mary waiting for him. This time, Mary must have described a speech she gave to the local Rotary Club and her frustration about having to arrange for rides as she still was without a car. Bill replied, "I know you must be anxious to broaden out in your work rather than having to wait around in Greenville as much. No doubt the Rotary boys were glad to have such a tasty speaker."

Ending his letter, Bill groused that, because his and Hal's room was such a mess, he was having to become a house cleaner. He quickly added, "Don't get any ideas, my sweet—the house will be your business except for odd jobs and a little dish wiping. And that only if you give me a kiss occasionally. Yours always, Bill."

Fortunately, Bill was over three thousand miles away when Mary read those comments.

By March 8, the snowfall accumulation in Stockholm had outpaced the street cleaners. With the added snow, Bill was giving skiing another try. "I'm going skiing again in the morning, so I'd better leave a line to tell you how many times I buried my nose in the snow." Luckily for Bill, the next morning, two young children were along, slowing the pace. As a result, Bill told Mary that "the ground and I were on little better terms today."

Apparently, the street cleaners caught up on the snow that afternoon, as Bill went to another concert that evening, this time Shubert's Stabat Mater with choir and orchestra. Ever the critic, Bill said, "It was pretty good, but not up to Bach."

He ended that letter much like the previous sixty letters, but, like

112

a piano composer, with yet another variation. "I miss you so much, Mary. A dozen times a day something comes up that makes me wish we were together. The time can't come too soon. I love you, Bill."

A letter from Mary's mother arrived on March 10. Bill had been nervously waiting for a reply to his letter to Mary's parents, promising them he would spend his life trying to be worthy of marrying their daughter. But when he read the letter, he realized that he had worried unnecessarily. He told Mary that her mother was "mighty sweet and understanding." "It makes me all the more anxious to know your mom and dad," he wrote. "It's wonderful how they have accepted me sight unseen."

That same day, Bill got another letter from Mary, disclosing that Betty was planning to marry Ted, the Methodist seminarian in New York Bill had met just before heading for Sweden. Bill quickly sent Betty a letter giving his approval. A few weeks later, Bill learned that Betty had canceled her plans to go to China as a Lutheran missionary. He told Mary, "I know Betty must feel pretty bad about having to tell the board that it is all off. She gets into more predicaments. I'm afraid Mama doesn't particularly like the idea of Betty becoming a Methodist. She is a dyed-in-the-wool Lutheran all right. I know Betty would be much happier marrying a Lutheran minister, but that seems secondary to me."

Bill thanked God that Mary was a good Lutheran and there would be no denominational asymmetry in his marriage.

Another letter from Mary arrived on March 12. "There was a mighty sweet letter waiting for me when I got home. You are awfully good about writing and I really appreciate it. It helps to cut down the distance when letters come through so regularly and often." Bill added, "It sounds as if your work is getting more interesting. I'm glad because I am happy only when you are. That's because I love you so much, Bill."

"Our anniversary" was the title of Bill's letter the next night, March 13, 1947. It had been exactly two months since his proposal was accepted. "I think this month has passed in a hurry—much faster than the first, but it seems ages since that evening when you said 'Yes.' It has helped to be in school and have my time filled up. I wish that we could go back and start all over though. About every other day would suit me.

It was a wonderful time, sweet Mary. I love you more all the time."

He then abruptly and randomly changed the subject. "Speaking of pies (who was?), my favorite is butterscotch mix. Betty usually makes one for me when she is around—did you get a piece when I was in Burlington? You needn't send a piece through the mail. It might get a bit mussed. God bless you, Mary. You have all my love, Bill."

Bill was a bad boy on Friday, March 14. He cut class that afternoon, but he had a good excuse. Having run out of meal rations, he had to get his next six-week supply of food to avoid going hungry through the weekend. He told Mary that he could get all the bread, butter, and sugar that he needed, but he had to go slow on the meat: "One small portion once a day."

He started his letter that night with yet another nickname for Mary. "Hi there, my brown-eyed sweetie pie!" He then described going to a Swedish movie with Hal and Gertie, a Swedish girl who lived in the same apartment building. Just as they were going into the theater, Gertie's fiancé, a Swedish soldier, drove by. As Bill described it, "Fire glinted from his eyes as he slammed on his brakes. Gertie must have calmed him down because he came on to the movie with us." In a later letter, Bill told Mary that despite the rough start, he became good friends with the soldier.

Bill also described a "masquerade ball" he planned to attend on Saturday. But he told Mary that they do things differently in Sweden. No dates. Men and women were to come separately. "They also invite a bunch of town girls, so that there are many more women than men. I hear that the chorus girls from the shows turn out in mass, and it generally ends up in a wild brawl. You would think that the University considers that part of a person's education is teaching students to drink. I think I'll stick to American ideas on that."

Even without a drink, Bill was happy that Saturday. Two letters from Mary arrived. One came in five days and the other in three days. "Quick service, I'd say! It is better if they came singly though because they last longer that way. I couldn't possibly leave one over until the next day. I suppose you are at home now, or maybe at an alumni dinner. I wish I could be with you—by your side and content with the world. I'll just have to crawl into bed with an order for a dream of you. Your

Bill."

On Sunday night, Bill wrote again: "My sweet Mary, it was a lovely day to take a stroll around Stockholm. You should have been here to give me the inspiration. Tain't no fun doing it by myself!" He described being impressed by Pastor Nils Bolander, the preacher at the main cathedral that morning. He had a "fine personality and a forceful, striking way of saying things," and the church was always full when he took the pulpit. However, Bill conceded that even with Swedish lessons, he "could understand only a little of what he said."

In one of her letters, Mary must have told him she had gone to Newberry for an alumni weekend. Bill replied, with a strong sense of nostalgia.

> You are probably headed back to Greenville tired out after a busy weekend. It's too bad I'm not going to be there to furnish a willing shoulder so you could cuddle up and go to sleep. Every once in a while, I think back to last summer and Thanksgiving when I wasn't sure what you thought of me and can't help but grin at myself. You were such a prim little lady! But it just made the first kiss that much more precious! Gee, but I love you Mary. God bless you always.

On Monday morning, March 17, Bill got a third letter from Mary in just a few days, including a report on a visit from Buck and Sue. Instead of waiting until that night, Bill quickly responded, "I'm just mad 'cause I'm not close enough to make it a foursome." He also commiserated with Mary concerning her search for a car. "You are certainly getting the run-around on the car deal. I hope something breaks soon. You can be sure that any kind will suit me, as long as a certain brunette goes with it. If you could have seen my old '34 Chevy, you would understand that I'm not so particular about what I ride in. 'Jasper' was a great little baby, though!"

Mary also must have mentioned the possibility of sitting for a portrait, as Bill closed his letter, "That business about your having your portrait painted sounds interesting. Naturally, I can understand and agree with her choice of subject. I never get my fill of sitting in front of your picture. With a hug and kiss, Bill."

As spring was in the air, Bill's next letter to Mary focused on an upcoming ski trip to Lapland over Easter vacation. He worried about the $50 cost of the ten-day trip, as his budget for a whole month was $65, but he told Mary, "I'm here to see Swedish life and customs and I don't think I ought to miss that." He planned to leave on March 31 and return on April 11, so he provided Mary with an address for her next two letters. He could not bear to go two weeks without hearing from her.

Bill's skiing skills had progressed, but he still had plenty of room for improvement. After a trial run on loaner military skis on March 19, Bill wrote,

> You should have been around earlier this evening to help me pick myself up out of the snow. Since we got the equipment from the Swedish army, we had to try the things out. Fortunately, we now live near a pretty nice skiing place, so Hal and I took off after school. The recent thawing had left a hard crust in the snow, so it was pretty fast. We took a few easy runs and then went up a pretty good size hill to try our wings. It really felt like I was flying! A couple times I made the run like a veteran, but most of the time I would wind up in the snow. A couple of times, I fell so hard that my skis came off and went sailing on down the hill by themselves. We had a wonderful time anyway. Fortunately, you are going so fast when you fall that the impetus eases your contact with the ground.

His letter that night also answered the question: What in the world is a Trafagel, the gift he had sent to Mary the prior month? "In Sweden, it is a kind of bird of peace. You hang it on the window shade or something and nobody in the room can say anything bad about anyone else."

Bill wondered if such a trinket would work in America.

After reminding Mary to study the two Swedish books he had sent her, Bill had another idea.

> When we get settled down in our home, I hope we can plan time so that we can do a little reading or studying together

116

along some line. I think it would be nice if we could find something that we could 'major' in as a sort of hobby. It might be nice if we set aside 10–11 in the evenings for various kinds of reading. A preacher needs it, and I'm too poorly acquainted with good classic literature. You ought to keep up on your public health work too."

He closed, "So long for now sweetheart. I love you heaps and heaps. Your Bill."

"Heaps and heaps" also described his efforts to "tackle a gigantic pile of laundry." He wrote, "As you doubtless know, this old man has been wishing all day that he had a wife to take over such chores. Of course, I know wives are good for more than keeping a fellow's clothes clean!! And I will be glad to buy you a washing machine! Sorry a preacher's salary won't allow a lot of luxuries, but I'll try to make up for it in other ways."

Bill also shared with Mary problems in post-war Sweden. The government had decided to ration coffee to half a pound per person until April 8: "That strikes right at a Swede's heart. The Social-Democrats are all-powerful, but they have taken a lot of criticism on the Russian trade agreement and the heavy taxes. Even though the people grumbled, there was no serious opposition until they started rationing coffee. Now a couple of the cabinet ministers are apt to get kicked out." He ended his letter, "Well, the iron is hot, and the bottom of the page is near, so I'll just have to wrap up a couple kisses and stick them in the corner and send them off to you. God bless you, my Mary. My heart is always with you. Ever yours, Bill."

That weekend, Bill went to a youth gathering at a large house a few miles outside of Stockholm. Despite his many social outings, in his Sunday night letter, he tried to convince Mary he was not a gadabout.

Dearest Mary, there was the nicest letter perched up on the table smiling at me when I got back from the weekend with the student group. I guess I'm getting old or something, because I think I would be perfectly content just to sit here in the apartment every night in the week. And with you at home,

I'm not sure that you could stir me with a stick. I'm just a home-loving boy!

He finished his letter, "And so to bed! I certainly do need you, Mary. I miss you so. Bill."

March 24 was a "hunky-dory" day, as it was a national holiday in Sweden. To celebrate, Bill and Hal hosted an American meal for Gertie and a few other friends. Bill spent a week's worth of meat rations to buy some steaks. His menu also included Southern-style rice, spaghetti, and cheese. For dessert he found a nice gelatin mold in his landlord's kitchen. "Goodness knows how it will turn out," he wrote Mary. Bill later claimed the meal was a success, but his rice "wasn't as dry and separated as I would like, and the cream for the jello wouldn't whip (how did I know coffee cream wouldn't work?), but we ate it with gusto."

Suffice it to say, Bill would never be much of a menu-planner, cook, or house cleaner.

Toward the end of his letter, he responded to Mary's last letter about her outreach to minority groups. "Does your work here have to do with negro health education as well as for the whites? I have been greatly interested in the negro situation in the last few years and would like to make that a major interest if I get a parish in the South. What are your ideas along that line? Any strong prejudices?"

Thankfully, despite being a Southern girl raised in the thirties and forties, Mary had no such prejudices. She had grown up with "Uncle Hince" and "Aunt Julia" at the Saluda County farm, being taught that they were also God's children and deserved to be treated with dignity, respect, and equality. They were part of her family.

At the bottom of the letter, Bill added, "Bye, bye, baby! It's time for me to go fill my gish! Wish you could tuck your hand under my arm and go along. All my love, Bill."

On March 27, 1947, Bill hit the jackpot. "Mary, lilla, it was a great day for the mailman today. I got a letter from every member of the family.... It was particularly good to hear from Clare and Betty."

Clare apparently had been snowed in for seven days, but Bill was more worried about Betty, whose engagement to Methodist minister Ted had cratered her missionary plans. "It's funny—Betty is the one in the family that you would expect to be very calm and collected about things, but she makes up her mind pretty quickly about some things. I'm a fine one to talk like that—but we did know a lot about each other's backgrounds and family. It's hard for parents to accept a complete stranger." Ironically, Mary's parents had accepted him even though he was also a complete stranger. The difference was simple. Like Mary and her parents, Bill was a good Lutheran. But Bill would always feel a bit guilty about not having gotten their approval before proposing marriage to their daughter.

As Bill's classes in the fall would be in Uppsala, a city approximately thirty-five miles north of Stockholm, he planned to travel there the next day to arrange his fall schedule. He promised Mary he would describe Uppsala once back.

The next night Bill opened his letter, "Mary, my darling, do you think you could blow me a kiss over this way? There is some nice music on the radio and putting me in a sentimental mood. And I can't say that looking at Hal's puss is much help. Saturday night is always a kinda lonely night for me, and I would so much love to be with you." He then described Uppsala as "a quaint old place," with a very impressive "domkyrka" cathedral, with its three dark spires and red-brick towers dominating the center of town and its magnificent organ beneath a circular blue stain glass window. A wedding was in progress when Bill visited the massive church.

> There were no attendants, male or female, and the bride walked down the aisle on the arm of her groom. It was a long walk—the cathedral is 100 meters (112 yards) long from door to altar. Brides in Sweden wear little crowns—two or three inches in diameter—which are beautifully worked in gold or silver and sometimes set with stones. Usually, they belong to the church or a family. It seems like a right nice custom.

Even in a strange land, over three thousand miles from his sweet Mary, Bill was already checking out marriage ceremonies!

On that Sunday, Bill and Hal went to hear Pastor Bolander preach again. Mentally taking notes, Bill told Mary that he hoped he could someday become a great preacher,

> I'm quite a booster for Bolander—he is my idea of a topnotch preacher. He hits straight from the shoulder and has a striking

way of saying things that is modern and impelling. Preaching is a tremendous challenge to me. I hope I can be effective at it. I feel that if a person is going to be a fit vessel for God's Word that must be the only consideration. That means that salary or people's opinion come far down the list. Do you think you will be ready to stick by that? It can mean a lot of unpleasantness at times, but I am convinced that the ministry needs such an attitude and that only God's Word can really challenge the church of today.

That evening, a group of students, including Bill, was invited to the home of a former Swedish consul general, a "tremendous man with white hair who is supposed to be a millionaire." The man's beautifully furnished house near the river was "filled with fine paintings and sculptures and a library filled with beautiful leatherbound books." Knowing that he was heading the next day for his Lapland ski trek, Bill feasted on "lamb roast, potatoes, beans and green salads, followed by lemon meringue pie—fallen but tasty—and chocolate cake." Not knowing when he would get his next good meal, he had two helpings of everything. He finished his letter to Mary that night, "It would be fun to have you along to struggle through those 18 miles of skiing with me. Guess you could make it? All my love, Bill."

Before heading for Lapland, the next morning Bill got what he described as an "army bunk" letter from Mary. It is not clear where Mary had slept on such a bed, but Bill noted that she "did not seem to speak too highly of the accommodation." Bill told her that since he had experienced army bunks for years, it was good she could also have that experience. He quickly added, "I'm glad I had my army years, but I'd certainly hate to go through it again."

This was a rare, passing comment from Bill about his stint in the army and World War II. He had survived it, barely, but he never dwelt on it—at least not out loud. It is uncertain how much he shared with Mary about his tour of duty before they got engaged.

With that letter, Bill also enclosed his monthly souvenir gift, this time a little pendant with Sweden's three crowns on it, writing, "My love goes with it, as it does every minute of the day for that matter. You are the best part of me now. Love always, Bill."

Chapter 25

Ski Trip to Lapland
(April 1–11, 1947)

Aptly, April Fool's Day, 1947, was the day Bill left for his ten-day ski trip to Lapland during spring break. Having hardly mastered cross-country skiing, Bill sensed that going on a trek of this magnitude was probably foolhardy. However, he almost never turned down an adventure.

The trip started with "a long train ride, a night on a baggage rack, and a four-hour bus trip" to a town called Saxuas. After a short pit stop, his group strapped on skis and headed out along the edge of a lake. After four miles, they cut across the ice for another five to six miles to a farmhouse where they went in for cocoa and buns. "We ate like ravenous wolves," he wrote Mary later that night. But they still were not finished. After leaving the lakeside farmhouse, they skied through the woods for another ten miles, finally arriving in the small town of Lorberg at 5:30 p.m.

"Dearest Mary," Bill began his letter that evening, "I don't know how I will be able to hold my eyes open to write much tonight. It has been a long time since I've been so completely exhausted… Every few minutes they would say that it was only a few more kilometers farther. I've had it!" He scribbled another half page the next morning so that he could get his letter in the mail before heading out for another day in the snow. "Can't let my little honeychile wait all that long for a letter." He told her that he "slept like a log last night and felt quite chipper" though he was still "plenty stiff."

After another exhausting day, Bill wrote again. "Mary, my sweet, it looks like all I will be doing the next few days will be skiing, eating, writing to you, and sleeping." That day, the group had slowly and steadily climbed a mountain, reaching the top at two p.m. "It was a beautiful day," he wrote. "The sun was out in all its glory and made movie scenery of all the mountains and the lake. All the mountains were covered with snow above the timberline and the beauty almost took your breath away."

But the trip down the mountain was the real adventure. Bill had taken the first gentle slope perfectly. But the next one was steep, long, and a bit rocky and "gave me my baptism of snow for the day—3 times." Then he hit a wooded trail which was "as crooked as a snake track." This was a major problem, as Bill had not yet learned how to turn. "After the first 100 falls, I stopped counting. It was funny how I always managed to bury my head. But the snow was so deep I couldn't hurt myself." Before he fell asleep that night, he finished his letter, "You should certainly be around to put my head on your shoulder. I'm very much afraid I would go to sleep though."

The next day, Bill and his group began to tackle an even steeper mountain. Looking at the snowcapped peak, he thought it would be impossible to climb on skis. However, he endured, finding it "wonderful to stand on top and see the world." By the time they finished, Bill was dead tired, but this time he told Mary it was a "pleasant kind of tiredness and I suppose I'll get over it eventually." He even suggested that when he got back to America, Mary would have to try it.

Bill really did not know his fiancée that well. Mary had many loves and hobbies, but none of them involved mountain ski trips or any other strenuous sports.

"Dear Mary," Bill started his April 5 letter, "I can't remember when I was so exhausted and sore as I was last night. I never thought I would be able to drag myself back to Lorberg." That day, with the air clear and the sun brightly shining, Bill and the group had gone across a lake and downward through a steep, wooded, and winding trail. "It was a photographer's paradise." In the afternoon, under a blazing sun, the group had attacked a series of ridges. Bill, soaked with perspiration, shed his jacket and skied in just a shirt. Several of the guys stripped to their waists, their torsos glistening in the bright sun. But at the top of the ridges, the brisk mountain breeze was freezing, causing them to add more layers. Bill was thrilled when he neared the top of one crest, but his excitement was temporary. "You can imagine my feelings when I got around the edge and saw that we were heading for a bigger mountain behind. I almost gave up! But after going so far, I couldn't stop. I'll never know how I finally managed it. And what a view! You could see in every direction. The beauty and the icy wind really took your breath away." The group finally made it back to Lorberg, with Bill collapsing in a heap on arrival, every ounce of energy sapped from his body.

The bright sun had taken its toll. That night he told Mary, "You should see my beet-red face." And just to make sure Mary knew how much he really wished she could see him, he ended his letter, "The mail goes out today, so I'll get my epistle off. I wish I could climb in the envelope and spend a while with you. I hope you will have a happy and blessed Easter, Your Bill."

That Sunday, Bill went to the local church in Lorberg, which had a Pentecostal meeting. Bill felt it was a "fine service, simple but sincere." He even knew a few of the hymns, including "Rock of Ages." For once, he understood practically every word, leading him to feel his Swedish comprehension was coming along nicely.

Despite his sore muscles and sunburned face, the biggest problem for Bill on this trip was a lack of letters from Mary. "It's been so long since I had a letter from you—a whole week as a matter of fact. I'm hoping that I'll have one when the mailman comes again on Wednesday. We start back on Thursday, arriving in Stockholm Friday morning." He added, "I miss you all the time, sweet Mary. God bless you and keep you well and happy always, Bill."

On Friday, April 11, Bill described the end of his ski trip.

In the hustle and hurry of getting off and coming down on the train, I missed writing you too. We had to get up at dawn to eat breakfast and get on our way to ski the 18 miles down the lake to Saxuas. I pulled a muscle in my heel the last day, so I wasn't too spry. However, the miles went pretty rapidly. The best part of getting to Saxuas was finding a letter from you. Hal had it for me.... All in all, the trip to Lapland was swell. It was fun trying to go up and down these mountains on skis even though I took plenty of falls doing it. Being in the mountains in wintertime was a new experience, and I know I'll never forget some of those wonderful views of the snow-capped fjalls (that's mountains, my dear). But I was too poor a skier to enjoy a longer stay—even though I was much more confident at the last and was beginning to stand up on a lot of spots that would have thrown me earlier.

Another letter from Mary was waiting for him when he finally got back to Stockholm. He had good news for her in response.

More and more when I hear from you, I am convinced that God was leading us to each other. You certainly fit all my dreams of what I want in a wife. I hope that we can always keep our lives as a partnership in all our work. And as the days go by, I think that perhaps it is best that you do have your contract to fill. Your work will give you a lot of ideas and experiences that will strengthen our work together.... I have already decided to cut my stay a month or two so I can get back about the time you quit work. Surprised? I don't imagine so!.... I love you, Bill.

Apparently, Bill assumed Mary would stop working when he returned to the United States, more proof that he did not know his fiancée that well when he proposed to her.

Chapter 26

Letters from Stockholm
(April 12–13, 1947)

Bill's first full day back in Stockholm after the ski trip was made special by yet another letter from Mary, which "started the day off right." Mary had just visited her brother. When Bill wrote her back that afternoon, he focused on marriage. "I know you must have had a great time with Buck and Sue—and I understand perfectly the feeling you got when you are around a happily married couple. It does something to you alright." He continued, "There were a couple of awfully nice, engaged couples up in Lapland with us, and Charlie and I would look at them and wish we were back in Utah and S.C., with our sweethearts. It was right hard to take sometimes. But we will have our day—about 1/6th of the time is up today!"

Nevertheless, Bill's social life seemingly went on unimpeded. "Hal has roped me into a foursome tonight with an American girl from the legation that was up at Saxuas. Her roommate is an English-Finnish girl. I hope it is not too boring." He reported on the evening the next day, making sure he let Mary know that he did not find the girls too attractive.

> Hi Butch! .... Last night was quite pleasant. We took in a queer English film with David Niven starring and then went to the girls' apartment where we had some sort of Russian pancakes and some delicious chocolate cake (home-baked). Coca Cola too—first in Sweden—thanks to the legation commissary. The girls were nice but nothing extra—one lisped and the other was the sedate, motherly type.

His critical eye continued in the next paragraph, in which he lamented that Gertie, the pretty fellow apartment renter, had quit her job to get married to her soldier guy. Her replacement was a "sad change from Gertie—bowlegged, over painted, and fresh from the country." But Gertie's replacement did not last long. Her boyfriend moved into her room without permission from the apartment proprietor who "wouldn't stand for such stuff." The next day, the girl did not show up for work and never returned.

Bill also sympathized with Mary over a series of shots she had received to deal with a persistent sore throat. "I trust you are over those shots by this time. They aren't much fun. In the five days it took me to get to England after I was wounded, I got a shot every four hours, and you would have thought my arms were pin cushions from all the holes. I hope that throat will be okay now."

Instead of moping in his apartment, Bill told Mary he was going to take a walk in the beautiful, sunny day. "I'll play like you are along swinging hands with me. It's good to have a good imagination. Always, your Bill."

The next day, Bill told Mary about an upcoming series of "Discussions on America" which included a final social event at a local zoo in Stockholm. Bill and three others were working up a singing quartet for a little entertainment. "It's been so long time since I've done any singing that I sound like a frog, but maybe a week's practice will help. It will be four anyway." On that subject, Bill told Mary he hoped to have a boys' or maybe a children's choir when he gets a church. "There is something about that kind of work that is exciting. The kids get a big kick out of it too when it is done right."

The following day, Bill attended a large youth gathering attended by four or five thousand people. The program dealt with the biggest problem churches face all over the world, i.e., how to reach young people effectively. They too often become missing in action after confirmation. Bill had a few ideas to deal with the problem, which he shared with Mary.

One thing I would like to work toward is a sort of family night at the church every week. That would be the night for all sorts of meetings and classes, choir practice, scouts, etc.... I think it would be possible for most churches to have more of a weekday program than they do. Gee, we have a lot of planning and work to do. We will be old and gray by the time we get through with all the plans we have stored up.

As he finished the letter, Bill could not help but point out that Mary's next letter was behind schedule. "A letter is a day or so overdue, but I hope you still love me a tiny little bit. My heart's still pounding away over here for my S.C. sweetheart. Your Bill."

Chapter 27

Greenville, South Carolina
(April 1947)

One Saturday morning in early April 1947, Mary got great news. Her long-awaited car had finally arrived. Her Greenville Health Department director was fully aware of Mary's need for transportation. Until then, she was having to find rides all over the county to press forward with the department's initiatives. Totally dependent on others to get her where she needed to be, she was getting run down with the effort.

Luckily, the director knew a local bank manager who arranged to keep his bank open on Saturday afternoon so Mary could pick up her war bonds to make her down payment. The loan was quickly approved. On the following Monday, Mary beamed as she drove the brand-new Ford to the State Highway Department to register it and pick up a license plate.

At the same time, this exciting event for Mary came with a substantial level of trepidation. Perhaps because of her father's endless farm loan obligations when she was a child, Mary did not like borrowing money. She cringed at the thought of being personally responsible for car payments. Worse yet, the busy Greenville streets, with cars honking at anyone going too slow, made her quite nervous at first. She had learned to drive on the isolated Saluda County farm, but she had rarely practiced her driving skills on real streets. Nevertheless, Mary, no matter how much she fretted, was up for the challenge. Soon, she was proudly driving her shiny Ford all around town and beyond.

Mary could not wait to tell Bill all about it. Bill had never owned a new car, so she knew he would be a bit jealous of her good fortune. She shared with him her concerns about the ongoing car payments, saying she wanted to have enough money left over to get married when he returned.

Bill quickly responded. "Hi, little sugarplum! So, you are riding around in a brand-new Ford these days! Good for you! I'd certainly like to be around to help you break it in. Don't bang up too many fenders, don't get too many parking tickets, and don't do any one-armed driving! You can leave that for me." As for the cost, Bill tried to alleviate her concerns.

And, silly girl, don't worry about what money or property you will have when we get married. You, yourself are the most precious gift any man could hope for. I keep pinching myself a dozen times a day to be sure that I'm not just dreaming that you are waiting for me way down in South Carolina. We won't have much to start with, and probably won't have much more at the end, but as long as we are happy together that's enough for me. We will trust that God will take care of our everyday needs.

Chapter 28

Letters from Stockholm and Uppsala
(April 18–May 24, 1947)

Henry Wallace, the thirty-third vice president of the United States (1941–1945), arrived in Stockholm in mid-April 1947 for an important speech. His Stockholm stop was part of a multi-country European tour intended to break through the so-called "silken curtain" and promote a "One World" foreign policy.

Wallace's speech was big news, so Bill naturally attended and told Mary about it that night. "Personally, I was a bit disappointed. He has a nice personality and is a very forceful speaker, but I thought his speech was rather weak. It's alright to be an idealist if you have a practical side to back it up. He didn't show that side last night. But I am convinced that he is utterly sincere in his program."

Wallace ultimately ran for president in 1948 but received only 2.4 percent of the popular vote after he was branded as a Russian sympathizer. In a 1952 article in *This Week*, Wallace later apologized for seeking conciliation with Russia and declared the Soviet Union to be "utterly evil."

On Sunday, April 19, Bill was thrilled to receive a package of goodies from his Aunt Ruth, including four big jars of peanut butter, his favorite food, along with bars of soap, boxes of Saya crackers and macaroni dinners, and three packages of dry noodle soup. He and his friends had quite a party sampling every item. That night, he told Mary, "My darling, you should have been here to play hostess tonight.... I always have an empty spot where only you could fill the bill. It's funny how I always miss you most when I'm visiting some place new and interesting or when I'm having a good time with friends—just whenever I'm particularly happy."

With spring having sprung, Bill was upbeat.

Bicycles have come out in droves. Now bright red, green, and orange awnings are going up on the dull, sickly-looking walls of the apartment houses to give them gay colors. It's amazing to see the change in the appearance of the girls, too. During the winter they were a homely, dismal looking bunch with their dark clothes, wool stockings, and heavy shoes. Now they have changed all that and are nearly as attractive as our American girls. Even the boys seem to spruce up a bit although they still stick mostly to their blacks, dark blues, and browns. They haven't cut their shaggy, messy looking hair though. It looks as if Swedish girls aren't the bosses in the family like they are in the U.S. You won't henpeck me too much will you? I'll promise to be good.

At the end of his letter, Bill reminded her, "Toot that horn a couple times for me. Your Bill."

The next day, Bill participated in the "Discussions on America," giving a speech on the South. He told Mary that he received some flattering comments, but, according to his roommate, not everyone agreed. "Hal was sitting behind a pretty girl, and being a bit of a wolf, he leaned over and asked her how she liked it. She replied, 'Americans are an arrogant bunch!' He realized she was English. Of course, she was right! But I think we are pretty decent people anyway."

The speeches behind them, Bill and three buddies rehearsed for his quartet's performance for the "Discussions on America" festival at a local restaurant, startling some of the stolid Swedes when they suddenly began to sing. Bill worried his voice was not in good enough shape to hit the high notes. "Goodness knows how it will turn out." A few days later, Bill finally reported his success. "I was right proud of our quartet. We sang five or six numbers and they got better as we went along. Maybe that was because the other fellows loosened up their voices with a few glasses of beer."

Despite his vocal success, Bill's enjoyment at the festival was muted. "I didn't dance all evening. Guess I just wasn't in the mood. It's funny how you can be in a place with good music and a lot of pretty girls, and then sit back and be merely an on-looker. I really think it was because you weren't there to dance with me. I wasn't in the mood to have substitutes.... Behave yourself, little rascal. Your Bill."

On April 24, after a lull in incoming mail, a letter from Mary arrived. "Mary, my sweet, that was a mighty welcome letter that was waiting for me when I got home this evening. Days always seem long and empty when a letter is a little longer in coming than I figure it should be. I guess I'm an impatient lover, that's all!"

Mary must have raised the subject of life insurance. Perhaps Bill's crazy ski trip adventures and wipeouts factored into her thinking. Bill assured her that he had a $2000 policy already in place and that he would consider increasing it by $3000 after returning to America, conditioned on his "right and privilege of seeing that you behave."

Bill then turned to an important new subject, Mary's potential engagement ring. Clare had spoken to Johnny's father, a jeweler. He had two diamonds, one in a white gold setting with two little diamonds on either side, and another that was unmounted. Johnny's father thought the loose stone was the better of the two, so Bill asked Mary to pick out the setting for it. Bill's preference was for a yellow gold setting, but he left it to Mary to make the final decision. "The only drawback to the whole business is that I won't be around to put the ring on your finger—but I'll try to do a quick and satisfactory job putting the wedding ring on when I get back."

He saved his best words for last.

"Sometimes at night when I go to bed, I lay there for an hour or so just thinking about you and how wonderful it will be to have you alone by me all the time, to dream and plan with, to work and play with, and to hold tight in my arms. It's going to be a great day, Mary, Bill."

A few days later, he wrote, "Sweet Mary, I was a bad boy yesterday—didn't write the whole day! Didn't do anything most of the day either." This was only the second day that Bill had not written Mary since he left her in Greenville. His excuse was the rainy weather and his problem getting clothes starched and washed. It was a pretty lame excuse given that he had found time to go see the film *The Jolson Story* that evening.

Not missing another day of writing, Bill started his next letter to Mary the following night, "Maria, lilla! Hur mar min sat flicka deuna le vall? Det har varit en mychet stilla dag, utau naget ovanlig. Ocksa megnada det hela dagen. Jag staunade hemma och studerade sasom en god papeu." He asked her, "Can you translate that?" then confessed, "It really doesn't make much difference since it doesn't say anything important. I'm not certain that it is correct Swedish anyway!"

This was the first of many paragraphs Bill wrote in Swedish, somehow hoping that Mary would translate it from two language books he had sent her. Whether Mary ever learned any Swedish or ever translated these paragraphs is unknown.

The next night, Bill was in "a very lazy and disagreeable mood for some reason." It was a rainy day, and Bill had spent all day in class. On top of that, there was no letter from Mary waiting for him when he got home. He told her, "I'll try not to bite your head off before I get to the bottom of the page. I get this way occasionally, so you may as well get used to it. You will have to furnish the inspiration for better things and all such stuff."

The rest of his letter was more positive. The last day in April was a party day for students, with May 1 being the Swedish Labor Day holiday. "The students will have a big blowout and get good and drunk, I'm told." For the celebration, Bill and a couple of his friends planned to ride their bikes up to Uppsala, a thirty-five-mile ride. Bill felt it would be good training for his summer bike trips to see other parts of Scandinavia.

The next day, Bill's ride to Uppsala took four hours, through a beautiful rolling countryside. The road ran parallel to the train track, with only a few steep hills. Bill got there just in time to watch Uppsala University's graduation ceremony, with hundreds of gown-clad students and faculty waving their white caps in the air as they ran down the hill from the campus library to the main streets of Uppsala. "That was all the excitement except that a few of the students fell down and were practically trampled to death, and a few of the dumber ones got a bit belligerent."

After the ceremony, the American students gathered for dinner at a restaurant in a refurbished eleventh-century jail, having a "swell time being American and singing the whole time." But Bill and his friend skipped the rowdier entertainment at another restaurant once they learned there was a cover charge. They were too tired to enjoy themselves anyway. Fortunately, they met some Mormon fellows who let them sleep on the floor of their apartment rather than having to take the train back to Stockholm that night.

Not being shy, Bill decided to show up the next morning, unannounced, at the home of the archbishop of Sweden on the outskirts of Uppsala. He was surprised to be taken right up to see him. Archbishop Erling Eidem and his wife, who were "quite cordial," had a very elegant house, with a big library and lots of paintings. The archbishop, while puffing on a big pipe, made Bill feel at home and seemed to take keen interest in his ministerial future. But the highlight for Bill was being asked to sign the archbishop's thick, leather-bound visitor book, realizing that the last four visitors were the archbishop of the Eastern Orthodox Church, a Lutheran bishop from Budapest, an important minister from Iceland, and Reinhold Niebuhr—"some big shots, eh?" Reinhold Niebuhr was an American Reformed theologian, a professor at Union Theological Seminary, a political commentator, and an author who wrote *Moral Man and Immoral Society* and who later received the Presidential Medal of Freedom in 1964. Bill had attended several lectures by Niebuhr when he briefly studied at Union Theological Seminary in summer 1946.

Bill's fellow theological students could not believe that he had been so bold as to visit the archbishop of Uppsala without any appointment or advance notice.

"Hi, my honeychile," Bill started his letter on May 2. He had waited to go to school that morning to see if the mailman would bring a letter from Mary. "And he did! That lifted my spirits to meet a rather gloomy, cold day." In her letter, Mary must have asked about the three crowns on the pendant Bill had sent her a month earlier. Bill told her that the "Swedes don't seem to know the real origin of the three crowns, but generally, it is thought to come from the days when Sweden, Denmark, and Norway were united into one kingdom." He suggested that the three crowns were to the Swedes what the bald eagle is to Americans, an impressive emblem of national pride. The same three crowns had adorned the *Gripsholm* stationery on which Bill had sent his first letters after leaving New York.

Bill finished that letter after midnight. That evening, he had gone to a "Swedish English-speaking club party." It was the "liveliest and most pleasant party I've been to in Sweden, I think. And best of all, there was nothing to drink." He had danced every dance for a change—to the music of a "little four-piece orchestra of high school kids...which was unusually good." After that, he had gone to a party at the American Legion post of Stockholm, but it was a "little too liquid." Regarding alcohol, Bill informed Mary that he probably would not join any veterans groups, primarily because most of them center around getting drunk. "I never feel right in such surroundings," he wrote. "I have no objection to temperate drinking, but too many fellows don't stop when they should." Bill also wanted to focus on the future rather than dwelling on or trying to numb the horrors of war with alcohol.

Instead, vacations and Mary's welfare were on Bill's mind. "Sweet Mary, you had better listen to the boss and take your vacation like a good girl. You know all about that 'all work and no play' business. Maybe you could take a week at a time, so you won't be away from the job too long at a time. I hope you and Betty can get together up at Dogwood Dell some time during the summer." As usual, he closed the letter more intimately. "The old moon was out in all her glory tonight. As I came home, I played like I had your hand tucked under my arm and we were strolling along as I dream about. I didn't sing 'There's going to be a great day!' but I was thinking it. Your Bill."

Bill's lunar and dream themes continued in his letter of May 5. "Hi little rascal, come over and take a peek at this big full moon! It isn't quite as yellow as the one you see in South Carolina, but we might be able to steal a kiss or two on a park bench just the same. It's spring all right." At the bottom of the page, Bill wrote, "Good night now, my little apple-dumpling. It's time to crawl under the cover and build us a few dream houses before I go to sleep."

The following morning, Bill responded to yet another letter from Mary. Mary's brother had taken a job in Jackson, Mississippi. Bill offered to ask his folks if they would take Marion and Sue in until they could find a place to live. Mary also must have been fretting about her apartment building being sold to a new owner. Bill commiserated, "I hope that you won't get thrown out of your apartment after getting so comfortably settled. It may be that whoever buys it will just let the apartments stay as they are. After all, I can sort of picture you as you are now and that helps when I start dreaming." That evening, Bill did not have to dream about what Mary looked like. She had included a photo in her letter. "Thanks for the picture, glamour babe," Bill wrote. "God bless you. Yours always, Bill."

Bill's next letter on May 7 started with another paragraph in Swedish. It is not included here, as he followed that paragraph with, "I hope you can translate that without too much trouble—it really doesn't say anything vital to the welfare of the world."

More vital was the progress on Mary's engagement ring. Mary had agreed to the loose stone and the yellow gold setting, so Bill was instructing his sister Clare to proceed. "Goodness knows when it will be ready, but we still have plenty of time. Maybe it will be finished for your birthday!" Mary's birthday was November 29, over six months later, so Bill was building in a big cushion for the ring to be completed. "Does the time seem to be rolling along a little faster now?" Bill asked. "I believe it feels that way over here!"

Bill's summer break would begin in less than a month and end his stay in Stockholm. So, Bill sensed that time was speeding by. Unfortunately, we do not have Mary's letters to see if she felt the same way. But she probably appreciated Bill's closing comment: "Goodnight, my own sweet Mary. I love you with all my heart. You fill my thoughts all day long."

In his May 9 letter, Bill reprised his theme. "Dearest Mary, another week has gone by—they are clicking off right regularly these days, little one. That suits me fine!"

One thing is clear. Mary was busy back in South Carolina, so perhaps time was flying by for her as well. She had been visiting numerous factories, checking on the labor and health conditions for the workers. A membership drive by the AFL-CIO had been successful in increasing the wages for the workers. With union membership came health benefits. She was trying to improve health conditions for workers, and anything that aided in that endeavor was greatly appreciated.

In her spare time, Mary had also been sitting for a portrait. Bill responded, "I'd like to take a peek to see if that artist is doing justice by you. It must be interesting to model for a real portrait painter. I guess we will have to frame you and put you over the mantel."

While Mary was working hard, Bill was hardly working, taking advantage of the warmer Scandinavian days. Earlier that day, he and Hal rode their bicycles six miles out of town to the king of Sweden's palace. It was in a "beautiful setting of inlets and woods." He described the south end of Sweden as a "mass of thousands of islands jutting out into the Baltic Sea. If I lived here I would certainly have me a sailboat and cruise around to my heart's content. And naturally, that would include having you by my side to enjoy the scenery and to cuddle up to our bright moonlight nights. So long, little rascal. I love you so much it hurts. Bill."

Sailing, cruising, biking, cross-country skiing, nude saunas and bathing, endless parties, visiting archbishops with no invitation, exploring various sights seemingly every weekend—was there no end to Bill's adventures? One can only wonder what Mary thought her future with Bill would be like when she read these letters. What type of minister had she committed to spend the rest of her life with? Something told her that life with Bill would never be boring.

On Sunday, May 11, 1947, Bill's Swedish water was hot! "That's always an event for rejoicing over! So, I washed out a few dirty clothes and took a leisurely bath. Wonderful thing, a bath!"

That afternoon, Bill joined the group from the Lapland trip for a "compass course" of cross-country skiing. "We were supposed to make a sort of circular trip with three small lakes at the points where we had to check in with fellows who were stationed there." They started out in five-minute intervals, with Bill managing to complete the "not too simple" course in an hour and forty minutes. Three fellows got lost and came in last, so they "took a ribbing." Bill added that, during the course, he "jumped a pair of deer which took off in long leaps through the woods with their white tails stuck up like flags," and later, came across several couples lounging out in the sun "without a stitch of clothes on."

Mary had asked about his summer calendar, knowing that he planned to attend the Lutheran World Federation's conference in

Lund, Sweden. Having only had a few lines left at the bottom of his page, Bill merely said, "I'm going to Lund the last of June and Oslo the last of July. I'll fill in the details later. Adjo sota Maria, Jag aloka dig. Bill."

Sounds like "My dear Mary, I dig you a lot!" But that's just a guess. Really, it means "good night" and "I love you."

In his letter the next night, Bill filled Mary in on his plans.

I'm going to head south along the east coast of Sweden the middle of June. I expect to be in Lund in a week or ten days. I'll be there then until July 6th. My plans from then until the meeting in Oslo are vague probably. I'll try to cycle up the west coast and around the central lake section. After the first of August, I'll try to see something of Norway if my money holds out. If I have no dough, I'll have to get me a job for a month. At any rate, I'll be in Uppsala by the first of September at the latest.

Bill's Swedish teacher was the subject of his next letter. They had been having "quite a discussion about the pros and cons of the German past and Europe's future." His teacher had "decided opinions, with a leaning towards Germany Nazism as a better bet than Russian Bolshevism and the Anglo-Saxon dabbling." Bill disagreed on that subject and on many other things, including his married teacher's apparent relationships with several single women.

This led Bill to comment on European relationships in general. "I certainly would think long and hard before considering marrying a European girl. They have an attitude toward life that is cold and impersonal that I could not stomach. There seems to be an atmosphere here in Sweden that allows too much hardness and impersonality in the relations we hold sacred." To complete his point, he concluded, "So, it makes me just that much happier that we have each other and have so much to look forward to in the years that are ahead. God bless you and keep you happy. I love you, Bill."

The next day, a Thursday, was yet another national holiday, this time for Ascension Day. So, Wednesday night was party time. Bill and Hal were invited to a fancy dinner by some friends of a girl who had come over on the *Gripsholm*. As before, all guests, except for Bill and Hal, were dressed in formal wear. The meal must have been amazing, as Bill described it in detail. It started with a smorgasbord of "pickled herring, radishes, potatoes baked in cheese, meatballs wrapped in onions, rolled fish, boiled small potatoes, egg omelets, something tasty rolled up in bacon, little Swedish meatballs, red beet salad, hard-boiled eggs and cheese," followed by a main meal of "delicious baked salmon, a green salad and more potatoes" and "a dessert of strawberry ice cream and orange sherbet." Of course, there was ample "schnapps, wine, and brandy." Dancing followed until around one-thirty a.m., when sandwiches, cakes, and coffee were served. Bill exclaimed, "These Swedes just don't know when to quit." He added, "It's never quite complete without you, sweet Mary. I have a good time, but there is just something missing. Your Bill."

Bill's letter on Saturday, May 17, was a full four pages. Bill felt good because he had just gotten a "nice, sweet letter" from Mary that she had mailed on Wednesday morning. Mary had negotiated for a silver serving set from her mother. Bill replied, "You must have had a happy time with all the family at home. I guess she must be rather fond of her daughter to start off that silver set with a bang like that. I'll bet you took it home, got out your best plate, and felt quite smug as you looked it over. I can't say that I would blame you though. I am a bit smug about it myself even at this distance. Give her a big kiss for me!"

Not to be outdone, Bill devoted two pages of that letter to his tour of a china factory in Gustavberg. Built in 1822, it was the oldest of its kind in Sweden. Bill described the different plates, including heavier pottery style, bone china, and flint china, then explained how the designs were applied, either with oiled paper or by hand-painting. Bill liked one set with an old English pattern in a rose color that he thought might be a good buy. But he parted with no money that day.

Before he signed off, Bill described a light opera he had gone to the night before—*The Merry Widow*. "I thoroughly enjoyed it! The settings were good but not elaborate. The singers were excellent and good actors and actresses as well. It's amazing what a town of 750,000 and a nation of 7 million can do in the way of art and culture." He finally said good night. "Well, I've been long-winded tonight. It's one of those nights when I miss you an extra bit. I guess I love you a little somehow. Bill."

Bill went to a service at yet another church that Sunday. His Swedish comprehension must have been improving, as he understood the whole service. The highlight, or perhaps the lowlight, was the baptism of five children after the service. "I don't think I've ever heard better lung work from babies. They squirmed and yelled the whole time."

The next day, Bill's Swedish class went on a field trip to see ancient rune stones in various fields, church yards, and woods outside Stockholm. Rune stones date back to the fourth century, or earlier, and typically involve inscriptions chiseled in a twenty-four-letter runic alphabet. On the bank of one lake, the Vikings had erected two red granite rune stones with poetic inscriptions. For Mary's benefit, Bill included in his letter that night a drawing of another moss-covered rune stone pulled out of a wall surrounding a church rebuilt in 1776. The stone was two feet high with inscriptions and a cross, indicating it was Christian. His professor interpreted the inscription, resulting in Bill and his fellow students being the first to hear a reading of that rune stone for probably nine hundred years. He closed the letter, "We biked about 36 miles, so I'm ready for bed. Night, night, lilla Maria. Jag aloke dig. Bill."

Good to know that Bill still dug his sweet Mary!

The subsequent night, Bill started his letter, "Kavasta Maria," followed by a long paragraph written entirely in Swedish—something about not neglecting his Swedish lessons ("svensk laxa") or being lazy ("lata"). In English, he acknowledged that he was delirious from "spending three hours translating eleven pages of Swedish." God only knows how long it took Mary to translate the one paragraph.

At this point, Bill was getting ready for his summer bike trips. Approval for a veteran's subsistence allowance came from Washington, taking care of his financial concerns. He still needed to get visas for Norway, and possibly Denmark, as he hoped to make a side trip to Copenhagen. He bought some pastel chalk crayons to try his luck at drawing some scenes he hoped to see along the way. "I figure it will be fun to fool around with some drawings during rest stops as I cycle to Lund and around this summer. I'm afraid Betty got the talent in the family, however." While talking about artwork, he followed up on a prior item. "How is your portrait coming along—or have you been back?"

Alas, the professional portrait apparently never materialized.

Bill ended that letter, "Bye, bye, sweetheart. God bless you always. You are constantly in my prayers. Your Bill."

"Hi Butch!" Bill started his May 23 letter. Now that she had her new Ford, Mary had let him know that she was going out on the weekends and being sociable. Apparently, she had also named her car "Jasper" and was enjoying her freedom. "You are getting to be as big a gad-about as I am," Bill responded.

What's the matter—won't "Jasper" sit in the garage over the weekends? It's okay with me. I wish I could be there to go along with you, that's all. You might as well do it now, 'cause we probably won't be able to do it after I get back. A preacher can't get away on weekends—or anytime for that matter. I'll try to keep you entertained though, my sweet. Can't have you running off to mamma!

He confessed that he had neglected Mary for the last forty-eight hours. Indeed, there does not appear to be a May 22 letter. He tried to make up for it. "It's high time I got around to telling you how much I love you. Of course, I've been thinking about it right along, but I didn't put it down in print."

In the "small world" sphere, Bill then described meeting some air corps officers who knew an "old high school pal" of his, a woman named Tootie Buchanan. She was now the wife of the base chaplain in Stockholm. "I had my first date with Tootie," Bill wrote, "so naturally I had to send greetings to her." Indeed, Bill's first date during high school was with Tootie at the junior-senior dance. But the date was marred by embarrassment when his parents rejected his plea for his first pair of long pants. He was the only knickers-clad boy at the dance and took some ribbing from his classmates. But Tootie had stood by him, ignoring the teasers. Their relationship never progressed, but Bill always appreciated her sticking up for him at the dance.

In the same letter, Bill mentioned another former girlfriend, this time when he was in the Advanced Specialized Training Program in the army. Why Bill felt the need to reference girls he had seen in the past is unclear. Apparently, he was comfortable enough with Mary's expressions of trust to be transparent about his prior relationships.

And he never hid his love and pining for Mary. As he reached the bottom of the page, he told her, "There was a nice new moon peeking over the rooftops as I came home, just asking for a couple lovers. I miss you awfully, Mary. Bill."

Chapter 29

Lynching Trial, Greenville, South Carolina
(May 1947)

In February 1947, in Greenville, South Carolina, a Black man named Willie Earle was arrested for allegedly robbing a taxi driver of forty dollars, a watch, and a ring, and then stabbing him. The evidence against Earle was sufficient for probably cause, but a conviction was not assured. However, at 5 a.m., less than twelve hours after he was arrested, thirty-one White vigilantes, all but three of whom were fellow cabbies, broke Earle out of his jail cell and promptly murdered him. Earle's body—beaten, stabbed and riddled with shotgun blasts—was found on the side of a rural road at 6 a.m. The cab driver died later that day. Earle's death is purportedly the last racially motivated lynching to occur in South Carolina. The trial of the perpetrators of the lynching occurred four months later in May 1947, with a jury of twelve White men acquitting the thirty-one defendants on all charges even though twenty-six of them had signed confessions and one of the defendants had been implicated as shotgun triggerman and leader of the mob.

The story of Mr. Earle's lynching and the acquittal of his murderers reached all the way to Sweden. Bill wrote Mary about it. "The trial of the lynchers of that negro in Greenville have made the papers here. Yesterday, the outstanding Swedish newspaper even had an editorial on it—not favorable as you can guess. Such things certainly hurt the U.S. I hope we can wake up one of these days."

In a subsequent letter, Mary responded with a greater description of the lynching. Though Mary's letter was not preserved, Bill's further reply is telling. He knew too well that prejudice against Black people was a significant problem that needed to be fixed, both in society and in the church.

Your comments on the lynching trial, in addition to what I have read here, make me sick. I can't for the life of me see how people can be so mean and prejudiced. And there are plenty of supposedly good church people who are exactly the same way. America and the church have a lot to answer for. Yesterday, in a *Newsweek*, I read an article about negro prejudice in California, which shared that it's not only the South that is to bear all the shame either.

When it came to civil rights and equal justice and dignity, Bill was ahead of his time. He hated racial prejudice and discrimination of any sort. He knew that prejudice and racial segregation was also a huge problem in religious denominations, including the Lutheran church.

He hoped he could do his part to remedy that practice once he was ordained and back in the States. Especially if he ended up in the South.

Chapter 30

Letters from Stockholm
(May 26–June 10, 1947)

Bill addressed his May 26 letter to "Lilla bov (det betyder 'rascal')!" and followed that intro with another full paragraph entirely in Swedish, this time mostly about the weather. Whether Mary ever translated it is unknown.

Because that Monday was another national religious holiday, this time for Pentecost, Bill and a friend took another bike ride to an inlet twelve miles outside Stockholm. The water was cold, but they took a dip, then "lazied around," stretching out in the sun. "The air was so fresh and clean that you couldn't breathe in enough." Bill then confessed that "these holidays are bad on my initiative and industry. I'm always good for nothing but bed when I get home."

The holidays also interfered with Bill getting letters from Mary. He had not gotten a letter from her since the prior Friday. He asked, "Ain't that a terrible long time to wait? But I'm greedy enough that a letter every day wouldn't be too much! Guess I'm in love with you, honeychile! It's too bad you are so far off I can't squeeze you till your bones crack, in a bear hug."

His greed was rewarded the next day with two letters from Mary. After reading them, he wanted more details about her upcoming vacation. "I couldn't quite figure out your plans, however. You mentioned going to Myrtle Beach, but you didn't say what day. You said you would take your vacation in June, but you didn't say when exactly. Now, honeychile, how do you expect me to keep up with you that way?" He promised to send his next letter to her parents' house in Cross, South Carolina, as she would be stopping there on the way to the shore. He concluded, "Have a good time at the beach, my sweet. I wish I could be along to give you a few good dunkings! Behave yourself—if possible. I love you, Bill."

While Mary was vacationing at Myrtle Beach, Bill attended a final dance at the business school in Stockholm, at the invitation of a girl he had met at the English club party two weeks earlier. Explaining why she invited him, Bill, in his usual self-effacing manner, told Mary, "I guess males are scarce in Stockholm," and described the woman as "a long-suffering girl who could put up with my dancing." Just to make sure Mary had no reason to be jealous, Bill added, "But enough is enough. The bad part though was seeing all the girls dressed up in their pretty dresses having a good time and you weren't one of them. Just t'ain't like it used to be before I fell in love!"

Bill was sure a letter from Mary would be waiting for him after he got back from church that weekend. But "the cupboard was bare!" In a letter on Sunday afternoon, he told her, "I think this has been the longest wait between letters since I got to Sweden. You better have a good excuse.... I miss you so much that when letters don't come on time, I am hard to get along with. I love you with all my heart, and every minute of the day."

He then described going to yet another "blowout for about twenty Americans and ten Swedes" at the invitation of Lela Douglas, the Mississippi girl with whom he posed for the newspaper several months earlier. "It was certainly pleasant. You really appreciate the informal, easygoing ways of American parties after the rather stuffy, formal affairs of the Swedes. I am looking forward to seeing the other side of Swedish life this summer and next year—so far, I've seen mostly the upper crust. It's pleasant, but I don't belong there."

In closing, he told Mary, "It will be wonderful when we can have our own home and build our life together. God grant that we have long years together. All my love, Bill."

Bill's outlook significantly improved on Monday, June 1. "I feel much better tonight, and you can no doubt imagine why.... There was a letter today! It was mighty welcome." He commented on her newsy letter. "I'm glad you had such a nice time down at the beach. I wish I could have been along—might even have shoved you in that cold water, sissy. Someday, I'll have to visit that part of the coast with you.... Be sure and fatten yourself up while you are eating your mother's good cooking—I want a good armful when I get back to S.C."

He also updated Mary on his recent purchases for his upcoming trip—"a couple of saddlebags for my bike, a pair of sneakers, and a sleeping bag." He was anxious to get started, but there was one big drawback: "It will mean not getting any mail from you for long stretches."

With the semester in Stockholm ending, Bill had to take final exams, be out of his apartment by June 12, and finalize his plans for the bike trip. In his Thursday, June 5, letter, Bill laid out his initial plans. "If I can manage it, I'm going to try to leave Stockholm on the 12th and spend a couple days seeing the island of Gotland before I go on down to Lund. It is supposed to be a quaint old place. All told, there are around 90 churches on the island that go back beyond the 13th century, so I'd like to see that. I'll tell you more details later."

On Friday afternoon, Bill got another "particularly welcome" letter from Mary. According to Bill's reply, she was "having a busy time working, enjoying the springtime, and keeping house." Bill was also busy. His exams started on Monday. Feeling confident, he spent most of Friday afternoon celebrating Swedish Flag Day in Stockholm, with military parades, flags, music, and the royal family. On Saturday he planned to go on an all-day sailing trip. And for Sunday, he accepted an invitation to spend most of the day at the "stuga," or summer cottage, of a couple he met at the party the prior Saturday.

Somehow, he kept assuring Mary that he was serious student!

Bill almost missed the boat on Saturday morning. He forgot to pull out the alarm plug on his clock. Luckily, he woke up just in time to dash across town in the pouring rain. He got there just before his friend Charlie arrived by bike. Both were soaked. "We figured it was a rather foolish day to go sailing—but!!"

The sailing trip got off to a bad start. The boat's anchor chain was all fouled up, taking ninety minutes for the boat owner and some other fellows diving down into the cold water to loosen it. After a few hours in the wind and rain, the weather improved and they sailed through beautiful archipelagos that stretched out from Stockholm, finally coming ashore at a little village where the group had dinner. As the sailboat was going further for the rest of the weekend and Bill had committed to a separate outing the next day, Bill and Charlie took a bus back to Stockholm—just in time to do some last-minute laundry.

Of course, despite being busy all day, he wrote Mary that night. "It's been a good day—the kind that makes you feel content with a job well done. Naturally, when I'm in a mood like that, you are very much in my mind. It will be wonderful when we can come to the close of happy days that we have enjoyed—together! I love you more every day, sweet Mary."

The next day he got another letter from Mary. Bill immediately replied. "Back again. And I love you just as much as I said yesterday…. I'm glad you had such a nice day."

Bill had also enjoyed a "swell" day. Early that Sunday morning, he and a group of about thirty students bicycled to the summer cottage of a Swedish-American/ French-Norwegian couple he had met at a party the prior weekend. The cottage, situated "high on a hillside overlooking a beautiful lake way out in the woods—perfectly secluded and quiet," had a sod roof, three chimneys, and a nice stone terrace. "A perfect type of rustic summer place," Bill wrote. For a change, he enjoyed an American meal—"hamburgers, deviled eggs, baked beans, lemonade, and a big bowl of Jello. It was delicious!"

As for his final exams, Bill took them one day at a time, briefly keeping Mary apprised of his progress. "Tomorrow we start tests, Swedish first. There isn't much to study for that, but I'll have to do a little work for the other two. God bless you, sweetheart. All my love, Bill." The next night he wrote again. "Sweetheart, one down and two to go! Swedish wasn't too rough. I don't imagine that I made 100, but I am not worried about it. Tomorrow is 'scientific development' which is more or less a big conglomeration of things, so that is uncertain."

The second final was not as easy, but Bill was not concerned. He wrote Mary right after he got back from the test. "We had a lulu of an exam this morning—of course your old man got by!" He told Mary he planned to spend the whole night studying for the third exam in his economics, government, and social policy class. He expected it "to be the roughest yet," as the professor for that course was "rather exacting."

How these social science courses fit into Bill's further theological studies is a mystery other than giving him a well-rounded education. It seems that most of his religious-based experience that semester was going to see ministers like Pastor Bolander preach on Sundays and making surprise visits to archbishops.

True to form, despite Bill's last-minute studying, the third exam "went fairly well." Fortunately, Bill always came through academically even when he was not too diligent in his studies.

One of Bill's letters during those exam nights covered his plans to visit Gotland. He would leave Stockholm on a train on Wednesday night in the "rugged" third class, then take a boat to the island. He mapped out a three-day travel itinerary, allowing him to circle almost the whole island, with a full day in the island's main town, Visby, before returning to Stockholm on Sunday or Monday night. He would then immediately take off by bike for Lund for the Lutheran World Federation conference. Bill warned Mary that he "may not get to write a note tomorrow in all the hurry," but he promised he would "scribble" from Gotland. After giving Mary an address in Lund for her next few weeks of letters, he signed off. "Don't work too hard these hot summer days. Can't have you running yourself down to skin and bones. God bless you, Mary. Your Bill."

Bill's final letter to Mary from the apartment in Stockholm on June 10, 1947, was titled "The last night at the old stand," and started, "I suppose you are quite fat and sassy now after those happy days at home. I'd give anything to have been with you there. Did you manage to put on those extra pounds?"

Mary must have been thrilled to have a fiancé who wanted her to gain weight rather than to stay slender! Perhaps he felt she was working too hard and skipping meals when on the road.

At 10 p.m., Bill climbed aboard the train for his next journey, leaving Stockholm behind.

PART V

BIKE TRIPS AND
CHURCH CONFERENCES

Chapter 31

Island of Gotland
(June 11–15, 1947)

On June 12, Bill woke up to the boat's foghorn as it approached Visby, the capital of Gotland, the large island off the southeastern shore of Sweden. The night before, Bill had taken a train to the coast and boarded the well-worn vessel for the overnight voyage to Gotland. Bill only had a "deck ticket," so he had slept in a six-foot space on the deck in his old army sleeping bag. Fortunately, the fog lifted just ten minutes before the boat arrived at Visby. As it docked, Bill was treated to "a fine view of the city." In his letter to Mary that night, he described the town: "Visby is certainly a quaint old place. During the Viking days, it was a lively town, and during the days of the Hanseatic League (remember your history?), it was one of the most important cities in the world. Now it is mostly a picturesque monument of the middle ages with a population of around 12,000."

Bill spent the morning walking along the "Mediltide," a medieval wall surrounding the old city, one of the best preserved of its type in the world. Then he took to the narrow streets, doing some sketching of the tiny houses and exploring over a dozen church ruins. In their heyday, the churches were magnificent, massive structures built by the rich inhabitants, but only a few were being restored. Bill climbed to the top of the tower in the cathedral for a "wonderful view of Visby clinging to the hillside."

Having "about walked my legs off," Bill hopped on his bike at about 4 p.m., heading south to start his ride around the island. He carried only his sleeping bag, with some pouches for food and an extra shirt and shorts. He avoided the main roads, stopping at several countryside churches. Some had Bible scenes painted on their interior walls, which he described as the "People's Bible of the Middle Ages." At 7 p.m., Bill stopped at a farmhouse, hoping to sleep in the barn. But the owners invited him in, welcoming him warmly. The family's grandmother, now eighty-five, had lived in America fifty years ago and spoke good English. Instead of starving and sleeping in the barn, Bill ate heartily and spent the night on a couch inside the house.

Gotlander hospitality at its best.

The next day was Friday, June 13. That night, Bill started his letter, "Hi, little apple dumpling! There must be something in this Friday the 13th business. This morning I woke up to the patter of rain. If there is anything less welcome to a cyclist, I don't know what it would be. It was lucky I had such a friendly, hospitable family to stay with." In fact, while the family members did chores, Bill was invited to play the piano. Then, he joined them for "pannkaka," which were very thin but filled his entire plate. By 10 a.m. the rain stopped. Bill said his goodbyes and headed out. But the rain returned, making the roads soft and muddy. In his letter that night, Bill griped, "They don't seem to have such things as paved roads in Gotland."

He had made the most of the dreary day. He biked from one ancient Gotland church to another, getting out of the rain whenever he needed to. Almost all the churches were over six hundred years old. Between the raindrops, he took time to sketch the ones he liked the most, some in pencil and some in colored chalk.

Bill, who was traveling by himself, told Mary, "It gets a bit lonesome, but I stop along the way when I see people that look interesting and strike up a conversation. It is fun and helps my Swedish, too. At least when you are alone you can do as you please. I'll be glad when the day comes when I have you to boss me and keep me straight. That's love!"

That night, it took Bill three stops to find a place to sleep. "Maybe I should have shaved," he told Mary, as he settled down on a nice pile of hay in a smelly barn at the third farm. The next morning, the farm's family did not offer breakfast, so Bill headed out, stopping at a few churches. Then, when his "stomach was getting pretty rambunctious," he picked out a few houses and asked if the owners could spare some milk and a few eggs. The first try failed, but he hit paydirt at the second, landing three eggs and all the milk he could drink. "The nice old lady wanted to charge me 15 cents, so I doubled it!" he wrote.

The rest of his ride that day was through wooded sections of Gotland countryside under blue skies. "Kinda lonesome," he wrote, but he especially enjoyed scarfing down a "great big meal at the little, thriving, modern town of Slite." After dinner, he found a tourist "vandraham," the Swedish version of a hostel. That day, he had ridden about seventy-five miles. He told Mary, "My legs are still strong, but my fanny is tender."

He was proud that his Swedish was now passable enough that most people he met in Gotland thought he was either Danish, Norwegian, or Finnish—"doing better, eh!" He closed his letter, "Behave yourself, my darling. Blow me a kiss before you go to bed. Bill."

Bill's last day in Gotland was a Sunday, so he slept in until 7:15 a.m. and then started back towards Visby. He visited several "unusually nice old churches," staying at one for a service. With only forty-five miles to go, he stopped to sketch several of the steepled sanctuaries. Despite his "dawdling," he arrived at Visby in time to go to the cathedral for evening worship.

Another magnificent day in Gotland.

At midnight, Bill boarded another rusty boat back to the mainland, his aching body stiffening on the hard deck, with only his sleeping bag for padding.

Chapter 32

Bike Ride from Stockholm to Lund
(June 16–23, 1947)

Back in Stockholm temporarily, Bill "rushed around like mad" trying to get a hold of subsistence money he expected to receive before his long bike adventure to Lund for the Lutheran World Federation conference. But there were no checks waiting for him. "I will just about make it until I get back to Stockholm, I figure," he wrote Mary. "At least it will make me watch my money very carefully." He found several letters from friends waiting for him, but none from Mary. For once, he did not complain. In his letter that night, he rationalized it. "You figured things too well and sent the mail to Lund just at the right time."

That day, Bill learned that his Gotland trip resulted in his "very conspicuous" absence from the closing exercises at Stockholm University. He ranked third in his class and won a scholarship prize but was not there to accept it. He visited the administrative office to collect it—"a beautifully bound (red leather book and corners) and illustrated copy of Selma Lagerlof's *Jerusalem*, one of the outstanding pieces of Swedish literature," signed by all four of his professors who added a "fancy spiel about his accomplishments in the intellectual field." Bill was "tickled pink with it," and that night, after biking south to the little town of Trosa by dusk, he told Mary that she could read it any time!

Surely, Mary was thrilled with that opportunity. The book, which tells the story of Swedish emigrants to the Holy Land and earned Lagerhof the Nobel Prize in Literature in 1909, was entirely in Swedish.

On June 18, Bill wrote a long letter covering the first two full days of his ride to Lund. The day before, he got up before 7 a.m., rode five hours by himself, then hopped onto a ferry to cross a bay, intending to find somewhere to sleep on the other side. However, on the boat, he met "a Swedish-Norwegian fellow of about 30, not too much to look at," who was also cycling south to visit relatives. The fellow, named Sixten, tagged along as Bill biked off the ferry. Bill was not eager to share the road, but Sixten was a fast cyclist and turned out to be "quite a guy—a jack-of-all-trades—a soldier, sailor, and now a farmer." They covered many miles, talking in Swedish all the way, before finding shelter at a "little farm out in the sticks." Bill was glad to have Sixten along when Bill suffered a back tire blowout the next day. They patched the tire, but it did not hold. After hitching a ride to the closest town, they found the hamlet had no cycle shop. Ultimately, they caught a bus to Sixten's relatives' town, where Bill rode Sixten's bike to a store to buy a new tire. In his letter that night, he told Mary, "Although I am a little freer and more comfortable by myself, I must admit that it's been good to have Sixten along." He ended the two-page letter, "So with a long-distance hug and kiss, I'll say goodnight. Your Bill."

"Sweet Mary," he wrote the next night from a coastal town called Oscarhamm. "You would have loved the trip today. The sun was out, and the weather was perfect." He had parted ways with Sixten after twelve miles, then spent the day riding along back roads full of trees, lakes, and rocky terrain. Oscarhamm was big enough to have a vandraham, so Bill cleaned up, "got his stomach full," then took in "some typical Hollywood musical" at the town's theater. He concluded the letter, "So nothing really exciting happened, but it's been a good day and one I would have liked to share with the 'gal I love.'"

Bill's next stop was a town named Kalmar, where, by happenchance, he ran into a girl he recognized from Stockholm. "She saw me and come over. It turned out that she had just come down to work in Kalmar during the summer. So, we took a couple of rides at the carnival and walked around town a little. I was tired and sleepy, however, so pretty soon I called it a night."

Before he went to bed, Bill lamented that he was missing Mary's letters. "It's certainly been a long time since I've had a letter. I am anxious to get to Lund and feast my eyes on your familiar writing. All my love, Bill."

The following day, Bill arrived at a town called Ronneby, on the southern coast of Sweden. The town had a church from the eleventh or twelfth century, built in the Moorish style, with a richly decorated interior. Just as he was leaving, people started arriving for a wedding. "I waited around to see the bridal couple. She was certainly a pretty one. Made me jealous!"

Because the weather was still pretty, he rode further down the coast towards Kristianstad that evening, stopping to help a family pick some strawberries, while saving a few for himself. Just before dark, he finally found a place to bed down for the night.

With only a short ride left to arrive in Lund, Bill was down to one page of air mail paper, so he limited his letter that night to a single sheet. "Mary, my darling. Guess what has been on my mind all day as I rode along—gardening. All you have to do now is to start canning the stuff I've raised. It must be some of the farmer blood I inherited from Mama. Or perhaps it was the influence of some of the fine farms I saw along the way. We will have a time carrying out all our plans." He closed the letter. "I'm getting ready to sleep in a smelly stable. I hardly expect to dream of you tonight."

What a romantic!

Chapter 33

Letters from Lund, Vadstena, and Stockholm
(June 24–July 13, 1947)

On June 24, 1947, Bill arrived in Lund, his destination for the Lutheran World Federation conference, a day earlier than planned. That night, at midnight, Bill was a happy man as he wrote Mary on a new set of air mail paper.

> Sweetheart, well I made it! I pulled into Lund about 2 p.m. and have been on the go ever since. I'm really a day ahead of schedule, but the last couple days I made a few extra miles—I guess it was the thought of mail waiting for me that kept me pushing. It was really swell to see the familiar envelopes and handwriting. I certainly did miss it the last two weeks. It's good to hear that you had such a happy time at home. Sounds as if you and the sewing machine stuck pretty close together. I'm glad to hear you are a "barefoot girl"—I still like to wiggle my toes in the dirt, too.

Though Lund is a sizeable town not far from the city of Malmo, which is directly across a narrow channel from Copenhagen, Bill described it as "a big country town set right in the midst of farmland." He "fell in love with it immediately." At the Grand Hotel downtown, Bill met with four American students and Carl Lundquist, a Lutheran minister who later became the executive director of the Lutheran World Federation, commonly referred to as the LWF. After two weeks on the road, it was "mighty good" to see them. They were planning a wedding anniversary celebration for Dr. S. C. Michelfelder, the executive secretary of the LWF based in Geneva, Switzerland. Bill was invited to tag along. "It was wonderful evening—quite an assembly of the Lutheran nobility," with lead pastors from all over the world. Bill was "certainly impressed by their spirit and power."

That night, he finished his letter, replying to a letter from Mary about her visit to see her brother. "And so to bed! It's been a great day— with the best part those letters from you. Buck and Sue had the same effect on you that happy young married couples have on me, I noticed. Will make them all take a back seat someday. I love you heaps. Your Bill."

Bill's role for the LWF conference was essentially head go-fer for the press office. He described the job as the "leg man (or rather the bicycle man)," telling Mary,

> There is a tremendous amount of work to be done for as big a conference as this. It's fun to be in a spot where you can see a bit of the inside and have a small part in it. The thing that has been most enjoyable and inspiring is seeing the generous, agreeable, warm-hearted way in which Drs. Michelfelder and Ralph Long, the LWF Executive Director, do their work. They are great men.

Fatigued from the busy work, Bill fell asleep while trying to write letters on the night of June 25. He completed two letters, one to his folks at home and one to a group of American students coming to Sweden. But he dozed off before his daily letter to Mary. The next day, he apologized. "Not a nice way to treat you after I got two nice letters from you." So, on June 26, he did "double duty," a two-page letter covering two days.

The bulk of that letter dealt with souvenirs. Mary had received the china slipper Bill had sent a few months earlier, but she referred to it as a "glass slipper." Bill responded, "What do you mean calling it a glass slipper? If it isn't china, I'll eat it!" He explained that the little blue mark on the bottom means that it is Dresden china. He then told Mary that his mother was sending $25 to him for his birthday and asked her if she preferred him to spend it on Swedish china, glass, linen, or something else. Mary must have also written him about some progress on her engagement ring, as he wrote, "I'm glad the 'ring complications' are being cleared up a little. Maybe it will be a birthday or Christmas present!"

By the time he wrote his letter, Bill had been moved into a private home by the accommodations committee. He told Mary that he came to the right place. When he returned to his room, he found "a bowl of fresh strawberries, a couple of sweet cakes and a pitcher of cream." He added, "Incidentally, there is a blonde here that knocks your eyes out—the daughter of house. She is as pretty and sweet-looking as any girl I've seen in Sweden. Don't worry, little one, she has an engagement ring on her finger and I'm not available either! It's still a pleasant atmosphere, mind you."

Bill reassured Mary that she had nothing to worry about. "It's bedtime and the end of the pages—just enough room to say what's always on my heart. I love you and wish you were here with me to share every hour. God bless you, Mary. Your Bill."

Bill's next letter to Mary on June 27 lends credence to the phrase, "It's a small world." To his surprise, a certain young woman from South Dakota to whom he had written letters in the war was also working in the press office for the LWF conference. He had not seen her since Easter weekend the prior year. Bill described her to Mary.

There has been another right interesting angle, too. Have I mentioned Norma? She is the other member of the publicity office with me under Lundquist. She has been studying for the past year in Norway. Back when I was in Germany, I began corresponding with her, sight unseen, through the prodding of Pauline Bresnahan in Washington who was always trying to make a match for me. We wrote for over a year and when I got back to the States, it got pretty often—serious enough so that over Easter holidays we met in Chicago—she from S.D. and I from Gettysburg. It didn't take—but we had a good time. I wasn't sure if she knew anything about you until yesterday when she asked me when I expected to be married.

Pauline Bresnahan, the failed matchmaker, must have given Norma the news of Bill's engagement.

The next day Dr. Lundquist was in all-day meetings, leaving Bill to his own devices. Bill spent part of the day at the student cafeteria, getting a free meal and meeting other students. He then took in a movie at the local theater. "It's a hot night, my sweet—not quite like Mississippi, but at least like S.C. Several of us decided to go to the nine o'clock show. It wasn't a good idea! The movie was the 'Northwest Mounted Police'—very old, but still interesting—but the theatre was hot and smelly. It's no wonder Swedish movies generally close down for the summer."

As he closed his letter, Bill described another nice tray filled with strawberries, cream, cakes, and milk. "Yum! Yum! Behave yourself, little sweetheart. I love you. Your Bill."

He most likely devoured everything on the tray before going to sleep.

The lull ended the next day. There were press releases to be sent out and arrangements for people still arriving to be made. Perhaps the most moving moment that day was the arrival of the German contingent of ministers on a bus—a big deal, as it was the first time they had been allowed to travel outside Germany since the second World War ended.

Bill's primary role during the conference was to help line up and carefully schedule key people to participate in a promotional movie for Lutheran World Action, so no time would be lost by the "movie men." Bill enjoyed "prowling around as much as possible to get to know the important personalities." He told Mary, "I am thankful every day that I've learned as much Swedish as I have, but today I was kicking myself for not being able to speak any German. I just had to stand around like a dumb dodo when any of the German delegates wanted anything. You will have to take me in hand and teach me, I suppose."

It is uncertain what expertise Mary had in foreign languages, but apparently Bill thought she could speak some German.

The LWF conference was in full swing by the next day, with six hundred delegates from thirty different countries.[3] Bill worked from 8

---

[3] The countries listed on the LWF stationery of this conference were Australia, Austria, Brazil, Canada, China, Czechoslovakia, Denmark, Estonia, Finland, France, Germany, Holland, Hungary, India, Iceland, Japan, Jugoslavia, Latvia, Lithuania, Madagascar, Porway, Noland, Rumania, South Africa, Spain,

a.m. until 1 a.m. that night. The highlight was attending a press committee dinner with the vice president of Gettysburg Seminary and bishops from Germany, Hungary, Argentina, and Finland. He also enjoyed
a special presentation by the president of the Chinese Lutheran
Church, who reported that, after a six-week evangelical program at a
Chinese university, two hundred Chinese students had become Christians—"quite an achievement." He closed the letter, "You should be
here, my sweet. Lund is a nice old town, and we could have a great time
together. I miss you! All my love, Bill."

Bill's next letter, dated July 3, was on LWF stationery. He must
have typed it in the press office early in the morning. He started it out
with an admission of guilt. "Dearest Mary, I have been neglecting you
terribly the past few days. This press and publicity office is a madhouse.
I am usually in the office by 8:00 (today 7:00 for this good reason) and
I climb into bed sometime after midnight."

Due to drizzly rain, Bill's carefully crafted schedule for the Lutheran World Action movie interviews had to be scrapped. Shots and
interviews would be taken whenever delegates could be present. This
created a "ticklish situation," as Bill did not want to interfere with the
archbishops' and bishops' more important duties. Thankfully, most of
them were patient and cooperative. Ultimately, Bill told Mary that
while he enjoyed meeting the dignitaries, he regretted being involved
with the movie because it turned out to be a "disruptive influence." Bill
was "plain disgusted" by the intrusion of the moviemaking during the
conference's biggest worship service. "You can't be mixing that stuff
with worship."

After another hectic day in Lund, Bill added a few lines of hand-
writing at the bottom of that letter. "I'll be ready to hit the road where
I can have some time to myself—don't have time to give you the time
I want to. Love always, Bill." As the conference was nearing its end,
Bill also told Mary to send her next letters to "General Delivery, Oslo,
Norway."

Sweden, and United States. These spellings are verbatim. Presumably, the "P" and
"N" in Norway and Poland must have gotten transposed. Prior conferences had
been held in Eisenbach in 1923, Copenhagen in 1929, Paris in 1935.

On July 4, Bill met with other students and Bishop Hans Lilje from Hanover, Germany. It was a couple of hours that he would never forget. Bishop Lilje told the group about his eleven-month experience in a Gestapo prison.

And if you can imagine it, he told of his solitary confinement, his five-day long grillings by the Gestapo, his scanty food, the terrible mental strain, in a way that made you laugh—and yet you could also sense that he thanked God for making it a time in which his convictions were strengthened, his soul enriched, and his mind could be disciplined in a way that will never be forgotten.

As Bill consumed "a bottle of pop and a couple of bananas" left for him by the woman of the house that night, he signed off on his letter. "It's high time I got to bed. God bless you and keep you happy, Mary. I pray always that our love will grow stronger through the days and that our years together will be useful and blessed in the work of God. Your Bill."

On the night of Sunday, July 6, Bill wrote,

My Mary, this is one of those nights when the thousands of miles between us seem to fade away, and you are very close to me. And just for that reason, I suppose, I'm missing you terribly right now. The week has been great, but it's been hectic and tiring as well. It's been fun working and playing with the swell gang of American students, but I think it has made me a bit homesick—something that is unusual for me. So, it was good to have a letter when I asked at the hotel this evening. And there you were, smiling so sweetly out of the car window. It makes things a little more pleasant, to see a new picture occasionally. I'll look forward to the others that will come later.

The next day, Bill finished his LWF work in Lund, tying up loose ends in the press office. When he got back to the house where he was staying, he found a farewell snack, with a "big bowl of huckleberries and cream and some delicious socker kaka." After gorging on the

Swedish sponge cake, he closed by telling Mary, "If you were here and gave me a great big hug and kiss, I might be persuaded to share with you. God bless you, my sweetheart. All my love, Bill."

Bill had planned to start his return bike trip toward Stockholm the next morning, but by the time he and a few buddies had packed up their gear, it was "raining cats and dogs." The downpour persisted until four o'clock in the afternoon, so they stayed in Lund for one more night. He told Mary, "It was nice to have a day for loafing after the hurry and hustle of last week." Plus, Bill was able to take in the Fred Astaire and Rita Hayworth movie, *You'll Never Get Rich*, which he found to be "plenty corny, but kinda funny—in the right mood."

The movie title was apt. He knew that he and Mary would likely never be rich.

The next morning, Bill and "a big gang" took the train out of Lund, heading to a town where they were supposed to meet two Swedish students who would take them on some side trips and then on to Stockholm. However, the two students never showed up. Bill was stranded with five non-Swedish speaking friends. He told Mary, "It's right much of a responsibility to be the mother of five—but I know how helpless they can feel when they can't speak the language, so I'm glad to be of help. Goodnight, once more! I love you, Mary. Bill."

In the morning, Bill and his friends improvised, taking a boat ride to a small island in Lake Vittern to see St. Peter's Church, then catching a bus and a train to Vadstena, to see its well-preserved castle. The moat-protected castle, with massive watch towers capped with green domes, was finished in 1430 after about a hundred years of work. Vadstena is also famous for its lacework, so Bill bought a little piece for Mary. Before he went to bed, Bill finished off his next letter to Mary. "So long, my sweet girl. I thank God every day for your love. Your Bill."

After finally arriving in Stockholm, Bill found two letters from Mary waiting for him. Mary had been to a wedding, and she included a few snapshots. "Naturally, that pepped me up heaps," he wrote her back. "You must have been a beautiful bridesmaid. I know if I had been around when you looked so sweet, I would have been tempted to make some 'hug-wrinkles' in the pretty dress."

Mary had also made another trip to the beach and to Charleston.

Bill replied, "I'm glad you had such a pleasant and restful visit to the beach. And as often happens, I wish I could have been with you in Charleston. I've always liked that place, particularly St. Matthews Church."

Indeed, as a child in the 1920s, in addition to climbing up inside the high steeple at St. Matthews, Bill used to scamper up the winding stairs to the highly raised, goblet-style pulpit in the beautiful sanctuary. From the pulpit, he pretended to preach, just like his father, though he was too short to see the pews below. Now, he was on the cusp of potentially becoming a theologian or a parish minister with his own pulpit and sanctuary to preach from every Sunday. He wondered whether the theologians and bishops at the LWF conference missed their parish ministries and regular weekly preaching. But spreading and organizing Lutheranism across the world could be equally important as developing churches or nurturing existing congregations back in the States. Bill pondered whether his ministerial road might someday lead in that direction. He hoped and trusted God would help him choose the right path at the right time.

On the evening of July 13, Bill wrote,

> My darling, do you realize that this is our sixth month anniversary?" It seems like 6 years instead of 6 months. It helps though when I figure that 1/3 of the time I'll be away from you is past now—one year to go! One thing I'm more certain of every day is that we are going to be mighty happy together. God has blessed us far beyond our deserts. I love you, sweet Mary. And since it is now almost 1 a.m., I'll turn in for a good night's sleep and a few dreams of you. Your Bill.

Chapter 34

Bike Ride to Oslo, Norway
(July 15–20, 1947)

"My sweet Mary, did you feel 'missed' tonight? You should have! Time after time I kept thinking 'Mary ought to be here, Mary ought to be here!' And yet you seem terribly close, as if you were sharing the whole evening even though there is a long stretch of water between."

It was July 15, and Bill had just returned from an evening with Carl Lundquist at Solong, one of the fanciest restaurants in Stockholm. Apparently, the fine dining, including delicious steaks, was a bit of payback for Bill's help at the LWF conference. Bill told Mary that night, "Every once in a while, you really enjoy such doings—it wouldn't be half as nice if you did it too often."

Luckily for Bill, he finally received his subsistence checks from Washington—for $138.67 and $65, giving him enough cash for his passage home at some point. But he was not heading back to America any time soon. He would study in Uppsala in the fall, then take additional classes in Lund in spring 1948. During the 1947 summer break, he planned to travel to Oslo for the interdenominational World Council of Churches conference, followed by a bike trip through Norway. But he did not want to miss any letters from Mary. He instructed her to send any letters after July 25 to "General Delivery, Bergen, Norway," and to hold any packages until after his birthday (August 11) and then send them to his student housing address in Uppsala. He ended the letter, "Stay sweet, my darling. I love you with all my heart. Your Bill."

On July 17, Bill began his bike ride westward to Norway, with two friends, Otto and Jim. Their first stop was Sigtuna, the first capital of Sweden. With a population of 1,200, Sigtuna had four schools, two of which were church-backed religious schools. A Swedish girl named

Gun, whom they had met in Lund, gave them a town tour, including several "fine old church ruins" and a "well preserved brick church" from the thirteenth century. "She is one of the most attractive girls I've known in Sweden and full of life," Bill wrote, quickly adding, "Otto really hated to leave, because he sort of got a crush on Gun, and I can't blame him for that."

However, to Otto's chagrin, they had to leave right after the tour, making another thirty miles before nightfall. The vandraham they found in a town called Härkeberga was a winner, with the woman in charge reviving their spirits with a big batch of sandwiches, milk, bread, and coffee. They also visited a nearby churchwhere the sexton invited them in. Bill told Mary that it was "the most interesting church I've seen in Sweden." It was "a plain, white painted, high-peaked one without any tower," but inside it was "most beautiful." The vaulted arches had paintings from 1480 that depicted "vividly imagined" Bible scenes in warm colors, and on the pews, Bill could see the "old markings where each man sat."

That night, Bill confessed to Mary that, with so much happening in Lund, he had gotten out of the routine of writing faithfully every day. But he promised to get back to the nightly routine. "Something is always missing when I don't get to put down on paper that I'm thinking about you." He concluded, "It's been a good day, Mary. All my love, Bill."

"Hi, little rascal," Bill started his letter the next night from Karlstad, Sweden. It was July 18, and Bill and his friends had biked to the town of Vasteras, stopping briefly to see the big cathedral there, with its single impressive spire and green roof, then taking a train to Karlstad, a large city near the southern coast of Sweden. Karlstad, which was built on the delta of the Klaralven river, the longest in Sweden, is considered the sunniest city in the country. Bill had planned one of the most scenic rides in Sweden the next day. "It's time to hit the sack! So long for tonight," he wrote that night. "I'll be day-dreaming of us before I get to sleep."

The cycling trio soon got underway the next morning, riding the sixty-five miles to Eda, a Swedish municipality east of Oslo. He described the trip to Mary that night. "It was beautiful biking—rivers and lakes the whole way. There were a lot of hills, too, unfortunately. About noon we stopped, took a refreshing swim and bath in a lake, and ate the crackers, cheese, and bananas we had bought earlier." He ended the letter, "It would be wonderful to have you here so we could go down by the lakeside and watch the last rays of light fade from the sky. Things just won't be right until that day comes, but even now it's wonderful to know that you love me as I do you. Bill."

The next night, he wrote Mary again, this time from "Somebody's barn, July 20." He, Jim, and Otto had biked another sixty-five miles, crossing the border into Norway. As it was a Sunday, Bill had hoped to attend worship at a church shown on his map, but there was no service. So, they biked on, along a big river and through wooded hills toward Oslo. As evening approached, Bill stopped at farms along the way, asking if his group could stay the night in a barn. His third try was successful. He told Mary, "Jim and Otto were a bit doubtful about the whole business, but now they seem quite satisfied and are bedding down for the night."

Bill described his view from the barn: "The sunset is beautiful tonight here in Norway. I'm sitting by a little window in the barn out over the rolling hills of grain and hay to where the sky is bright over the hills. In a few minutes I'll be snuggled down into the nice fresh hay for the night."

Chapter 35

Letters from Oslo, Norway
(July 22–29, 1947)

On Tuesday, July 22, Bill wrote Mary from Oslo. "I am a bad boy again—didn't get a single word written [on July 21]. And I had two letters waiting for me here, too!" He confessed, "I wasn't in the mood when I got ready to go to bed." So, he wrote a two-page letter to make up for his laziness the night before.

Bill and his friends had arrived in Oslo at about noon after a morning of climbing "some pretty stiff hills which seem to circle the city." They quickly found the headquarters of the World Council of Churches conference, a huge affair with over seventy countries represented by about fifteen hundred delegates. They checked in as visitors, then headed to the railroad station to retrieve their bags.

Bill had "a time finding a place to stay." Norwegians did not use the term "vandraham" for their hostels. Instead, unknown to Bill, the Norwegian term was "ungdenherhergets." Eventually, Bill found a suitable one at the end of a blind alley.

He shared his first impression of Oslo with Mary.

> I couldn't quite put my finger on it, but something was missing. I've felt that way about Oslo generally as a matter of fact. There is an entirely different atmosphere in Norway. Of course, part of that is due to war conditions—things are apt to be dirty and unpainted. But it's more than outward dilapidation. You can sense it in the people too. In a way, it seems that they are lacking in pride and spirit. I hope my opinion will change—I'd hate to feel that the comparatively unharmed condition of Sweden would give me a bad impression of Norway.

That afternoon, Bill went to a choir practice session "with about 250 voices present," followed by the opening session of the conference and a service at the "damkyrka" cathedral. The cathedral, built in the late 1600s, had a massive but well-worn clock tower topped by a multitiered green spire out front.

The conference's opening session was stifling, mainly because it was held in an un-airconditioned auditorium with no ventilation. After sweating through several boring introductions and speeches, Bill escaped to get some cooler air. But Bill found the bishop who preached at the service at the cathedral that night to be "powerful and impelling. His sincerity and Christian convictions were very apparent. It was one of those occasions when you can say, 'It was good to be there!' Now for bed. I love you, Bill."

On Wednesday, July 23, after finding "one of those new blue [air mail] jobs waiting for me," at the post office, Bill wrote Mary from Carl Lundquist's room at the Grand Hotel. He said he felt "anxious for the summer to be over so I can get back to Uppsala and a regular schedule with mail and study, etc. I'll try to 'answer' your letters, at least, instead of scribbling about what I am doing all the time."

Apparently, Mary had written him about some new initiatives at the public health department. He replied, "It always makes me feel better when I hear that you are happy and encouraged in your work. It sounds as if that X-ray program is really going over the top. The South has certainly needed something like that. I wish they could start a similar project to combat venereal disease, too." Indeed, Mary had successfully convinced reluctant factory foremen to participate in having their workers receive X-rays to detect cases of tuberculosis, resulting in many workers and their families being treated or protected.

Bill's letter-writing was interrupted by Carl Lundquist coming back to his hotel room and "chatting away." After he left, Bill resumed writing, telling Mary about that conversation.

> He said to tell you "hello"—they have all heard about Mary, of course. We finally got around to talking about finances for Lund. All in all, I'll get about $75, which takes care of my expenses nicely. I hope he doesn't wait another two weeks to pay me now. We also discussed that watermelon you

mentioned. You realize, don't you, that the whole subject was a cruel suggestion in this hot Oslo weather? Every time my mind wanders to a juicy, ice-cold watermelon, I long for the good old Southland.

Growing up, ice-cold watermelon on a hot summer afternoon had always been one of Bill's favorite treats. Typically, the watermelon would be chilled in the cool spring water above the house at Dogwood Dell, then carved into large chunks for all the children and adults present. Everyone came running in response to his father's gleeful shout across the mountainside, "Watermelon!!!"

But his love for watermelon was not limited to his childhood. In a letter he sent to Pauline Bresnahan several years earlier while in the army and roasting in the heat and humidity of the Louisiana summer at Camp Claiborne, he wrote,

> The general pulled a stinker yesterday. He sent down an order that we were to buy no more watermelons. That hurt because we have been eating thousands. However, it hasn't stopped me completely. I was sent on an errand yesterday, taking some prisoners to regimental headquarters. On the way back, I saw a watermelon truck. Yeah, I couldn't resist! The fellow who was with me and I ate the whole thing before we got back to our area. My tummy was first cousin to a balloon, but I had much higher morale. Right now, the officer's orderly and I have one more hidden in the bushes. We will cut it after it gets dark.

For Bill, watermelon would always trump orders, even those by a general!

In Oslo, Bill finished his reply to Mary's blue air mail letter by saying he was "glad you liked the Vadstena lace. All of us would have liked to buy the stores out when we were there."

Because he was only a visitor and not a delegate, Bill was not allowed to attend the afternoon sessions, so he and some friends hiked up to the top of the hill above Oslo to see the famous Holmenkollen ski jump, "which takes your breath away just to look at it." That ski jump facility was built in 1892 and was used in numerous world championships and in the 1952 Olympics. Fortunately, Bill did not attempt a jump.

Instead, he got back to town just in time for choir practice. "It's a real treat to sing with such a group and such an interesting director. He really can handle the musical end and the singers as well. We sang the last number rather well, and he stopped rather abruptly and closed with prayer. You felt it!"

Bill wrote his next letter on July 25 immediately after he attended a farewell party for a friend from Lund who was leaving to work in Germany: "Sweet Mary, I've just gotten back from a party!" Then, in the essence of transparency, he explained the party was hosted by Norma, his prior platonic pen pal, at her "big attractive apartment, so we had a swell place to gather." Norma was studying in Oslo and seemed to be showing up wherever Bill went, first in Sweden and now Norway.

Good thing Mary was not the jealous type.

All was not perfect in Oslo. Bill's living quarters were "the most unpleasant part of the business. I never know when I go back at 11:00 whether I'll have a cot, chairs, or the floor to sleep on." He claimed he was not complaining, but he told Mary that he planned to find a hotel room for the remainder of the conference. "I could do a bit of washing too."

To keep Mary's letters coming, he advised her to send all letters after the first of August to "General Delivery, Trondheim, Norway." Bill was almost ready to hit the road on his bike again. He closed his letter, "Behave yourself, my sweet. I love you heaps. Bill."

Bill started his next letter while sitting in a crowded pew. "My Mary, perhaps it isn't right and proper to write letters in church, but I can't think of a finer place to think of you and talk with you. The delegates had to be in the church at 10:15 to get the places which were saved, so that leaves 45 minutes until time for service." He then described the sanctuary, which was closed off to one half of its internal height. The "temporary" ceiling had been there for eleven years while an artist was painting the ceiling. "The bishop said it will be a beautiful addition to the church, but I couldn't quite imagine one of our churches allowing such a rather oppressive situation for a dozen years. Time has a much different place here, where the churches themselves go back for hundreds of years."

Later, Bill continued his letter, expanding on his prior impression of Oslo.

> I really can't say that I like Oslo. Outwardly, it seems to be drab and dirty. There are some nice parks, and the outskirts of town are pretty, but it is certainly not attractive downtown. But most of all, I've somehow felt a spirit of cheapness and lowness ever since I've been here. Maybe it is the contrast between Norway which has suffered and Sweden which escaped. Norma, who has been here a year and is of Norwegian extraction, seems to have the same feeling, however. I'm anxious to get into the country and see what it is like.

One can only think Mary was getting a bit tired of hearing about Norma.

Bill had received another letter from Mary the prior day. He thanked her for telling him that his letters brightened her days. "It always makes me feel better to know that you are happy and getting along well in your work," he wrote. "I don't need to tell you that your letters have the same effect on my day that you say mine do."

He had also received a letter from his mother, indicating that Marion and Sue were still living with Bill's parents in Mississippi and joining their church there. Bill predicted that his parents would soon go to Dogwood Dell for cooler weather. And before closing, Bill again chastised Mary about a prior comment. "One thing you should never have mentioned, Mary, is that ice-cold watermelon. I've been thinking about it these last hot days in Oslo, and my mouth has been watering for a great big slice. Stay sweet, my love. Don't get into mischief. Your Bill."

Bill wrote Mary two more times, on July 28 and 29, while at the conference in Oslo. The whole week had been "awfully hot," he wrote. "It will be good to start biking where I need only a pair of shorts."

At the World Council of Churches conference, Bill attended a series of talks on traditions and unique factors in different religions—Anglican, Roman, Orthodox, Reformed, Free Church, and Lutheran. Though Bill was disappointed in the Lutheran presenter's talk ("it stunk"), he was still convinced that "we have a combination of qualities that come nearer the Biblical and historical basis than any other." He thought that Bishop Neal of India was "a powerful Christian" who gave a "concise and clear" presentation. "It was a joy to listen to him," he wrote. Bill's review of the Chinese YMCA secretary's speech was not so favorable, telling Mary, "It was a flop." For Bill, the last day of the conference salvaged the gathering. Ten or twelve delegates had been selected to give brief summaries of the discussion groups and their personal reactions. "They were of a real Christian humility and sincerity. I'm awfully glad it ended on that note. I would have left with a big feeling of disappointment otherwise."

Once again, Norma appeared in his letter that night. After the closing worship service, she invited a bunch of Lutheran delegates over to her apartment for a "bull session." While they thought the conference did not accomplish much, they all agreed they had "a much larger conception of the worldwide significance of the Christian Church and the challenge to strive for closer understanding and cooperation among Christians." Bill's takeaway was that it was up to the youth to "take a leading part in trying to bring the Lutherans together." He told Mary, "It is a silly thing for us to be so bullheaded when you come down to it."

Mary's likely takeaway was that she was glad Bill was finally leaving Oslo and the ever-present Norma behind.

Bill closed his letter, telling Mary that he would leave Oslo on Thursday, two days later. He stayed one more day to hear Martin Niemöller speak. Niemöller was a prominent German anti-Nazi theologian and pastor, the founder of the Confessing Church, and president of the World Council of Churches. He was also a naval officer and commander of a German U-boat in World War I before becoming a theologian. His talk was both an interesting and inspiring end to the Oslo conference.

"Goodbye for this time, sweetheart. All my love, Bill."

Chapter 36

Bike Ride from Oslo to Bergen, Norway
(July 31–August 9, 1947)

"August 1, out under the sky," appears on the top right corner of Bill's next letter. "Maria lilla, it's wonderful to be out on the open road again, with only my own whim to guide me. Tonight, there wasn't a vandra-ham handy, so I found a nice fir forest and have my sack ready for the night. Not a care in the world! But the best part of it is that we can be 'together' once more without anyone to interfere."

Bill had enjoyed the past few weeks with the gang from America, and he was grateful for the friendships he had developed with Jim, Otto, and Carl Lundquist. But his time had not been his own. He was ready to explore the fjords and Norway by himself, pretending at times that Mary was with him, if not physically, certainly spiritually.

That day, Bill had ridden sixty-eight hilly miles west from Oslo, having to "buck a headwind a good part of the whole way." Fortunately, most of the roads were paved and the scenery was spectacular. "Part of the road was along the coast of one of the less impressive fjords, but the scenery was beautiful. Even with the little I've seen of Norway, I'd be willing to say that it has much more picturesque scenery than Sweden."

In that letter, Bill reminded Mary that his parents were planning to go to Dogwood Dell in August and that his sister Betty and her fiancé, Ted, would be coming down as well. He hoped Mary could get up to Hendersonville when everyone was there. He gave no hint as to why he wanted her to be there at that specific time.

At the end of each month so far, Bill had sent Mary a souvenir or keepsake of some sort from Sweden. This time, however, he had nothing to send. "I didn't send you anything from Oslo. Everything I saw looked souvenirish, so I decided I'd look around in some of the out-of-the-way places. God bless you, Mary. I love you, Bill."

By the end of his bike ride the next day, August 2, Bill knew he was in for a rough time. "Sweetheart, another fine day is almost over—and I am dead tired. I've had a firsthand experience to demonstrate the fact that Norway is mountainous. It almost seemed that I was doing as much walking (uphill) as riding." But the scenery was magnificent—"picturesque and primitive." Bill had passed at least twenty-five lakes of all sizes and shapes, climbing the hills at the end of each lake, and dropping down to the next one. He was so thirsty at the top of one hill that he stopped at a farm and asked for a glass of water. Instead of water, the farmer's wife gave him a whole meal of "some sort of cheese—meal combination—soft and eaten with sugar and cinnamon. It was good!"

The next day, a Sunday, was a Norwegian holiday. Bill's letter that evening started, "This is King Haakon's 75th birthday, so I hope you have duly celebrated. I think they must have put out all the flags in Norway—I never saw so many anywhere else." That day, Bill had biked to a "quaint town of Arendal," where he attended a service at the "big brick Gothic 'almost cathedral'…on a little hill overlooking the harbor." There were only about fifty people present.

Bill griped about having dealt with a headwind most of the afternoon. But he had enjoyed "joining forces with a nice young Norwegian 19 years old" after passing through the town of Grimstad. After supper with the young man, Bill biked on alone until dusk, picking out "a convenient field…to settle down for the night." Though it looked like rain was coming, he was willing to take the risk. "If I get wet, I won't complain."

Bill biked two more very pleasant days before his next letter. On Monday, he reached Kristiansand, a seaport town on the southern tip of Norway, with twenty thousand people and an old charm and appearance. "The houses in most of the town are tiny one-story wooden houses," he wrote, "and the streets are red cobblestone." For once there was no large cathedral dominating the skyline. Bill spent the afternoon window shopping "without buying a thing." Later, he hunted up a youth hostel and got a "good ice-cold bath" and a shave. "After the barber got through with me, I was ready to face the world."

A girl named Marianne, who hosted several social events in Stock-holm, had given Bill the name of a friend to look up in Kristiansand. But Bill was unsuccessful in connecting with her. Instead, he took in a movie, "*A Yank in the RAF* (in which the heel got the girl)." To his surprise, Marianne was in town visiting her friend and Bill found them attending the same movie. He described Marianne's friend as a "bird," saying, "She was 45, I guess, the dean of a teacher's college, and as full of fun and the devil as anyone I've ever seen. She was tied up with the underground during the war, and her apartment was used regularly as a radio station. Some experiences!" Bill ended up spending the night in the "bird's" brother's house.

On Tuesday morning, August 5, Bill took a walk through the Kristiansand town park—"the most unique one I've ever seen. It is at the foot of a tremendous rocky cliff that sits right across the peninsula where the town is and there are little lakes and fountains and paths and flowers and everything to make it perfect."

He left town at noon, heading north towards Bergen. After dusk, he stopped at a farm, asking the woman there if he could buy some milk. The nice lady said he could have some—"just as soon as she milked the cow." Bill waited patiently and eventually was rewarded with a bowl of milk that "must have held a quart still warm." Luckily, Bill had some food to eat with it. "Usually, the warm milk doesn't sound particularly inviting, but tonight, with my bread and marmalade and cheese and sardines, it was delicious."

That night, before he settled down in the farm's barn, Bill finished off his two-page letter to Mary, covering the last two days.

> Sweetheart, I'd give most anything to have you sitting here by my side watching the sunset over the mountains. My "hotel" for tonight is an old farm and my bed a soft haystack in the barn. But you couldn't beat the view for a million dollars. The farm is on a gentle slope that stretches down to a big lake. All around are massive, towering stone mountains with a few trees clinging in the crevasses. It's Norway at its best! So, here I am scratching out, "I love you, I love you," by the last rays of the sun. Your Bill.

Twenty-four hours later, he wrote Mary again.

"Hi, little apple-dumpling! This has been a day straight out of *National Geographic*. For scenic beauty, Norway was really blessed by the gods." He had woken to the "patter of rain and the sweet smell of mountain grass for perfume." After coffee and "some luscious coffee buns" at the farm, he had waited for a break in the rain to head out on his bike.

> It was still a bit misty and foggy, but that didn't mar the beauty of the road at all. I was riding right along the Byglands fjord, an inland lake, really, which is 30 miles long and only a couple hundred yards wide at the most. On each side, the tremendous rocky cliffs and mountains went up about 200 yards, almost vertical at time…. At one place, the road was literally dug out of the mountain side. The rock cliff was so vertical that they just blasted out a hole, so it gave you a queer feeling to know that there were thousands of tons of rock hanging over your head.

Little farms were tucked away between the mountains, with log houses that must have been hundreds of years old. "Many of them were in the quaint Norwegian (Alpine type) style."

At some point, Bill saw a sign spelling out "SYLVSMED," which means "silversmith." He stopped, picking up a souvenir to send to Mary—a week late. Always wanting to create some suspense, Bill did not tell Mary what silver piece he had selected.

That night, Bill pulled into a small settlement with "tourist homes," where he "had a delicious meal to fill the aching void—good country-style food that can't be beat." Rather than asking for a room, Bill opted to "wander along to the most promising looking barn." Fortunately, he ran into a farmer biking home. "It's a nice barn," he wrote to end his narrative.

The next night, Bill, dead tired from another tough day of biking, still wrote to Mary. He had climbed steadily all day, stopping briefly at a little white seventeenth-century log church with "vividly painted walls, altar and pulpit," in the tiny town of Bykle. The decorative folk artwork in the chapel was known as rosemaling, or rose-painting, popular in the region in the 1700s and 1800s.

With thighs and calves tight as a drum by the evening, Bill spotted a shed full of hay and "plunked himself down." Just before dark, he finished his three-page letter.

> I'm getting anxious to have a letter too. It will probably be Monday before that happens, however, since I won't get to Bergen before Sunday. I'll be glad to hear if you are going to be able to squeeze time in to go up to Dogwood Dell. If you do, you might ask mother about the possibility of our having one of the beds she brought from Tennessee.... Got to get our furniture in line! Your Bill.

On August 8, Bill was up early and on his bike by 6 a.m. "The sun was shining brightly, the air was crisp, the world was wonderful!" He quickly reached the top of a long hump of a hill he had avoided the night before, only to learn that hill was the first of three. He was now well above the tree line and could see big patches of snow, with "sparkling little lakes to reflect the majesty of the mountains." Shortly after reaching the top of the series of climbs, Bill saw some women milking goats at one of the "little shacks tucked in amidst the rocks." Referring to himself as "nosey me," he watched the women "milking them—the goat's head tucked between the women's knees as the women straddled them. They were milking 110 goats—it only took a couple minutes, however, for them to finish each one."

Late that afternoon, Bill descended to the village of Roldal, then endured another climb of twenty-five hundred feet over a span of six miles. He finally made it to the top in two hours, pushing his bike part of the way. At the top, he threw a couple of snowballs for Mary. The final fifteen miles downhill on the other side of the pass was "pure coasting." Bill wrote Mary that night, nestled in the hayloft in a barn at a fruit farm near a fjord. He described his view, consisting of "waterfalls of all sizes and shapes that come tumbling down the sides of the rock cliffs from the snow above" and "towering snowcapped mountains on each side" of the fjord.

He planned to bike the rest of the way to Bergen the next day, but the day was hot and the mountains steep. By the afternoon, Bill hopped onto a bus, later telling Mary, "I was a bit tired of my bicycle." That night, in Bergen, Bill found an unusual place to stay. "Now I'm sitting on top of Bergen—almost literally. The youth hostel is on a high cliff overlooking the city and bay. I came up by way of the inclined railway that goes straight up the mountainside. We are in an old German barracks, which, unfortunately, is now in the process of being made over into the hostel. And how I need a good bath!"

He closed his letter, expressing his constant longing to hear from Mary. "It's rough waiting until Monday to get those letters. All my love, Bill."

Chapter 37

Letters from Bergen, Norway
(August 10–11, 1947)

With his mind squarely focused on anticipated letters from Mary, on Sunday afternoon, August 10, Bill wrote Mary again.

> Mary, my love, I'm perched on a rock overlooking the city and harbor of Bergen and way out to the waters of the Atlantic. I'm sorry to say I can't quite see all the way to Greenville, S.C., but my thoughts are there as usual. The sun will soon be setting, so I may sit here for a while and try to do a bit of drawing. It's hectic to have to sit right here in Bergen without being able to get any mail. You can bet that I'll be down there bright and early in the morning to help the postmaster open up. Have my letters been off schedule when I'm way out in the sticks? Goodness knows when the mail goes out of some of the spots I've been in.

Before exploring Bergen that morning, Bill had gone to church at the over eight-hundred-year-old cathedral downtown, with its white stonemasonry and green spires.

> It's an interesting place. You can see where a section of several blocks had been bombed—the wreckage is still there. Bergen has some old parts, where the narrow little streets don't have room for a car, and some new modern sections. And it has enough water and parks to make it a good place to live. It's good I didn't only see Oslo, or I would have had a very false impression of Norway. I've loved every place else. And I'll love Bergen particularly when I get your letters in the morning.

The next day, Monday, August 11, was Bill's twenty-ninth birthday. Up early, he went straight to Bergen's post office. "The best birthday present I could have gotten was the big batch of letters which were waiting for me at the post office this morning. I just let the rest of the world go by while I read away to my heart's content. Now that I've finished a big chicken dinner in celebration of my 29th birthday, I'm in very much of a mellow, happy mood—at peace with the world."

He then turned to a "serious matter." Bill finally revealed why he asked Mary to join his family at Dogwood Dell later in the month. He had heard from his sister Clare. The engagement ring for Mary was ready.

Bill had a plan.

Dad writes that he hopes to have the members of the family out to Dogwood Dell on the 26th of August when they would announce Betty and Ted's engagement. It would be mighty nice if you could get up there for the occasion and make it a double event. I've written them to that effect. Clare will write you the details. I don't know of a better time or way to do it when I'm so far away. I wish your mother and father could be there too. The best time will be next summer when we can maybe tie the knot on the anniversary. You know I love you and will be mighty happy when the ring is on your finger even though I can't put it there myself.

That same day, Bill sent what can only be described as a cute, colorful postcard with a little Swedish boy smiling and gesturing at a Swedish girl on a couch on the front. On the back, Bill wrote a very special "formal proposal":

Bergen, Norway—August 11, 1947. This is far from a fancy way in which to make a formal proposal to the girl you love, but since our courtship has been a bit unusual, perhaps this is in keeping. At any rate, the young fellow on the opposite side is no more earnest and ardent than I am—and Norway seems to have no suitable card to fit the situation. You can be certain, Mary, that when the ring goes on your finger, it only seals the love that I have had for you for a long time. May God bless our engagement and marriage to come. Bill.

Chapter 38

Trip to Trondheim, Norway
(August 12–22, 1947)

On August 12, Bill found himself lounging in the cool air and fading sun on the *Nordfjord I*, cruising through the beautiful Sognefjord. He had boarded the boat on the night of his birthday, his destination being the town of Sogndal. With an estimated time of arrival at 8 p.m. the following day, he had ample time to write another letter. "Sweetest girl, it's been a nice easy, lazy day! Now it's evening and while the boat is tied up to get rid of some freight, I'll enjoy some time with you. Beautiful hazy-blue, snowcapped mountains are all around, so there couldn't be a better setting."

He had spent that day comfortably basking in the bright sun on the open top deck. The trip to Sogndal was an all-day affair because the boat constantly pulled into lakeside docks and dropped off freight. Each stop took about an hour, just long enough for Bill to walk around the towns and get a bite to eat. But his thoughts remained on the events back home. "Since there has been plenty of time, I've read all my letters over a couple of times to let everything sink in. I get a queer, and happy, feeling when I think that in a week or so you will have my ring on your finger. I can imagine there will be some people who will cock their eye at our long separation. I hope you and the family can get an evening arranged."

He then caught up on some "back items." The first was Mary's car, Jasper. "It sounds as if Jasper is really getting a workout. I thought I was pushing my old Chevy pretty hard when I put a thousand miles a month on it for 15 months, but you've got me beat. Don't run him to death before I get a ride—and 'be careful on the cross-streets.'"

The second item involved new skirt hem lines, which Mary

apparently mentioned in one of her letters. Bill responded, "I agree thoroughly about those 1920 styles—so don't let those skirts out too far. When I get back, I'll be bossy and make you satisfy me and not Dame Fashion. I suppose the dressmakers have to keep changing styles to sell their stuff."

The third item was all about letter logistics. His letters on his bike trip had been mailed haphazardly, resulting in him receiving fewer response letters in Bergen than he anticipated. He hoped they would show up in Trondheim. Then, for all letters after August 25, he gave Mary his Uppsala address, "S:t Johannesgaton 13, Ovra Fjullstesta Studenthemmet, Uppsala, Sweden," where he would be living for the next four months in the student housing.

Mary, probably wondering what type of wild man she was marrying, must have asked him about his penchant for sleeping in barns. He replied, "And the barns—they are quite comfortable, thank you. I don't sleep in the stables, you see, but in the hayloft (of which US barns have the same). The ones over here are much like the ones in Pennsylvania with an incline to the hayloft. So, they really are comfortable." In his letter, Bill even drew a small picture of a barn with stables below, with an arrow pointed at an incline up to the hayloft above.

The last item was Mary's ongoing collection of household items. "You must be a mighty busy girl getting so interested in china and silver. They should have more of the Edmonton pattern within the next year, so there is plenty of time. We can't get everything at once anyway."

He ended the letter by inviting Mary to dinner. "My stomach tells me it is time to eat—come and join me. I have bread, cheese, preserves, sardines, and nobody to eat with me. All my love, Bill."

Bill resumed his bike trip in the direction of Trondheim on August 13. He rode a pleasant sixty kilometers out of Sogndal, stopping at a tourist station for lunch. It was a "gingerbread sort" of house with "a waiting room chockfull of the ugliest Victorian age bric-a-bracs and pictures you can imagine." However, after a long wait, he savored delicious onion soup, fish with melted butter and potatoes, rich roast beef in big chunks, carrots, cabbage, and a dessert of fresh currents and cream. "I stuffed and stuffed" and "sat back, full as a tick, willing to pay whatever the lady asked." Amazingly, the bill was only "a little less than 80 cents."

After lunch, Bill discovered that the road beyond was straight up a steep mountain. He "could see the road winding up, up, up." A bus showed up, but it would not take his bike. He "was fit to be tied!" After two hours walking his bike up the mountain and dripping sweat all over the road, Bill was able to hop into a taxi with his bike. The taxi used low gear up to the summit and dropped Bill off at another tourist station. However, as it was already 9 p.m., there was no room at the inn. Bill finally found an empty construction crew shack and "gratefully crawled in for the night." It was too dark for him to write his usual evening letter.

The next day he conquered even steeper mountains, but he forced himself to write another letter regardless of his exhaustion. "Hi Butch! It is amazing how foolish and ignorant a person can be! When I planned my route, I just looked at a map and then took the roads that suited me. Sometimes that worked out well, sometimes it is almost disastrous! Yesterday was the 'almost disaster' sort." He had clearly underestimated the steep, mountainous roads, but the scenery had been incredible: "Jagged, rocky, spikes stuck up on all sides out of blankets of snow. The rivers and lakes ran full with water, which was gray from the rock dust which the ice ground up and the water carried off. There was not a sign of vegetation for miles—just rocks and moss and snow and water." He ended the letter, "So long for now, my sweet. I miss you terribly when I am alone and thinking of you all day long. All my love, Bill."

Bill had better luck the next day, writing his nightly letter from yet another barn, the first one he tried. This letter was entirely upbeat. "All that uphill stuff that I was worrying about turned out to be duck's soup." The first part, along a slow-moving river, went up gradually for about twenty miles. He biked it with ease. When the road got a bit steeper, it was a "good grade that I could do most of it without getting off to push." Then, just when the road got too steep, a lumber truck gave him a ride. He had ended the day with a descent down the "tiniest and curviest" road he had ever seen. "My brakes are a thing of the past; they catch at the slightest touch." But the "four or five waterfalls tumbling down along the way made it a musical ride."

The following day began with another fjord boat ride through a narrow gorge with towering mountains, dozens of waterfalls, and little farms and houses "tucked up out of this world." Once off the ferry, Bill rode another thirty-three miles to Ålesund, stopping twice to gorge himself on patches of "huge and delicious" huckleberries.

Ålesund, with a population of twenty thousand, was "quite an attractive little city." With major parts built on a row of islands, every available square inch was filled with streets and buildings. Because the entire city was destroyed in a fire in 1904, all the buildings were rebuilt in a colorful Art Nouveau style, making Ålesund feel more like a central European city. The key natural feature for Bill was the Fjellstua, "an abrupt hill," up 418 steps and overlooking the city. Of course, he climbed to the top to watch the sun go down. That night, Bill "found a convenient spot to sleep in the abandoned garden of a big house" on the road to Trondheim—"not too comfortable, but decidedly cheap."

In the morning, Bill boarded another boat headed to Trondheim. The weather and waves got "a bit rough when we hit the open sea." Rather than hanging over the rail and getting doused by the churning waters, Bill opted to quell his nausea by staying inside, telling Mary that "I'm not a good sailor so I took to bed instead."

Trondheim is famous for its magnificent Nidaros Cathedral, built over the burial site of King Olav II, who reigned from 1015 to 1028. Completed around 1300, the massive gray stone church, with dual towers and an ornate façade full of sculptures in front and a soaring green spire in the middle, took approximately two hundred thirty years to be constructed. Expansions were added at various times over the next seven hundred years. It remains the northernmost medieval cathedral in the world and is still used for the consecration of new kings of Norway.

Bill arrived in Trondheim at 8 a.m. on Sunday, August 17, following his rough boat ride. After a bite to eat, he went directly to the cathedral.

Mary, my darling, it was easily worth the long trip north to Trondheim just to see the great cathedral here. It is without a doubt the finest in Sweden and Norway, and I wouldn't doubt but what it is the finest Lutheran cathedral in the world. The first thing I noticed was the magnificent rose window—tremendously rich with its deep blues and reds. As I walked around the dim corridors with their beautiful stained-glass windows, a calmness seemed to spread right through me. There was one niche with a nine-foot statue of Thorvaldsen's Christ (I don't think it was the original). The chancel is quite unusual—almost enclosed in an octagonal chapel column and screen work.

He drew a detailed picture of the floor plan of the cathedral for Mary.

As it turned out, Bill was there on a special occasion. Just before the service, hundreds of soldiers filed in and filled the entire new end of the cathedral. After a "good sermon," the soldiers and most of the people left, but "then followed one of the most solemn and inspiring communion services" Bill had ever attended. "The whole morning was tremendously impressive."

After lunch, Bill walked the town and spent time drawing one of the old chapels. "It was funny to have curious heads peeking over my shoulder" as he worked to capture the scene with his pastels (one of these drawings adorns the cover of this book). Then Bill went back to the cathedral to spend another hour, learning that much of it was newer than he first thought. Renovations had started in 1869 and were still going strong. Fifty men were employed full-time just to do the stonework involved in the colossal task.

"And tomorrow—more mail!!" he wrote, knowing that Mary had addressed her letters to Trondheim for the last week or two. Indeed, in the morning he found a trio of letters from Mary at the post office. He immediately wrote her again. "I've just finished reading three swell letters. It's wonderful to hear from you, Mary—every letter is a cherished event. It sounds as though you have really been in a whirl this summer, flitting about all over the state. I'm glad it makes the time go faster for you."

With summer ending, the formal engagement weekend in Hendersonville was on his mind. "I'm wondering what has been decided about the trip to Dogwood Dell—if you can stay for the 26th, or whether Dad decided to make it earlier. At any rate, I'm happy that you will be there with the family. My heart will be right there even though my body is thousands of miles away."

Bill initially planned to leave Trondheim the next day, but no boat was available for three days. At the end of his letter that night, he told Mary, "It's funny, but I'm getting anxious to get back to Sweden. I suppose I feel more settled there than here in Norway." He added, "I'll be back tomorrow, but I have no idea where."

This time, Bill's night was not over. Right after finishing his letter, he was summoned outside by the owner of the hostel to look up at the sky. "It was quite a sight. At first, there was a sort of ring of greenish-yellow shimmering light, something about the size of a rainbow. Then it began to shift and squirm in a snaky pattern with parts of it becoming very bright and then dying out. They said it was an omen of good weather." It was Bill's first view of the Northern Lights—the Aurora Borealis.

Indeed, the next morning, the weather was perfect. Bill leisurely biked out of Trondheim, heading south. The road followed a river surrounded by rolling hills and "fertile, prosperous farms," with sod-roofed buildings. Bill's destination was the town of Roras. Though the road was narrow, he made good time. Around 5 p.m., Bill met a farmer walking along the road and was invited to stay in the farmer's barn. However, because the night was so pretty, Bill decided to "bed down in a little grassy birch woods instead." For dinner, Bill found a spot filled with "raspberries, huckleberries, wild strawberries and a load of lingonberries, which taste something like cranberries." But he told Mary, "I'd swap them all for some of those peaches in S.C.—particularly the one I love. Always yours, Bill."

"Hey there Browneyes!" Bill wrote early on Thursday morning, August 21, from the town of Roras. The prior day's ride had been eventful. As he topped one ridge, Bill instantly applied his brakes with a loud screech when he encountered a huge bull moose with a four-foot spread of antlers in the middle of the road less than fifty feet ahead of him. The startled moose glanced in Bill's direction, then bolted into the woods so fast that Bill was unable to get a photo. Later that day, Bill came upon a series of houses with flags flying at half-mast. A lady hailed him and asked if he would help raise her flag again. It turned out that she had hosted a funeral service for her neighbor's twenty-one-year-old son who had drowned while in military service. She rewarded Bill for his help with leftover cheese and cakes from the funeral reception.

Roras was a unique silver and copper mining town with no paved roads. Half of the houses were red or dark-stained log cabins with sod roofs, creating an almost medieval feel, yet it was a thriving city featuring a working three-hundred-year-old copper mine and a big smelter. Bill wandered through a row of rustic iron and copper crafts and souvenirs shops, then visited several wool mills and furriers. In the evening, he biked two miles out of town to visit the town's pastor. The pastor was not home, but his "motherly, gray-haired wife was very gracious," inviting him in for coffee and cakes. Bill always had a knack for finding free food and enjoyed talking with pastors' wives, getting some inside information about ministerial life.

Bill spent most of the next day in Roras walking around and doing "a bit of drawing." He told Mary, "I can't say that I'm getting any better at the latter, but it's fun!" In the afternoon, he slowly rode the final twenty miles to the lake on the border between Norway and Sweden where the boat would depart the next morning. He found some nourishment along the way; as he described it, "the huckleberries really interfered with my progress—it will take me days to get the blue off of my teeth."

Bill finished his letter to Mary that evening from the dock. "There is hardly a ripple stirring on Lake Fernund tonight. The only noise is the chirping of a few birds in the woods. The only thing at this end of the lake is the boat and the house where the captain lives. But I'm all ready and waiting for the 10:10 a.m. whistle tomorrow."

After chatting with the captain, Bill was invited to spend the night on deck. He wrote, "If it gets cold, I'm liable to move down into the cabin. The mosquitoes seem pretty bad too." The next morning, Bill added to his letter. He did end up sleeping in the cabin when the temperature dropped precipitously that night. Luckily, the captain invited him to have coffee and cakes for breakfast, so he was not hungry on the first part of the twenty-four-hour voyage. He also hit the jackpot for dinner on the boat. "The lady who was at the house last night has a little kitchen aboard…and asked if I liked fish. 'Nuff said! It was free too! What's more, I was the only one that got a real meal besides the crew. I was especially grateful because we are in a rather desolate country and won't land until it's too late to buy stuff. And my box of food is empty."

Bill then cited a single disappointment. "There is one thing I regret about leaving Norway. Ever since I've been here, I've had my eye open to find one of those beautiful, hand-knit sweaters with the Norwegian motif to get for you. I saw a couple about a week ago, but they were too expensive. Since then, I haven't seen a one I really liked. That seems to have been a favorite purchase for all the tourists this summer."

Bill closed his letter with one final thing on his mind. "Tomorrow you will be heading for Dogwood Dell. I'd give my right arm to be along. I know it will be rather tough on you when Ted is with Betty and I'm not there. All this week, I've felt like picking up and heading for the States and you. It's time I got to Uppsala and to work!! I love you, Bill."

PART VI

THE FORMAL ENGAGEMENT

Chapter 39

Hendersonville, North Carolina
(August 23–30, 1947)

Saturday night, August 23, 1947:

> Mary, my brown-eyed sweetheart, you are no doubt in the
> bosom of my family at this moment. That makes me feel
> good, even though I'm not there with you. I'm awfully glad
> that you won't have to "break into" a strange family when you
> marry me. And I'm glad for Mom and Dad that they know
> you well. It generally takes Mother a good while to accept
> someone into a close relationship, but you were in her good
> graces long before she knew I would enter the picture. I only
> wish that I had had time to visit your father. No parents could
> have been more understanding than yours though, in spite of
> my being a stranger, more or less.

Bill was back in Sweden, writing his letter from an old log cabin,
on a century-old desk with huge heavy drawers and massive planks for
the desktop. Once off the boat, he had biked eighty-five miles that day,
"riding through scrubby pine woods on a dusty dirt road." The ride was
interrupted by two flat tires, resulting in lengthy delays. Fortunately,
there were nearby huckleberry bushes to keep him occupied. He was all
alone as he wrote Mary, sad that he was not back at Dogwood Dell to
give her the long-awaited engagement ring. He hoped his father would
come through for him.

Mary arrived at Dogwood Dell in time for lunch on that same day,
Saturday, August 23. That afternoon, on a hike up to some nearby falls,
Bill's sister, Clare, filled Mary in on the plans for the formal engage-
ment weekend. The events of Sunday, August 24, are detailed in a letter

on light yellow stationery that Mary wrote Bill on the morning of Monday, August 25.[4]

> Bill, my dearest, yesterday was a highlight I shall never forget…. Sunday morning just before we were to leave for Sunday School, your dad led me down the hill before the others were ready—and then presented me with the most beautiful engagement ring I have ever seen. It's the "order" to a "T." We had a nice talk and he made me feel every bit a member of the family. 'Course I was left somewhat speechless—and as I read your note, I was so far away from here—somewhere in Norway—perhaps on top of some mountain—realizing what a beautiful life together there is before us and how I can ever live up to it all. In about another year, we'll be taking that final step which will bring us together for always. It's wonderful to look forward and plan for—God has been good to me and I shall never forget it.

> I'm as happy as I can be without actually having you here with me. And this afternoon, the double affair comes off. Mom and Dad are coming. Ted, Betty, and I went over to Saluda yesterday to see them. Mom says tell "her other son, hello." We all think that this is the best time to make "our" announcement. This is the only time probably that the two families will be together. So, it will be as complete as I can be without you present. Bill, my love for you grows deeper day by day. That's a wonderful feeling.

Mary could not finish her letter without trying to describe the ring to Bill.

"I do wish you could see this ring. It is beautiful. I'll see what I can do in describing it. It is a beautiful single stone set into a perfectly plain yellow gold band—has a four-post or square appearance. I haven't done a very good job of this. You'll just have to see to see it for yourself. If I find a picture anything like it, I'll send it to you. It's just what I've always dreamed of."

---

[4] The third letter Bill kept over the years.

Before completing the letter, Mary slipped in some comments on her soon-to-be nephew Henry, Clare and Johnny's third child and first son. "I wish you could see Henry. He is walking all over the place and is as cute as can be. Knows no stranger and always wakes with a smile." She closed the letter, "I'll have to tell you the rest about my visit in the next letter. All my love to you—Mary."

Meanwhile, on that Sunday, Bill completed his lonely bike trip by cycling the twenty-five miles to the town of Mora. He had been invited to spend a week working at the Zorn Museum by one of his Stockholm professors, who was also the "boss" of the museum. Most of the summer interns were leaving, so Bill jumped at the chance to make some money before the fall semester started in Uppsala. He looked forward to learning about Anders Zorn, "Sweden's gift to the art world." Zorn had such international acclaim that his portrait subjects included presidents Grover Cleveland, William Taft, and Teddy Roosevelt.

On Monday night, August 25, Bill wrote Mary again, still in the dark about the events back home.

> My Mary, I've been wondering tonight whether you have yet got that ring on your finger. I never heard whether Dad changed the date to suit your convenience. At any rate, I just celebrated—a big glass of milk and four fancy cakes down at the local kandita. I suppose I'll have to wait until Monday, or perhaps later, to find out what really happened. I blew you a kiss to go with the ring—hope it arrived on schedule.

He told Mary about his mundane work at the museum, mindlessly sorting postcards by country. He added his impression of Zorn's artworks, including quite a few nudes. "I like his work immensely," he confessed.

Bill's work at the museum got tougher on Tuesday. Rather than sort postcards, he was assigned to dig up a tree stump outside the building. He and another guy got half of the stump out that sweltering day, then jumped into a local lake to wash off the sweat and dirt. Surprisingly, he told Mary, "It's a funny thing—I have managed to become a fair swimmer, even a senior Red Cross lifesaver, and worked one summer at a camp as a lifeguard; but I've never really liked or felt at home

197

in the water. Give me a sailboat and I'm perfectly content, but swimming doesn't interest me in the least. I enjoy an afternoon on the beach, but pools aren't for me."

He ended his letter that Tuesday night, yearning for more letters from Mary. He knew that none would come to Mora. "Next week this time, I'll be settled in Uppsala and the old mailman will start regular deliveries. That will be wonderful! I love you, Mary, Bill."

On Wednesday, August 27, Bill wrote to Mary and Mary wrote to Bill.[5] The letters were quite different. Bill's letter, which was addressed, "Hi Butch!" covered life in Mora, the rest of the stump removal, and a trip to the local theater, where Bill had watched *The Apache Trail*. Bill thought it odd that the cinema was filled with almost all guys and no couples. "You would think that with such a nice spot, and the only one open at night, couples would use it as headquarters. Sweden's odd in such matters!"

Mary's letter, written on light blue stationery, covered the formal engagement party on the evening of August 25 back in North Carolina.

> Bill, my darling, it's all announced and everything's right with the world. I've met all the in-laws—on your dad's side. How I wished for you with everybody gathered 'round—and when your dad announced that the gathering wasn't just an ordinary gathering—but a special occasion. Then he asked Dad for his announcement. And Dad was so sweet making the "one" announcement of his life. Then came Betty's and Ted's announcement. Uncle William then had a betrothal service which was beautiful. Then all the "oohs" and "ahs" and best wishes and shaking hands. This was all followed with a delicious supper. How you would have enjoyed that!

Mary's special day was not over though.

> After a little while, we went over to Aunt Florence's—Betty getting us lost twice before we got there. While there, your dad projected the slides you had sent. They were gorgeous—and I like one especially well. Could you guess which one?

---

[5] Her fourth and final letter in the leather portfolio.

We just "partied" and "partied"—but one thing was missing—'Course one William [referring to Bill's uncle] was there—but somehow he didn't quite take the place of "the" William. We've got lots of places to visit if we accept all the invitations extended.

Then she posed a question. "Since we made the occasion one of a double announcement, don't you think it would be wonderful to make it a double wedding too? If so, you'll surely have to use your influence on your sister. We all talked about it—but I still think it will take some compromising…. My love always, Mary."

Of course, while at Mora, Bill had not yet received either of Mary's two letters about the engagement ring or party. He had nothing much to talk about in his next letter. He had read a *Time* magazine article about prices soaring in America, so he asked Mary to start pricing "stoves, Frigidaires, washing machines, etc." He ended his letter that afternoon, "Days are beginning to drag already. I think it is because I am so anxious to get mail from Stockholm and Uppsala. So long, my love. Your Bill."

Bill continued the theme the next night in Mora:

Sweet Mary, there is a big full moon shining on Mora tonight—just the time to take a long stroll or tuck your sweetheart tight in your arms. Woe is me!! Sometimes all your good intentions and all your dreams can leave you feeling mighty lonely. Maybe it wasn't a good idea to hibernate here all by myself for a week. It will be better in a couple of days when I have some mail in my hand.

On August 30, still in Mora, Bill could not believe his luck. "Maria min, the most wonderful thing happened this morning—I got 8 letters, 4 of them from you. I have no idea how it all happened." As it turned out, the letters had been delivered to Stockholm University, then forwarded to Mora after one of Bill's friends informed the university of Bill's whereabouts. Bill immediately scribbled off another letter to Mary. He described the mail adventure as "a roundabout trip, but you can bet I was mighty happy to see those sweet letters."

But Mary's backlogged letters were all written before her big weekend at Dogwood Dell. Frustrated, Bill responded,

> In the last one you were just getting things cleaned up at the office to run off to Dogwood Dell, so I still don't know yet how things turned out. I'm glad you seem to have gotten together on Monday night as I thought you would. That was the evening I celebrated anyway. But best of all, I am glad that your parents were so close. I'll be mighty anxious to hear if they were present.

He then offered an apology. "After I had written you about plans for the announcement and all, I began to think I was out of place. It is you and your parents who should decide such things. The occasion seemed so perfect, though, that I thought you would like it better that way."

He ended the letter, "Good night, my sweetheart. God bless you always. I am always sending my love to you. Your Bill."

PART VII

SEPARATION IN UPPSALA

PART II

SEPARATION APPEALS

Chapter 40

Letters from Uppsala
(September 1–October 8, 1947)

"Sweet Mary, here I am at last! It really feels good to be in a place where I can settle down for a while. The charm of Uppsala has already been working on me in the few hours I've been here. It should be a pleasant and interesting stay here."

Bill spent most of his letter on September 1, 1947, describing his new living quarters at the student housing in Uppsala, complete with a drawing showing the locations of his bed, closet, radiator, and bathroom. He had hoped to find a letter from Mary in Uppsala, but none had arrived. Bill closed his letter, "One of the best parts of being here, sweetheart, is that I can get the mail on a regular schedule and get your picture where I can see you every time I come in. I guess I'm head over heels in love! Always yours, Bill."

Late the next day, the two letters from Mary about the engagement ring and announcement party finally came. Bill immediately wrote his sweetheart.

Hi there, fiancée! Now I know that it has actually taken place—it's wonderful, just wonderful! Of course, from this distance it doesn't make quite as much of a change as it does to you. I've been "engaged" ever since one night in Greenville last January. It makes me mighty proud though to have everybody know that we belong to each other now and always. I'm awfully glad that your parents were able to get up to Dogwood Dell and make a real announcement. It must have been quite a fancy, and yet solemn, occasion. And as for that double wedding, I'm all for it. In fact, I had mentioned that to Betty when she first wrote that she and Ted had matters settled. I rather imagine that she would be a hard one to change though. Any time in August would suit me, but I can't see how it could be any sooner than that.

Bill then interjected some confusion into the wedding plans.

You realize of course that I talk of marriage when I have absolutely no idea how I'm going to support you. I'm hoping and praying that there will be a place for me to work when I get back, but you know that a minister's life is rather uncertain in the matter of a "call." Next spring, I will write some synod presidents and some men at seminary and tell them I'm available, but I'm a long way off and they may not want to take me blindly. So, if I have to wait a while after I get home that may make a wedding date uncertain too. Personally, it wouldn't make any difference. We could live at Dogwood Dell a couple of months if worse came to worse. I'm not worrying—there is always work to be done if one is willing to do it.

He closed the letter, "So, the day ended perfectly. The room is full of junk, I'm tired out, but all's right with the world cause I'm in love with you. Your Bill."

With his bike trip done and the excitement of the official engagement over, on his first Friday night in Uppsala, Bill admitted to Mary that he was struggling to reorient himself: "Mary, my love, my eyes are drooping. I think it will take a while for me to get used to this indoor life after a summer in the open air. About this time of night (10 p.m.) I'm ready for bed—barns don't usually have electric lights and modern conveniences. I'll have to make up for it by getting up with the chickens. That is hard, too!" His Saturday night letter followed that theme. "Maybe Saturday night is the loneliest night in the week—I must say that there has been no excitement about this one. We eat midday at 4:30; that takes an hour at the most; and how many hours are left? I wasn't in the mood for a movie, so I just came up to the room and have been reading Swedish up until now. Ain't that fun!"

To perk up his mood, Bill spruced up his dorm room with a Zorn print of "Dalorna-dressed girls," some fresh, bright orange daisy-like flowers, and an original painting Bill made from one of his sketches in

Norway. "So, I'm getting fancy! One more picture and I'll be set." Bill also told Mary about the dorm's housemother, who had a strong motherly instinct. He added, "But I am ready for a different kind of caretaker—a wife instead of a mother. It will be wonderful when you take over, sweet Mary. All my love, Bill."

On Sunday morning, September 7, rather than attending church at the large cathedral in Uppsala, Bill opted to go to the smaller Holy Trinity church next to the cathedral. Interestingly, Uppsala's Lutherans were divided into two parishes, but the two churches were side by side. Bill described Holy Trinity as "a beautiful, small church with parts going back to the 1100s—much more 'homey' than the massive cathedral."

But when he wrote Mary that night, his mind was still focused on her.

Hi Butch! I wonder what you are doing tonight. Things are mighty quiet around this neck of the woods, and I could certainly use some company. Come on and join me! Your health camp must have kept you busy this week, as a letter is a day or so overdue. I hope the camp was a big success and that your labors were well rewarded. You know something? I have not heard one word in any of your letters or from home as to your opinion of my new brother-in-law-to-be. I only saw Ted for a few minutes before I sailed for Sweden and would like to hear something about him. You can be frank of course. You better be all the time, or I'll turn you over my knee!

The next night, Bill had still not gotten a letter from Mary. "I was doomed to disappointment as far as the mail was concerned—nothing of any description came for me today. Better luck tomorrow I hope."

Without much news to report, Bill noted that some Hungarian students had arrived at Uppsala University, having just gotten back from a month in Finland. They reported that Christianity in Finland is "strong and vigorous—quite a contrast to Sweden and Norway." Bill indicated that he hoped to get over to Finland for a week sometime in the fall.

Not long after Bill arrived in Uppsala, the summer warmth waned.

On September 10, Bill wrote, "My Mary, I think the weather has finally broken. Last night we had a shower and this evening we had a cloudburst. On top of that, it is quite cool now…. Today for the first time, I have a feeling that fall is in the air. I always welcome the changing seasons, but I can't say that I'm looking forward to a long cold winter." In his letter, Bill had one request. "Mary, my love, would you be sweet and stick a couple of teabags in a letter occasionally—just ordinary mail. They don't seem to have such things here and it will give a variety to my coffee diet. It's too much trouble to send and get a package, the duty office has a lot of red tape."

Mary fulfilled his order within two weeks.

The next day, Bill spent a few hours with Gyorgy, a student pastor from the Hungary group. According to his next letter to Mary, Gyorgy told Bill that "the central European lands expect tremendous things from the US, not in a material way, but in spiritual and moral leadership." Bill was "afraid the average American doesn't feel the responsibility that the US has as the power of western civilization," adding that "Russia is bombarding the lands under her influence with all kinds of propaganda with definite aggressive programs, while we are more apt to want to keep our hands off and let the nations shift for themselves." Gyorgy, who had also spent time in the US that year, felt that the vitality and future of the Lutheran denomination depended on the Finnish and American churches rapidly developing young pastors. Bill wrote Mary, "I hope and pray that we can measure up."

Bill knew he had to make some money if he intended to travel that winter. He met with a university official about possibly tutoring students in English. He told Mary,

> It would help a lot to have a few kronor coming in on the side. I won't need it particularly here in Uppsala, but I must do a bit of figuring if I want to go to Belgium next Christmas, travel a month or so next summer, and still have enough money for that passage home. And of course the latter is the most important since I have so much to go home to. I get awfully lonesome for you sometimes, but your love comes right on across the waves. It's wonderful! I love you, too. Bill.

"Min lilla, it is time to take a break from reading about Plato, Aristotle, Stoicism, etc., and think about something pleasant—such as what my brown-eyed sweetheart is doing about this time. You are probably working your head off as usual," Bill wrote on September 12. He had just gotten a letter from Mary and was glad she got back from a health education camp "without any broken bones, jigger bites, or poison ivy."

He had also received a letter from his mother, leading Bill to feel that his parents were still uncertain about Betty's fiancé, Ted. "Of course, they would never say anything directly, but I just have that feeling. In a way, Betty was much closer to them than Clare and me, and perhaps they feel more deeply concerned about her. Betty seems happy though and that is what counts. It will be a different life in the Northern Methodist Church, but she will adjust."

With the weather cooling, Bill tried to get his only jacket—his beat-up old green army overcoat—dyed brown. "But the dyers said the material was too hard and heavy. So, I guess I will smother my vanity and wear it just so as I did last winter. Warmth comes before beauty here in Sweden."

Speaking of beauty, in that same letter, Bill revealed that he had gotten a "long-overdue" letter from Greta, the "Scottish lassie in Edinburgh" he used to visit when in Glasgow towards the end of his military duty. As Bill described her to Mary,

> She is a cute little blonde and one of the most interesting friends I ever had. I think I was her first contact with religion, altho' she had high ideals and principles. I used to have "fish and chips," that her mother was expert in fixing, almost every Sunday night I was there. She was an inquisitive little thing, and we had some lively discussions. I rather think her family were communists—at least they had a picture of Joe Stalin in the living room.

He added that he had not gotten any letter from Greta in over a year.

Why Bill received a letter from Greta more than a year after he said goodbye is unknown. Given his penchant for writing letters, Bill probably wrote to tell her he was happily engaged. Thankfully, Bill kept his description of his Scottish lassie and her communist parents to a minimum. Norma and Greta were in his past—temporary relationships with no lasting attachments. His heart was only with his brown-eyed sweetheart back in South Carolina.

On Sunday, September 14, Bill wrote Mary again, noting another anniversary.

> Sweet Mary, do you realize it has been eight months since I caught the train out of Greenville that night in January? They have been blessed months, not only because of my experiences over here, but because I feel our love has had time to mature and grow richer. I have wondered in these months if we will feel a bit strange with each other when next summer comes around and we are together again, but somehow, I feel that it will be perfectly natural and as if there had been no long separation. I still can't help feeling amazed often though at the way you let a "stranger" win your love. Or had you some idea how my mind was working all the time? Did you realize that in the time after we first met in Jackson, I dreamt of the possibility of your becoming my wife? I would never have started writing you otherwise! I'm mightily grateful other distractions were never strong enough to keep that dream from coming true.

Bill realized that Mary was the only girl for whom he had enduring dreams. Technically, it was not *love* at first sight, but it definitely had been *interest* at first sight. Bill was thankful he had allowed his interest to grow slowly and steadily until Mary and he were both ready for their dreams to come true and to last.

The next night, Bill wrote Mary again after getting her belated birthday package.

> I got a letter and the box today. Thanks heaps for the book. It will fit perfectly with what I'm studying now—and be a lot easier to read than Swedish. The handkerchiefs are always welcome, and I was particularly glad to get the tie because I had forgotten to bring a plain blue one with me. And be sure

to thank your mother for me for letting me have the picture. It's quite pert and glamourous.

He closed, apparently responding to something Mary said in her letter. "It looks as if I just got that ring round your finger just in time to keep these 'mama wolves' off your doorstep. Well, everybody can't be as fortunate as I. Always yours, Bill."

Indeed, until the formal engagement announcement appeared in the papers and Mary had a ring on her finger, she was still "available" in Greenville social circles. There were plenty of mothers out there who thought Mary would make the perfect wife for their sons. But in Mary's eyes, she was unavailable, ring or no ring. Nevertheless, it was nice to have a diamond on her left hand to leave no confusion among her friends and possible suitors.

Bill thanked God that he had managed to stir up the courage to ask Mary to marry him before he left for Sweden, getting her informal, private commitment before he departed. Now, with the formal announcement and ring, their future was publicly sealed. He felt blessed and secure in his love for Mary and their future together.

However, as each day passed, he found himself feeling lonelier and lonelier.

Bill's program at Uppsala University in fall 1947 was less than stringent. He was auditing or merely sitting in on lectures for several courses, including religious ethics, while supplementing his continuing ministerial education by studying various church services and liturgies on his own. His Swedish had improved sufficiently to understand almost all the lectures, and he was now able to help teach English to some nurses to make extra money.

On one weekday night, he joined hundreds of students for a "high church" service at the cathedral. The boys were required to sit on one side and the girls on the other. Everyone was constantly kneeling and genuflecting. Most of the liturgy was a cappella from chanters. He told Mary, "It was all reverently done, but I couldn't help but feel out of place. I'm liturgically-minded myself, but when it goes so far, then it seems to me to be cold and unnatural."

Bill found that he increasingly disliked the highly structured practices of the more conservative and traditional churches. He preferred a more informal, intimate setting in which all congregants could sing and participate in a personal, joyful way, whether they were on key or tone-deaf. The more he experienced "high church," with its elaborate vestments and limited congregational involvement, the less he liked it. The organ music in the large churches was wonderful, but, for Bill, if it drowned out the regular attendees below, it defeated the purpose of the individual and collective worship experience.

Ten months of visiting dozens, maybe hundreds, of churches of all shapes and sizes in Sweden and Norway was slowly but steadily influencing Bill's vision of his future in church ministry. He was narrowing his thoughts about where he wanted to be and what type of church he wanted to lead.

On September 16, Bill got a letter from Clare, leading him to tell Mary a little more about his older sister.

> This morning I got a letter from Clare, telling me her version of the events at Dogwood Dell. She writes four or five times a year and her letters are always so much like talking to her that it is wonderful to get them. Since we grew up together, we have been mighty close. Of course, there was the time during high school when I couldn't stand her, but that changed in a hurry after we got to Newberry together. I guess I had as many dates with her as with any other girl in college. She has turned out to be a mighty fine wife and mother, too.

Bill hoped that someday he could match his older sister's parental skills.

That Thursday, Bill got another letter from Mary about recent happenings at her job in Greenville. He responded, "No doubt you are by this time all settled down in your new office—probably playing the big woman executive in great style. I wouldn't dare to disturb you in such a setting, I'm sure. It is nice that they recognize quality and give you the best office!"

Mary also mentioned a silver pin Bill had sent her from Bergen. Now that she had received it, he told her how he came to purchase it. "The pin came from Norway in the Schesdal Valley north of Kristensand. One day when I was riding along, I saw a sign and a display case of silver, so I stopped. It is handmade and typical of Norway. At least half the females you saw had a pin of that sort—not that small, however. Usually, they are three times that size…." He quickly explained that the larger ones simply cost too much.

Bill's next two letters described his plan to get a visa in Stockholm for his anticipated trip to Finland. But his trip to Stockholm was delayed when he attended a meeting at which he ran into Ulla Larssen, who had been the archbishop's secretary at the Lund conference. "She is a striking, six-footer and is getting married tomorrow afternoon. She invited me to the wedding, so that's one reason I think I'll wait until Monday for Stockholm. I have to see how these things are done, you know. I'll be imagining another day and another bride no doubt. Gee, but I love you, Mary. Your Bill."

The next night, Bill told Mary all about the wedding.

Sweet Mary, I did venture out long enough to see Ulla's wedding. It was pretty, solemn, and dream provoking. Getting married is a serious business, isn't it? You realize it more and more all the time when you know that it won't be too long before you are walking down the aisle yourself. But you can't help but be thrilled at the thought of sharing in the life of the one you love, day in and day out. Ulla was a beautiful bride. Her husband is just as tall as she, so they made a striking pair. Here in Sweden, they walk down the aisle together—I guess the groom is afraid she will get away.

Having described the Swedish version, Bill turned to another wedding on his mind.

You have never said anything about where you figure on having the knot tied or what kind of a wedding (now that chrysanthemums probably won't be ripe). I haven't heard from Betty, but I rather doubt if they will wait until I get home. If you have any ideas about attendants and stuff, you will have to let me know in plenty of time to scare up some fellows. All my friends are scattered from here to yonder.

The next evening, a Sunday, Bill mistakenly wrote on the back page of the folded stationery instead of the inner second page. He came up with a good excuse. "Looks as though I got a bit tangled up with this piece of paper and started at the back. Guess I got all confused thinking about you." In that letter, Bill told Mary he had received a letter from his Uncle William, who had been at the Dogwood Dell formal engagement weekend. "You made quite a hit with him. I could tell he was happy at my good fortune. He has been wonderful to me."

Bill finally went to Stockholm the following day, in the pouring rain. He got soaked trying to find the Finnish visa office, only to learn that it was a stone's throw away from his old apartment in Stockholm ("Dumb me!"). The clerk took his application and said he would send the visa and Bill's passport back later. While in Stockholm, Bill also booked overnight passage to Finland for the night of October 9. He planned to play hooky for at least a week in October to accommodate the trip. Ever the less-than-diligent student, Bill told Mary, "It's nice not to worry about classes, isn't it?"

On the afternoon of September 24, Bill had his first session teaching English. The leader of the program was a "friendly gray-haired teacher in the nursing school." The students included "a red cross lady, the receptionist for the nursing school, and two nurses—one a typical buxom Scandinavian blonde and the other a right attractive brunette." Fortunately, they were only interested in learning simple conversational English, as Bill had not found any good book on how to teach proper English to non-English speakers.

Having made some money that afternoon, that evening Bill took in the movie *Humoresque* with Joan Crawford and John Garfield. "It was great! The music was wonderful—I've always had a soft spot for the violin, always wanted to substitute that for the piano, but never succeeded. The love story was dramatic for a change and not the usual Hollywood mush."

On September 25, Bill got two letters from Mary, one written on September 20 and the other on September 22, just three days before. With one letter, Mary included a colorful pen and ink sketch of her, drawn by a friend who was an amateur painter. Candidly, Bill did not think the portrait looked much like Mary, but he told Mary to thank her friend.

In one of her letters, Mary must have wondered out loud whether Betty had acted as a matchmaker. She asked Bill if Betty knew Bill's thoughts about his possible future with Mary when she invited Mary to come to Burlington the year before. Bill responded, "Not definitely, but she had a good idea! You must remember that I hadn't seen her for nearly two years by that time. She was probably doing some wishful thinking." Bill shuddered to think how different his life would be if his little sister had not brought her roommate into his life, not once but twice.

Bill enjoyed the cathedral in Uppsala much more than its counterpart in Stockholm. In his letter to Mary on September 26, he told her why. He was going to "inspiring" Friday night services with special organ music (all J. S. Bach), a hymn, scripture readings, and a prayer. "The organ is wonderful, and the organist matches the instrument. When the full tones began rolling through the massive cathedral and echoes rang about the columns, it gives you a real lift. Things like that are what make Uppsala a hundred times better than Stockholm."

Bill also enjoyed the bells ringing almost all the time at Uppsala. Three clocks rang every fifteen minutes, specifically: "The town hall's clang, Holy Trinity Church's silvery bong, and the cathedral's deep dong. They ring for funerals, weddings and after services, so it's quite a musical town. When the hours get to 10 and 12, they have a gay time of it. It's pleasant and you don't need a watch—just wait fifteen minutes!"

But not everything in Uppsala was good. That same day, Bill was treated to a Swedish delicacy called "surstromming," loosely translated as "sour herring." In his letter, he told Mary, "I would be more apt to call it 'rotten fish.' I tried one—that was more than enough. The worst part of it is the smell. Even now at eleven o'clock the house smells to high heaven. It really is a sort of pickled fish, with only the head removed. That's one I won't try again!"

Bill ended the letter, "Mary, you have seemed mighty close the past couple weeks. It's wonderful to have mail so often and regular again. I love it and you. Yours always, Bill."

On September 29, Bill got a "nice letter" from Mary's mother, with another report on the engagement party. The only missing report about that day was from Betty. Bill wondered how Betty felt about the idea of a double wedding and hoped she would weigh in soon.

It being the end of the month, Bill sent Mary a little box with a "bit of glass," a candlestick he had bought at Orrefors back in June. He also included a souvenir from Mora. None of these gifts were expensive, but Bill wanted to make sure Mary received something from him at the end of every month. He also told Mary how famous she was getting to be in Uppsala. "Everybody is getting to know you around here. They recognize your letters and most of the fellows have been in the room and admired you from the pictures. They have been very much interested in the tinted picture and the fancy frame, as well as the beauty of the dark-haired 'flicka.' Of course, I beam with pride and say 'Yeah, that's my Mary!' I love you, Bill."

His pride was surpassed only by his nostalgia for the last time he had seen Mary. His September 30 letter started, "My sweet Mary, there is a big full moon shining tonight—but it is shining out of a mighty cold looking sky. I'd have to hug you awfully tight to keep you warm on a night like this. But if I remember correctly, it wasn't particularly warm one night on a squeaking davenport in Greenville—and that was the beginning of a world of happiness."

Curiously, Mary must have told Bill that she planned to go on a trip to Atlantic City in New Jersey. Why she was going there is unknown, but Bill wrote a full paragraph about it in his letter of October 1.

> It's too late for you to get in on the Miss America business so I don't see why you should go to Atlantic City. I'll bet it is cold there now anyway. Not that I have any say in the matter of course—you may already be there by the time this letter gets to the States. I wouldn't want you to let S.C. down at any rate. As a matter of fact, I've always had a soft spot in my heart for Atlantic City. Way back in the days before Uncle William was married—when I was just 10 or 11—he used to go there for a week or so after Easter each year, and he always sent a box of saltwater taffy. I loved it!

He followed that paragraph with another unusual comment about several of Mary's colleagues getting engaged. "It sounds to me as if the public health program knows how to pick the attractive girls—if the acquiring of rings is any indication. They are liable to start signing you up for five years instead of two, or accepting only cross-eyed, pigeon-toed applicants."

Thankfully, Mary's reactions to these comments were not preserved.

On the night of October 2, 1947, Bill wrote,

I'm inclined to be a lone wolf. Did you know that? I enjoy being with people, but I'm just as content by myself. For example, so many of my friends couldn't understand how I could take off this summer all by my lonesome, but it never occurred to me. In a way, it's selfish because I don't want to be bothered by what someone else wants to do. I have never had the least qualms about picking up and leaving a place where I had many friends and ties and heading for somewhere entirely new. I have always hated to have ties and claims on me. Strangely enough, you don't seem to come under such a category at all. Love does that, I suppose! But maybe it is good that you know a few things like that. I doubt if there is any couple that don't have some adjustments to make. I hope and pray that ours will always be treated with love and understanding.

Bill's next few letters demonstrated that though he had frequently picked up and moved on, he never left friends or acquaintances behind. That morning he received a letter from "Aunt Katie," a woman from Charleston from his childhood. "She had read in the *News and Courier* of our engagement and was happy to see I had been smart enough to get a South Carolina girl. Katie is quite a gal—used to take Clare and me with all her little nieces and nephews to play in Hampton Park when we lived in Charleston."

Another four-page letter had come from a buddy named Bob, from pre-Gettysburg days.

He finally got his Ph.D. from Yale last spring after struggling on his dissertation for over two years. Now he is assistant pastor in a big church in Sunbury, Pa., where he seems to be mighty happy. "Tootie Belle," his sweet and beautiful wife who is also a good friend of mine, is especially happy to be settled down after five years of wandering. I spent a weekend with them in New Haven, Conn., when I was at Union summer before last. They were sweethearts from grammar school days. We have a lot to make up for, sweetheart. I love you. Bill.

How these folks from Bill's past knew to send mail to him in Sweden is unclear. The most likely explanation is that Bill wrote them first.

"Hi, sugar plum," Bill started his letter on Saturday night, October 4. "Not a darn thing has happened to mar the quiet of today. I haven't gotten a thing worthwhile accomplished—laziness, visits interfered. With the system of education they have here, I can see it is easy to let things slide. There is never any work that really presses until you get along toward examination time."

With another letter from Mary, she enclosed a Newberry alumni bulletin clipping, presumably announcing their engagement. "It would be fun to see the expression on some of my old classmates' faces when they read that," Bill responded. Thinking about Newberry, Bill's letter that Saturday evening focused on college football, which was never Bill's sport. "I had completely forgotten about this being football season until you mentioned the games for last Saturday. I've averaged about one, or less than one game, a season for the last six or eight years. Last fall was an exception—I saw one at Gettysburg and then proudly squired you to Clinton." Bill would never forget that game in which he and Mary shared their first kiss. He was getting more and more anxious to resume that practice.

The possibility was getting closer and closer. Mary had tentatively chosen a location for the wedding. Bill concurred with her choice. "The Greenville wedding idea suits me perfectly. I had rather imagined that you would like it there. It will probably be as convenient as any place, if your parents don't object to it being so far from Cross. We can probably wait a couple of weeks to figure out the details!"

Before he signed off on his letter, Bill returned to his ongoing theme of being semi-lazy in Uppsala. "Now it is bedtime. I'm going to try to get up at seven o'clock in the morning. I have an awful time crawling out of bed before 7:30 or 8:00 since breakfast isn't until 8:45. But it's silly sleeping so long. Come on over and give me a good kick out of bed. Your Bill."

Bill was not too lazy to miss any important musical opportunities. On October 6, he attended a concert by Yehudi Menuhin, an American-born violinist considered to be one of the best of the twentieth century. Bill's critique was mixed. "The big auditorium was only half filled, but the audience was enthusiastic. Menuhin is a bit overpowering with his violin skill and technique, but I can't say I was lifted to the heights. I'm a plain common type that needs an appeal to the emotions as well as to the intellect. He was plenty good for any man's money though and I was glad to have the chance to hear him."

Bill devoted most of his letter to Mary that night, however, to the plight of a certain young lady from Heidelberg, Germany.

> I got a letter from Lore Schmitt[6] today—the first in months. I don't know whether I ever mentioned her or not. There were 8 or 9 of us living at her parents' house in Heidelberg for a couple of months the summer after the war was over. She was married to a prisoner in the British zone and had a little boy a year and a half old. Lore was 22 then, I think, and we became good friends. I met her husband later. He had studied in Chicago several years and was a mighty nice fellow, but he was 15 years older than Lore and I don't think things went too smoothly. About a year and half ago, he was killed in an accident in the rebuilding of his family's paper mill. Lore and her parents were run out of their house last summer to let an American couple move in. Lore says they even requisitioned the garden and wouldn't even let them have the fruit and vegetables. The wife is French, so I suppose she is a German hater. The occupation has been a mess as far as I'm concerned.

Bill only had three lines left on the page after the long narrative

---

[6] Lore's last name is uncertain. In his letters to Pauline Bresnahan during the occupation, Bill spelled her name "Schmidt." In his letter to Mary, he spelled it "Schmitt." Small point, but perhaps a telling one.

regarding Lore Schmitt. "All that talk," he wrote Mary, "and I hardly have room left to tell you I love you. I'll send my love from Finland with the next letter. Your Bill."

How Mary felt about Bill still being in touch with a woman who had been a "good friend" during the war is unclear. She steadfastly trusted her fiancé, no matter how many women kept cropping up in his letters. Norma, Greta, Lore. She wondered how many others were out there were, potentially pining for her fiancé.

But she rested easy. None of them had his ring, his unconditional love, or his commitment. She had all three.

Chapter 41

Bill's Trip to Finland
(October 9–19, 1947)

Two days later, Bill wrote Mary from aboard the *Ragne*, a small but comfortable ship bound for Finland. The day before, Bill had finished classes at 3 p.m., taught the English class with the nurses until 4:45 p.m., and caught the train to Stockholm at 5:10 p.m. He had spent the night in Stockholm with his friend Hal, who had put together a fancy dinner with several other friends. Because they talked until 2:00 a.m., Bill did not get a chance to write a letter that night.

The next morning, before heading to the pier for his boat trip to Finland, he joined the rest of Stockholm in welcoming the new king and queen of Denmark to town. King Frederick IX had just assumed the Danish throne following the death of his father, King Christian X. He, his wife Queen Ingrid, and their three children were making their first visit to Sweden. It was a big occasion, with the appropriate pageantry.

Boarding the ship ended up being quite a hassle, as Bill had agreed to hand-deliver two packages to Finland to the husband and mother of the woman who managed his last apartment in Stockholm. Unbeknownst to Bill, the lady put in some new shoes, sheets, and towels in one of the boxes, items banned from export due to post-war restrictions. This caused serious problems getting through customs. Luckily, Bill made it on board after the officials let the woman retrieve her prohibited items rather than confiscating them.

Bill closed his letter by telling Mary that the nurses let him off next week, so he would be staying in Finland until October 19, ten days hence. "I have no exact plans of where I'll be yet. I'll miss your letters. I love you lilla Maria. Bill."

Once off the boat in the seaside town of Abo, Finland, Bill struggled to find his way. Instead of the archbishop's office, the taxi driver took him to the archbishop's home, where he was welcomed by the archbishop's wife. "There is nothing like barging in on almost strangers unexpectedly," he wrote Mary. "She received me like an old friend however." Bill finally found the archbishop's office in Abo later that afternoon, where he had a nice fifteen-minute chat with the archbishop himself. "He speaks good English and is very ecumenical in outlook."

Of course, Bill also visited Abo's Turku cathedral, the only medieval basilica in Finland, which he described as having been started in the late 1200s and having "grown by bits to a massive and beautiful cathedral in the plain and stately style." The sanctuary holds fourteen hundred people and is adorned by sculptures, a beautiful painting of the Last Supper, stained glass windows, and a multi-sail model "votive" ship.

Bill's day was completed by giving an impromptu talk about American churches and church music to the local choir. All in all, it was a busy day in "drizzly" weather.

The next day, Bill caught the train to Helsinki. "The six-hour ride was through good farming country with well-kept and rich looking land. Harvests were much better here than in Sweden and Norway." Bill arrived after dark and headed to the address his Hungarian friend, Gyorgy, had given him. It turned out to be a home for theological students, so Bill was well-cared for. Ending his letter, Bill told Mary, "It is often hard to be wandering around seeing things and meeting new people, and not have you to share it all. I miss you, Mary. Your Bill."

Bill's first Sunday and Monday in Finland were a blur of visits to various churches, services, religious "revivals," and more unscripted talks about America at several of Helsinki's four large churches. Bill found the Finnish Lutheran churches to be much different than the Lutheran churches he knew in America, in that they have their "spiritual life in revival movements." The Finnish services were packed with enthusiastic congregants who publicly shared their personal beliefs in front of the assembly, quite a contrast to the Lutherans back home. It reminded Bill a bit of some evangelistic Baptist churches in the States. Between services, Bill managed to fit in visits to the modern stadium

Helsinki had built for the 1940 Olympics. The Olympiastadion, with its landmark tower soaring over seventy-two meters, had never been used due to the war.[7]

Bill's October 14 letter closed, "I must say that coming to Finland was a great idea. There is no doubt in my mind that Christianity is stronger here than anywhere else in Scandinavia. All my love, Bill."

Scribbled in pencil, Bill's next letter on October 15 was almost unreadable because Bill felt "in the mood to commune with his 'better half,' so I won't bother to hunt up some ink." Despite the continued dreary weather, Bill had managed to get a tour of the University of Finland. "It is easily the finest and most attractive that I've seen in Scandinavia. It is the largest too. The equipment and facilities are the latest modern types. During the war, a bomb fell on the main building and did a lot of damage, but it is almost repaired now."

That day, Bill had delivered the first box of stuff to the husband of the Stockholm apartment manager. He was "an interesting fellow with the biggest law firm in Finland and an intense patriotism and national pride." The man treated Bill to lunch, which included the luxury of meat. Meat, though not rationed, was terribly expensive in Finland. Coffee, sugar, and chocolates were strictly rationed, with Finns getting only two pounds of coffee since the war, a half-pound of sugar a month, and small portions of chocolate in the last two years. Bill immediately asked Mary to buy a box of Hershey bars and send it to the Student Theological Home in Helsinki, knowing that such sweets would be greatly appreciated.

The most interesting item in that letter was Bill's Finnish roommate's reaction to seeing a photo of Mary.

> You may be amazed to learn that you were the cause of a horrible shock to my "roommate." When I was writing to you last night, he asked if I had a picture of you. Naturally, I was happy to show him the sweetest girl in America. Then in a tone of amazement and horror, he said, "She uses paints!" I admitted that such was true, and he could hardly believe me. Only bad girls use rouge and lipstick in Finland. It is

---

[7] It later hosted the opening and closing ceremonies for the 1952 Olympics.

completely unheard of that a Christian girl would use them. I explained that things were a bit different in the US and that we preferred a little more color in life. I'm not sure he is convinced that you will do for a pastor's wife—I am though. All my love, Bill.

On October 16, Bill took a bus to a town called Jarvenpaa. A young Finnish pastor who Bill had met in Lund was waiting for him and took him home for lunch with his family—"a friendly, lively wife and three children." Bill and the Finnish pastor had "a continuous discussion the whole five or six hours about Finnish church life, American problems, 'revivalism,' Lutheranism, etc. It was intensely interesting. In between breaths, we had a fine lunch and a Finnish bath, complete with a heating with birch twigs. Of course, it was raining!"

Later that afternoon, Bill caught the train to Lahti, the gateway city to Finland's lakelands. There, he dropped off the second box with the Stockholm apartment manager's mother, "a wonderful, white-haired, motherly lady" who was the rector of the local Christian school for high school students. For a change, arrangements had been made for Bill to stay at the local hotel, where Bill would sleep in a "real bed." As Bill had only two days left in Finland, he told Mary, "I'm longing for those letters in Uppsala."

The next day, after giving a short talk about America to the student body at the Christian high school, Bill caught a train to Tampere. Halfway there, the train had a two hour stop. Instead of waiting, Bill "was dumb enough to climb aboard a local instead of the fast train," resulting in arriving in Tampere two hours late. He missed meeting the archbishop, but he was shown around by the pastor of the inner mission, "a young man with fresh, vigorous ideas."

In the morning, that young pastor took Bill to the town's cathedral, which was only fifteen years old. Bill described it to Mary. "I've rarely seen such a hideous church. The outside is fair—massive gray granite with a red roof and funny spires. Inside I wanted to scream. There were fantastic symbolic paintings—death's garden—fallen angels, etc. The windows were terrible, cheap-looking glass with more surrealistic designs." Bill's negative opinion regarding the cathedral's frescos was not unique. When first revealed, the paintings had drawn considerable adverse reactions, especially the winged serpent on a red background at the highest point in the sanctuary, which some religious scholars interpreted as a symbol of sin and corruption. Bill was happy to move on after less than fifteen minutes inside.

By the afternoon, Bill relaxed on the aft deck of a ship, admiring the views as it worked its way through the thousand or more islands along the coast of Sweden. Late that night he arrived back in Stockholm, ready to get back to the academic grind.

After a nice breakfast and hot bath and shave at Hal's place, Bill finished a letter he had begun on the boat the afternoon before. He told Mary that he really enjoyed gorging on bacon and eggs at Hal's, as he had cut down on food in Finland since meat, sugar, and other staples were scarce and expensive there. He had shared all his extra sugar and soap with the final families in Finland.

In that letter, Bill noted that so many of the Finnish families had a lot of children, "in a hurry." He told Mary, "I don't particularly care for the hurry, but I like the big families." He did not say how many offspring he had in mind, but he wondered how Finnish pastors could manage to have such large families, pointing out that inflation in Finland was terrible and pastor salaries had not kept pace.

With his ten-day trip to Finland over, he closed his letter, "Don't get into too much mischief. I long for you more than you know. God bless you always. Your Bill."

Chapter 42

Letter from Uppsala
(October 21, 1947)

Bill's loneliness and yearning for Mary during his trip to Finland, which had been growing stronger day by day for quite some time, led to a critical decision. He could not wait to tell Mary. On the night of October 21, he put it all down in words. "My Mary, I skipped writing you last night for a rather special reason. I had been thinking over something for several weeks and the big batch of mail that was here waiting for me brought it to a head. Brace yourself—you are going to be surprised! I figure on heading for the States sometime in January!!!"

Bill had planned to stay in Sweden for another semester under Professor Anders Nygren, a particularly brilliant theologian in Lund, returning to America in summer 1948. But a convergence of events and his already long separation from Mary changed his whole perspective.

"There are many reasons why I've made that decision—the last 24 hours have made it definite," he wrote Mary.

> Naturally, you have a big place in it. It is no fun being separated from the one you love so long. I've felt it more than ever this fall, and I feel from your letters that it is the same with you. Then it isn't so pleasant to think about coming home and getting married immediately without being assured of a way to care for you or a place to work. If I can receive a call in February or March, I can begin to get things together and ready for a married life. One of the factors in deciding was my letter from Betty about the double wedding. I can't quite figure all the angles yet, however. I don't like the idea of marrying and then having to be separated. When is your contract up? Could you work a sort of terminal leave business that would save a few weeks? Betty's plan is not definite I gathered,

so we could maybe get them to compromise on a little later date. Of course, a lot would depend on where I could get a call. It wouldn't be too terrible I suppose to be separated if I wasn't too far off.

Indeed, if Mary was still working in Greenville after the wedding and Bill could only get a call in North Carolina or Virginia, he knew there would be another separation. He wanted to avoid that at all costs.

Bill then shared his other considerations.

I have never pretended, even to myself, that I'm a "student," and the prospect of five or six months of studying something that I'm not particularly interested in is not too hot. I think I was cut out for plain pastoral work, if anything, and I may as well be about it. I had looked forward to studying under Prof. Nygren in Lund, but he is going to America in January and won't be there anyway. I might have gone there this fall if I had made these plans earlier, but that is water under the bridge now. I think I've gotten about as good an idea of Swedish church life and spirit as I would if I stayed longer, so that's no reason for staying. It's not particularly inspiring anyway. And, not least, there is the financial situation. Right now, I'm not certain that I have enough to get home without writing for a check. If I get home and work, I can be better able to start married life.

So, the decision was made. Bill would come home after a year instead of eighteen months. He would not position himself to become an academic theologian or a religion professor. He had no desire to be a "big shot" in the Lutheran World Federation, at least not to start. He wanted to be a "plain" old parish minister in a small, personal, family-oriented church without the overly symbolic trappings of "high church." Though the details still had to be worked out, his whole life and ministerial future was suddenly coming into focus.

Now was time to come home and get started with it.

However, because it would be almost impossible to book passage from icy Sweden before March, Bill planned to leave Uppsala in the middle of December, spend Christmas and New Year's Eve with the

Bourguignons in Belgium, then try to book a voyage home from a more southern port such as Antwerp, Belgium or Southampton, England. He figured that if he got to Antwerp in early January, he "could take a chance on a freight passage, or better yet, get a job working his way home."

Either way, his goal was to be back in the States by February 1.

He told Mary that he would immediately write the presidents of the Carolina and Virginia synods concerning a pastoral call. He figured they might need to fill some vacancies before the Easter season, though the timing would not be ideal for a pastor to start at a church. One way or another, he hoped to line up something before he got back to the States.

Bill had also received a letter from Clare, in which she disclosed that she was pregnant with her fourth child. He told Mary that Clare "was complaining that her children will be nurses for their future cousins with Betty and me so far behind." Clare figured that a total of four children would make a well-rounded family. Bill agreed. "I rather like the 'four' business myself—preferably two girls and two boys."

Having probably overwhelmed Mary enough in one letter, Bill mercifully ended his letter with a final paragraph. "Well, this ought to give you enough to think about for one time. I don't know whether the thought of seeing you in a few months will make me study harder or waste my time daydreaming. I'll try to make it the first, but it will be hard. I love you Mary. God keep you in his care. Yours always, Bill."

Chapter 43

Letters from Uppsala
(October 22–25, 1947)

Bill started his October 22 letter to Mary, squarely focused on coming home.

> Now that I've decided to cut my stay short, I've had a lot of things to think about. My studying will suffer this week I know. I've been wondering about what type of church I may get, what kind of program I'll have to plan for Lent, how I'll manage to live until you take over, and dozens of things along that line. Have you thought any more about what our furniture situation will be? I gather that you didn't have time at Dogwood Dell to talk to Mama and Betty about such things. It will be a mess gathering possessions together from the Carolinas to Mississippi. It will be wonderful to have time to talk to you about such things.

Unaware of Bill's new plans, Mary was busy on her end, generally planning for the wedding. Apparently, she told Bill about it in a letter, as Bill responded the next day, "You are being a mighty industrious young lady buying material for your wedding dress and getting ready to start sewing. I thought that was 'mother's job.' What has Betty said about the double wedding business? She only said she would like it in the mountains, but I gathered that she has rather definite ideas and maybe plans."

Bill suspected Mary had not yet received his letter announcing his early return.

> Naturally, I'm impatiently waiting to hear your reaction to the thought of my getting home six months earlier. I've hardly

gotten used to the idea myself, but it gets better every time I think about it.… I love you, sweetheart. It will be wonderful to have you close in my arms once more. Yours always, Bill.

With time suddenly running short, Bill added two new English pupils, sisters, one of whom worked at the post office. Both sisters hoped to improve their English for a trip to England. He told Mary he needed to earn more money for passage home, adding, "It's too bad I didn't get started two months ago."

While making extra money, Bill was also being benevolent. He received another letter from Heidelberg. "It was from a family I didn't stay with, and they asked if I would send some things for the children. So, I got some milk powder, cooking oil, etc. I hope it arrives safely. Unfortunately, they were always in the society circle and now they suffer more than those who had worked hard."

Almost as an aside, Bill also mentioned to Mary that he was sending Lore Schmitt a couple of pocket-size English books to read, then repeated his hope to get permission to visit his Heidelberg friends after Christmas.

Mary was a patient woman who was not easily rattled. But her fiancé kept mentioning other women friends, and now he seemed intent on visiting one of them in Germany before returning to America. One can only imagine that her trust was being tested.

One thing was clear. It was time for Bill to come home to her and to leave Europe behind.

Chapter 44

Letters from Uppsala
(October 27–November 1, 1947)

On Sunday, October 27, Bill received a letter from his mother, indicating that Clare and Johnny were moving to a church in Blacksburg, Virginia. Bill could not wait to get his own ministerial plans set. He ended his letter to Mary that night, "I think, after all the running around rushing here and there…we will probably be quite content to sit in one spot and relax for a while. What do you think? Love Bill."

"Sweet Mary," Bill started his next letter three days later, "I was a naughty boy and neglected you since Sunday night, so I will scratch away this morning before the day's routine begins and get a letter in the 'Post lada.' I had all good intentions to write you last night, but it was 1:00 a.m. when I got back to the room, and I crawled into bed instead."

His late evening was because Bill had met with a group of friends from India, Hungary, and England, starting at 9:30 p.m.

> I don't know when I have spent a more enjoyable and thought-provoking evening. There were two things that struck me particularly—the Indian problem and the Anglican attitude. In South India now, the Protestant churches (with the exception of the Lutheran) have joined in a union…. The question is whether the Lutherans will join or not. There are 10 Lutheran church groups in India, and they are attempting to unite also. Which union is most important is a real problem for the Lutherans.

As for the Anglican attitude, Bill noted that Anglicans strictly follow apostolic succession and closed communion practices. Bill was never thrilled about such restrictive church traditions. If a person believed in Jesus Christ and professed him to be their savior, Bill felt they should always be welcome to the communion table, regardless of denomination.

In other words, Bill believed in inclusion rather than exclusion.

Meanwhile, Bill got another letter from Mary. She had received the glass candlestick Bill had sent her but insisted that candlesticks should be in matching pairs. Bill teased her in response. "And you are getting mighty sassy not being satisfied with one candlestick. Just like a woman—always wanting things to match and conform. I bought the one at the 'second' shop at Orrefors, and there was only one. I'll be a good boy and look for another though. I will send you a souvenir from Finland this week—don't open it until your birthday. Your Bill."

On October 29, Bill, still anxiously awaiting Mary's reaction to his new plan, wrote again: "Mary my love, I wonder what you are doing way down in South Carolina tonight. I'm trying to wait patiently until there has been enough time for a letter to come after you get mine about coming home. So, I try to picture you running around to your meetings or busying yourself around the apartment."

The next night, Bill once again lamented that he had not gotten "the" letter he was expecting from Mary. "It will be late tomorrow night probably before I get the letter that ought to come in—that's bad. Yours always, Bill."

He did not have to wait much longer. On November 1, Bill wrote, "Mary, your answer to my sudden news came today. I had been anxiously waiting for it, and it makes me feel better. May God grant that we can come safely together in a few months." However, Mary's letter raised more issues than Bill probably expected. He replied, "I see that there are a couple of things that we will probably need to do a lot of thinking and talking about." The first issue was the wedding plan. Bill quickly deferred to the ladies. "You and Betty will naturally have to do some planning and compromising about the wedding. Whatever you decide, and wherever you want it to be, will be alright with me."

The next issue was Mary's intent to continue working after Bill got home. Somewhat surprised, Bill answered,

I will have to do some thinking about your idea of working. Frankly, the idea doesn't appeal to me at all at the moment, but I can see that it will depend on several other matters. One reason I'm coming home is to ease the financial situation. If I can get a place to work fairly quickly, I should be able to help with the car payments. You realize of course that ministers are poorly paid generally, and we will probably have to live together on less than what you are getting right now. However, most ministers' families manage. So, your working will have to be considered in the light of what work I'm doing and where we are.

Bill, a traditionalist, anticipated he would be the breadwinner in the relationship. But he realized Mary loved her job and was making more than he would make as a minister. Having two incomes could come in handy. So, he wisely left that issue open for further discussion.

Another major item was Mary's discovery that a Lutheran mission church was being organized right there in Greenville. Bill must have wondered how he got so lucky to fall in love with a woman who not only wanted to work for good money, but who was also helping him find a potential job. He responded cautiously.

As for Greenville, I'm interested, but again there are many things to be considered. I would have no idea of pushing myself into a call, and under no circumstances would I want you to do anything along that line. I would, however, appreciate it if you would find out just how far things have gone in the matter of organization, "pastor-calling," financial backing, and the relation to the Greenville Church and the synod. I will work only through the official channels of synod, however.

Mary also told Bill that her parents were considering selling their home in Cross, South Carolina, to relocate closer to Greenville. Bill was less certain about the wisdom of that move. "You had never mentioned before that they were thinking about moving up your way. Do they realize that their daughter is apt to be leaving those parts in the not-too-distant future? I can't blame them for thinking about that section of course. I like it too."

Things were suddenly getting very real for Bill. All at once, there were heaps of issues to resolve. Wedding plans, job prospects, parents who might move, a wife who wanted to keep working, furniture, salary, and just trying to get back to America in winter—a huge list of things to think about.

Bill's return voyage had yet to be resolved, and his trip to Stockholm to check on possibilities for passage had not been fruitful. The American Express office had no information about ships from Belgium. There were vague possibilities for passage from England or Holland, but nothing certain or affordable. Despite his tendency to get seasick in rough waters, Bill continued to consider the possibility of working his way home on a freighter.

His effort to visit friends in Heidelberg was also hitting a wall. He told Mary, "A visit in Germany will be impossible. You just don't get permission for a friendly visit. The wife of one of the American students works in the American Legation office and she said I'd better give up that idea."

Most likely, Mary was not too disappointed about that impossibility.

Bill finished his letter by giving her the address of the Bourguignon family in Belgium just in case she wanted to send a Christmas present there. But he added, "My real Christmas celebration will come when I get that long postponed hug and kiss."

Chapter 45

Letters from Uppsala
(November 2–18, 1947)

"Hi Butch!" It was another Sunday night, November 2, on a dark rainy day in Uppsala, where electricity was being rationed. Still, Bill was writing another letter to Mary by lantern light. He had just gotten back from a musical service at the cathedral for All Saints' Day, followed by a lengthy gab session with Gyorgy. Visiting Hungary was out of the question now that Bill had decided to come home early. But he didn't mind: "What is waiting on the other side of the Atlantic will make up for that and a thousand other things."

Bill spent the next day writing letters to presidents of the Carolina and Virginia synods. "I have no idea whether anything will come of them, but it is worth trying, I think. I can't imagine a congregation taking a fellow sight unseen when he is 3000 miles across the ocean. It would be wonderful though if I could have something tentative at least when I get home."

"Sweet Mary," Bill penned on Tuesday that week, "one more day marked off the calendar, and one more day nearer the time when I'll be heading your way. With all the hustle and bustle of the Christmas season, the time will probably go by in a hurry."

Bill had spent much of that day blackening his hands putting a new brake thing-a-ma-jig on his bicycle. The old one not only wouldn't hold but screeched to high heavens. He didn't know what he would do with the "faithful old creature." He had grown fond of his only mode of transport, but he knew he could not bring it back to America.

He then told Mary about another letter he had just gotten.

This morning, a letter came from Mama—the first since she found I was planning to come home earlier. I've been rather amused at both her reaction and Dad's. I almost believe they figure I ought to stay until next summer—in spite of the fact that Mama has mentioned time and again that she would like to see me settled in a parish. Even if you weren't in the picture, I think that it is the thing for me to do to cut my stay short. If I were intellectually inclined, things would be different.

As he closed his letter, Bill told Mary that he had still not heard anything from the American Express office about any boats from Belgium. "I hope it comes soon so I can rest easy. Love always, Bill."

In his Friday night letter that week, Bill suggested that he and Mary must have "a little mental telepathy running over the Atlantic," as Mary had asked for his Christmas address in Belgium on the same day that he sent her the Bourguignons' address from his end. For good measure, he asked her to send more pictures of her. "I can always find a place to put up a new one. It's nice to see you smiling at me wherever I happen to turn in the room." He added, "Don't get into too much mischief till I get back to help you. Yours, Bill."

Twenty-four hours later, he wrote her again. "Sweet Mary, it is past midnight, but I guess the bed will keep for a few minutes. Can't let my little honeychile play second fiddle to a little sleep." He had finally gotten his Christmas packages sent out that Saturday morning. Bill was amused that he had listed two "china pitchers" on one box and the translator had put it down in Swedish as "Chinese pictures." Either way, they were now on their way to America.

On Sunday, Bill went to a gathering of Swedish and German students, several from a youth leadership training center in Hamburg, Germany. After that meeting, he wrote Mary to tell her, "There is a faint possibility now that I may be able to get an invitation from St. Michael's House and thus have a little time at least in Germany. I don't know whether it would be possible to get to Heidelberg though." Despite yet another reference to Heidelberg, Bill's last two lines that Sunday night showed that he was thinking only of Mary. "So now it's bedtime, and as usual, I will spend my last waking moments with you. I love you, Bill."

With final papers and exams rapidly approaching, Bill started "hitting the books heavily." His religious ethics class syllabus required him to read fourteen books. Bill had gotten through just six. Of the other books, only one was in English. Bill had the easy option of simply auditing the class and not taking the exam. But at the last minute, he chose to take the test, for better or worse. He would try to bear down for the next month.

Despite the uptake in his studying, Bill continued to enjoy social events, including yet another nice evening at the home of one of the professors. "I can't help but be amused how formal everything is here in Sweden. I can't imagine a bunch of students in the States being so solemn and dignified."

Knowing that Mary's birthday was coming up, he closed the letter, "You can bet I'd love to help you celebrate the birthdays. Doesn't it seem ages since your last one?"

The next day, Bill wrote again. "Winter is here, little apple-dumpling. It snowed most of the day. It didn't stick, however, so it is only a memory. For a few hours though, the snow was really coming down." For the first time in months, Bill included in his letter a full paragraph in Swedish that Mary would be unlikely to decipher. "You thought I had forgotten to scribble Swedish, didn't you? It's nothing important— but this is: jag alsker dig. Your Bill."

Bill still loved her, regardless of which language he used.

The next day, a Wednesday, was a full study day, but Bill still found time to go to a movie.

> Dearest Mary, I just played hooky and went to a movie— *Margie.* I had been hitting the books all day and about 8:00 p.m. came to the end of a rather dull one, so I decided to have a little relaxation. The movie was silly but entertaining—just what the doctor ordered. For the life of me though I can't see why it is necessary to smear the paint on so thick in techni- color pictures. It certainly can't be necessary, and it is anything but natural or artistic.

In the same letter, Bill told Mary that his roommate at Newberry College was arriving in Uppsala to teach at the university. "He is a Doc now. Funny, back about 1936, we made an agreement that we would pay the other $25 if we got married in 5 years—and figured there was some possibility. He got married a bit over a year ago. One never knows!" Luckily, Bill's friend had not gotten married within the five-year window, as Bill needed every dollar available to pay for passage back to the States. Clearly, Bill had not met the five-year deadline—not even close.

Meanwhile, Mary had visited her parents and sent Bill a letter describing furniture available for the taking. At the end of his letter, Bill responded, "Sounds as if we will need a big moving van to get all those things you're collecting moved. It is hard to be patient about making plans, but there will be plenty of time after I get home. All my love, Bill."

Finally studying in earnest, Bill failed to write again until Saturday night. His letter described an American pastor and his wife who had arrived in Uppsala. The wife, "a little attractive woman with a non-stop tongue—fun though," had just bought some drapes from a Swedish shop and suggested that Bill buy some to take home. Bill asked Mary, "What do you think? I don't know what we could do about size or number. I doubt if they are cheaper, but they would be different. Color is another question."

Something tells us that Mary was not too comfortable about Bill independently picking out draperies in Sweden!

Sunday afternoon, November 16, saw yet another letter from Bill to Mary. Bill had gone to an unusual service at a "free church" that morning. The sermon was good, but Bill was disappointed that the service had no liturgy. Nevertheless, he was fascinated by the "funny chancel arrangement," with the organ and pulpit directly behind and above the altar, which was not used at all. Always an illustrator, he even drew a diagram of the arrangement, complete with floor plan and side view.

Bill ended his letter by noting that the fiancée of a friend of Bill's was in town for the weekend. "She comes up from Stockholm occasionally. They seem to have so much fun together. It always makes me envious. They plan to get married about the same time we do. Great day!! Love always, Bill."

On November 17, Mary came through again, with a letter and a Coca-Cola print photo. Coca-Cola prints, with photos of young women sitting on Coca-Cola coolers, drinking Cokes, or holding Coke bottles, were popular at the time and are now collector items. Unfortunately, this Coca-Cola print of Mary seems not to have been preserved. But Bill was excited to receive it.

> Sweetheart, the picture that came in the morning mail is quite a contrast to the way things look outside the window. It snowed most of the morning and things look cold and dark. But then I take a look at my little, brown-eyed beauty and the world is bright and gay. It is a good picture; brought you close in a hurry. Thanks! I haven't had a cola print like that before. I think Clare had some once that she sent to Johnny when he was overseas, but they were of a different sort.

Bill had spent all day getting ready for a paper and seminar presentation he was lead the next day, but household issues were on his mind when he wrote Mary that night.

> It looks as we are going to have silver and table linen without dishes or table at the present rate. And bed linen without anything to use it on. I can see that I'm going to have to get busy when I get home. One thing that I'm not looking forward to by coming home early is the months I'll have to "batch" for myself. But it will be better doing that than living with some "good lady" of the church, I suppose. That may be necessary for a while though until I can get the bare essentials together.

The following day, Bill nervously presented his paper and explained to Mary why he took it seriously. "I was especially glad to get rid of that paper for class. It really wouldn't have been necessary for me to have it, but since I'll be taking my exam from the professor who has the seminar, I thought it was wise to volunteer."

With his paper presented, Bill was free to go see Laurence Olivier's *Henry V*. His critique? "I thoroughly enjoyed it. The acting is superb, and the production is unusually well done."

The news was still foggy concerning passage back to America. Gyorgy had determined it was impossible to get any ship from Sweden.

So, he was looking into going to England and taking "one of the Queens" back to America. Bill told Mary, "Maybe I'll wind up on one of the Queens too…. A five-day trip on one of those big babies will probably be pretty nice." He added, "I won't mind what I'm riding on though, as long as it is heading your way. The hours will creep those last few days, I'll bet. I miss you. I love you, Bill."

Chapter 46

Letters from Uppsala
(November 19–25, 1947)

Bill must have gotten another letter from Mary on November 19, because he started his letter by saying,

> Don't tell me you are making my Christmas present with your own dainty little fingers! I thought that style had gone out long ago in the States. Over here in Europe, the females still busy themselves with such useful labors, but the girls in America don't seem to find time for useful work like that. Maybe I'm just jumping to conclusions about that Christmas gift at any rate! You know I'll be happy that your love is with it.

Speaking of Christmas packages, Bill warned Mary that Clare was sending her Christmas package directly to Mary. "If a package comes in from her, you will know why."

He also disclosed to Mary that he had sent "a package of stuff" to Lore Schmitt in Heidelberg because she had written him about particularly tough times in Germany. Lore had also advised him that "a young doctor was courting her pretty steadily, but she's not so sure she wants to get married now."

Mary's reaction to that letter is unknown, but she probably hoped Frau Schmitt would marry the physician and leave her man alone.

On Friday, November 21, Bill, while "holed up studying all day," got a letter from his mother about a visit to Jackson, Mississippi, by Johnny and Clare and their three children, who drove down from Blacksburg, Virginia. As Bill described it to Mary,

Their old car gave out three blocks from the house. I gather Johnny canvassed the town the next day and came back with a Plymouth, probably "black market." He probably paid plenty, if so. Mother said Henry is a live wire—pulled all the pots and pans out of the cupboard, played in the flour, and ate raw potatoes. She wonders how Clare manages—forgets she was in the same boat once.

Bill wrote Mary again on November 24. "Mary, my sweet, another day is almost over, and I have time to concentrate on the best part of every day—when you are the center of everything. I can see that it would have been 'might nigh' impossible to have gotten any work done in the States the past year if I could have been anywhere close to Greenville. I wonder how it will be until spring!"

The *Drothingholm*, another Swedish-American transatlantic ship, was due to arrive the next day. Bill hoped the ship would bring letters from the synods. So far, his efforts to arrange for a pastoral call before he returned to the States had been unsuccessful. But Bill seemed even sadder about another loss in his life.

My faithful old bike and I have parted companies. I hope it serves someone else as well as it did me. A couple German students (the two in Heidelberg) are going to start back for Germany tomorrow, so I gave my bike to them to take to the student pastor in Heidelberg. They seemed tickled at the idea. It is almost impossible to get a bike in Germany now, of course, and they have no Swedish money to buy such things.

Bill was also almost broke. He had to cash in his last subsistence check to send the Christmas packages that afternoon. He had bought $100 in traveler's checks and had about 125 kroner left. "I don't know what is holding up my October subsistence check. Dad is going to send me a check for reserve. I hope I can get work from Antwerp, so I won't have to use it."

Meanwhile, Bill was finishing up his reading for the ethics course.

I guess I can sleep with a good conscience tonight—I finally managed to wade through that 460-page ethics book in

Danish. Of course, I must confess that I don't know everything that's in it. I'll have some reviewing before I go up for an exam. That will probably be between the 8th and 15th of December. You make arrangements with the professor when you feel you are ready. The worst is over now, I think, as far as the reading goes.

Uppsala was becoming increasingly depressing. Daylight was short, with dawn coming around 8:30 a.m. and darkness returning by about 3:00 p.m. Snow and ice made any trips outside dangerous. On his way back from teaching English, Bill's feet slipped out and he went down hard on his rear. Luckily, after a few days, the bruises cleared and the pain subsided. Broke, bruised, bikeless, and buried in books in the icy, dark conditions, Bill wondered if he would muddle through. Despite his studying, his mind kept wandering back to Mary and his trip home.

On Thanksgiving Day, 1947, Bill was in an especially nostalgic mood.

My Mary, I am certain that Thanksgiving Day will always be much more for me than just a day for Thanksgiving for material blessings. It will always be a reminder of the time when our love began to bloom. I'll never cease to be thankful for that! Now, after a whole year has gone by, I realize more than ever the happiness that began then. There are a couple memories of those days that I will always hold precious—the first kiss! Remember how bashful you were? The slight tremble that went through your body when I told you that I loved you! I'm sure I realized then the tremendous seriousness and responsibility of that moment. Thanksgiving Day at P.C.! The curious looks we got! Then the way you said, so surprised, that you never would have dreamed that "it could happen to you" like that! I also remember how impatiently I waited during the next few days for letter from you—afraid that I had been dreaming all those wonderful things.

He kept going.

It hasn't been an easy year, has it? As nice as it is to get letters, it is a far cry from the actual thing. It will be wonderful to have you near before too many weeks have passed. I'm pretty sure that we needed the time for our love to grow. Things happened so fast for us that we might have put the cart before the horse. I'm certain I would have been mighty tired of being a "bachelor preacher" in a short time. At any rate, I am happy to be able to look into the future and pray that our time apart will go quietly and that we can make that wedding "soon."

As for his job prospects, Bill remained nervous, but hopeful. "The *Drothingholm* didn't carry those hoped-for letters from the synods. Guess maybe you will have to marry a ditch-digger or something. No, it's not that bad! I'm not worrying. God will use me somewhere in His service. I'm content for the place to be in His hands. God bless you, Mary. I love you. Bill."

Chapter 47

Letters from Uppsala
(November 25–December 10, 1947)

It was a typical Friday night for Bill on November 28. He had enjoyed the organ music night at the cathedral, "as usual." He was looking forward to another concert on Sunday—a Bach Christmas oratorio.

The news of the day was his letter from his parents. "Dad and mother finally managed to find time to write—the house must have been in an uproar with Johnny and Clare being there. Mother was still worrying about Clare's managing 'sa mange barn,' but I never remember Clare worrying about that."

Regarding Bill's ministerial future, his father advised him to "not worry about a call." Thinking long-term, he suggested that Bill "wait until something would challenge ten years of service." Bill's dad had moved around a lot in his first years as a pastor and questioned if a short-term call would be the best approach. Bill wrote Mary, "We have a lot of talking and deciding to do when the day comes that we can sit down together instead of writing across all those miles of water."

Bill spent much of his letter to Mary talking about Sweden's Advent season. Two young ladies had invited Bill to an Advent tea. "I learned several things that we will have to introduce to our home. Advent has a special candle season. They have two special types—like this." He drew two pictures, one showing four candles and a star on what looked like a round plate and the other with four candles on a rectangular board with moss and flowers at the base of the candles. In addition, the girls served "a plate with one long sandwich—a sort of three in one—each with a burning, small candle stuck into the sandwich."

The next day, in a letter with the words "HAPPY BIRTHDAY!!"

written in red pencil at the top (Mary's birthday was November 29), Bill told Mary about yet another trip he had fit into his busy study schedule. He and his friend Ted had a "wonderful weekend" in Sigtuna, the nearby town where there was "a people's high school (a boarding school for 18–25-year-olds), a guest home, and a 'humanistisk lavoverk' (a sort of prep school, I suppose you would say)." They had a "whale of a time" at a social evening at the high school, with folk dances, a choir, and girls wearing colorful national costumes. "The students love it, and the spirit is contagious."

Back in Uppsala, Bill told Mary that it "hardly seems possible but there are only three weeks left of my stay in Sweden…. I will have some pretty steady studying the next couple weeks, and I'm not at all certain that I can get enough knowledge crammed into my head to take an exam." However, he was thrilled that "the time won't be too much longer before I'll be seeing you again." In that regard, Bill had gotten a letter from one of Mary's friends. "Sounds as if she approves of our plans and assures me that you act like you are 'in love.' I sort of felt that way over here!"

Bill ended his letter by again complaining that he still had no letters from the synods. "I'm anxious to hear and see what encouragement there is for me to find you a home. Love always, Bill."

Meanwhile, despite a major snowstorm, Advent Sunday had been a standing room only affair at the downtown Uppsala church. "Parents even brought their children—something that is rather unusual over here." The Swedes had four candles for their Advent decorations. "One is for each Sunday in Advent. The first Sunday, they light the first and then add one on the following Sundays. Nice custom!" Apparently, this Advent custom, which began in sixteenth-century Germany, was not common in America in 1947 or Bill was not familiar with the Prophecy, Bethlehem, Shepherds, and Angel candles, representing Isaiah's prophecy of Christ's birth, Mary's love, the shepherds' great joy, and peace for all people. In some traditions, they signify hope, love, joy, and peace, respectively.

That Sunday night, Bill enjoyed a traditional Swedish Advent dinner, with a smorgasbord and a "tremendous ham as the 'piece de resistance' with God Jul written across the top." He told Mary, "Ham is the Christmas dish of Sweden. I really stuffed myself!" But he wasn't too stuffed to attend the Bach's Christmas Oratorio at the cathedral, which involved a full orchestra, choir, and organ. He wrote, "It was great!"

He also updated Mary on his studying. "I can see the end of my reading now. I have 13 of the 14 under my belt now and expect to finish the last one by tomorrow night. I figure on taking a week to review them and then go up for the exam." His last paragraph summed it up. "Well, December is here! That doesn't make me a bit unhappy. It will be great to start my travels again when I know who is waiting at the end of the journey. I love you, Mary. Bill."

On Tuesday, December 2, Bill wrote, "Mary, my love, two letters today! First time that has happened in a long time. One of them was a bit late coming—it must have gone by way of Copenhagen. The other took the usual amount of time."

Mary must have renewed her concern about adequate household furniture. Bill replied,

> I don't guess we need to cross that "furniture bridge" until we come to it. Things will probably work out okay. If worse comes to worse, we can rob Dogwood Dell of some of its cast-offs to tide us over. Did you see those two bedheads Mama was working on up there? I think there are a couple extra pieces of furniture knocking around in Jackson, too! But with Betty getting married maybe we will have to draw straws. Or do the Methodists furnish their parsonages?

Bill closed that letter with instructions for Mary to send any further letters to the Bourguignon family in Marche, Belgium, as he would be on the move soon.

On Thursday, December 4, Bill finally got a reply from the American Express office about sailing from Belgium. He gave Mary the details. "They only mentioned one, however, the *Marine Juniper*. That is a troop carrier that they used last summer for students—primitive, but fairly cheap, I think. It sails Jan. 10th. I'm going to Stockholm Saturday to dinner at General Konsul Lamm's, so I'll inquire more about it then. It might at least be good to have a reservation to fall back on."

The rest of Bill's letter described his favorite teacher at Uppsala—Docent Linderkag, the assistant professor in his New Testament class, who was "a peach of a guy." Bill was particularly interested in this professor's lectures because the man was being recruited to go to Gettysburg Seminary. "I certainly wish he would go. He would make a real addition to the faculty. He is about the only one on the faculty here that I would really recommend."

By Friday, December 5, Bill was "starting to have cold feet" about taking the ethics exam. "I'm beginning to wonder now how I'll ever manage to get through that exam to the point of being able to answer questions on 14 books at the same time. The trouble is that I've read without concentrating too much—a typical trait of mine. There is always too much to think about." However, Bill was encouraged by one of classmates having managed to get through the exam that morning. "So, maybe I can 'shoot the bull' and come out okay," he wrote. "I will try to answer in English so that will give me the upper hand to a certain extent. Keep your fingers crossed for me!"

He closed his letter, "God bless you, Mary. The time can't go too quickly now until I'm home with you. Bill."

Bill traveled to Stockholm on December 6 to check on passage on the *Marine Juniper* for January 10, but he did not buy a ticket. When he wrote Mary the next night, he explained he "would have had to shell out $135 here in Sweden." That did not appeal to him. "It looks as if I'm going to have to take my chances of getting work or a passage after I get to Antwerp. Maybe I'll have to be a stowaway to make it to the States by February 1st."

Bill had been a hobo on a train in America. Why not stowaway on a boat across the Atlantic? No adventure was out of the question. Even getting to Belgium would be an adventure. He told Mary that he would "leave Stockholm the night of the 16th, spend the next day or two in Lund, the next couple in Copenhagen—and, if possible, Hamburg—and get to Marche, the 22nd."

Meanwhile, despite his "cold feet" and focus on getting home to America, Bill was still planning to take the ethics exam. "It was a pleasant visit to Stockholm, even if it did interfere with my studies. The time is drawing closer, but I can't say I'm worrying too much about it now.

I'll do my best and let it go at that." He added, "I was disappointed when I got back this afternoon and found that this old man had no mail. I hope they soon get this crazy plane strike cleared up. I don't like to have them interfere with my mail. Maybe they will be good to me tomorrow. The days don't go right when a letter is overdue." He closed the letter, "Well, it is time to get back to the books. Woe is me! It won't be long now, honeychile! Love always, Bill."

Twenty-four hours later, Bill rubbed his brow, practically sweating over the impending ethics oral exam: "My Mary, tomorrow night this time, it will all be over—for better or worse. 'Blomman' took his exam in ethics this morning and came through easily, so my hopes have gone up. It was high time 'Blomman' got through. He has been studying for his bachelor's degree for eleven years now—it should take four or five."

Bill was also waiting for another letter from Mary. "I got four letters this morning—but none from you. Tain't funny, McGee!" One of the letters was from his mother. He told Mary that his mom was still "having a letdown feeling after being run ragged by Clare and Johnny and their kids for 2½ weeks. A Christmas card came from her saying that my Christmas present—a violet stole—is waiting for me at home. They gave me a green one a year or so ago."

Another letter was from a woman named Inge. A German diplomat's daughter, she claimed to have once had lunch at the White House. Bill told Mary that his spirits were lifted, because "it was the first letter I've gotten from any one in Germany that had not a single word of complaint. She even sympathized with the Americans that had to stay there and rule."

On December 10, Bill wrote his next letter to Mary, practically giddy with glee.

There are at least three reasons for this being a fine day. 1. Two blue letters turned up in the mail this morning. Since a week had gone by without a word from you, you can imagine how welcome they were. 2. The exam is all over and done with—he had me sweating over that crazy Danish ethics book for nearly 45 minutes, but I got through. 3. The sun is shining brightly for the first time in over two weeks.

With his exam behind him, Bill was ready for some fun. He planned on "getting things packed up ready to head for Denmark, Belgium, and you; loafing for the first time in a couple months; visiting a few people I've been wanting to see and haven't gotten around to; and generally taking things easy."

Another reason Wednesday was great was that Bill received a Christmas letter from his Uncle William, promising to send $50 to help defray his travel costs. Apparently, Mary had also written to Uncle William, as Bill wrote that "Uncle William appreciated the letter from you." Perhaps Mary told Uncle William about Bill's plans to return to America and his difficulty affording the passage. Hint, hint!

Despite their separation, Mary was always looking out for her fiancé. Bill was indeed a lucky man.

PART VIII

YEARNING FOR HOME

Chapter 48

Letters from Uppsala, Stockholm, and Lund
(December 11–17, 1947)

After a fun celebration at his apartment on Thursday night, December 11, 1947, Bill scribbled a note to his fiancée. "Sweet Mary, my room is a mess right now. Tonight, I had a bunch of friends in for coffee and a little farewell get-together. There were eight of us in all—the room was full. Now it's after midnight. Chairs are scattered here and there, dirty dishes are piled high, and everything is topsy-turvy. We had a good time—they are a nice bunch of fellows."

Bill confessed that since the last exam, he had done little other than "writing letters and getting some odds and ends finished up." He had also taught his last English classes. At the end of their last session, the sisters invited him to have a glass of "glugg," a "Christmas drink of wine, liquor, raisins and almonds—quite strong and served hot."

To freshen up his French, Bill also bought a small French grammar book. He would need to be able to speak French in Antwerp to arrange his passage and keep track of his luggage. "It is a job getting everything packed. I'll be glad when I can get the bulk of my stuff through customs and checked onto a train to Antwerp. That will be a load off my mind."

In his last three lines, Bill looked to the future. "It is high time I went to bed, so I'll blow you a kiss and dream a little about the happy days ahead. Your Bill."

Bill's last night in Uppsala was on December 13. He wrote Mary a three-page letter to bring her up to date. "I sweated and struggled today getting my books and trunk through customs and down to the station. It was a mess—almost a two-hour job. It is going to cost me about $15 to ship them to Antwerp, but I am glad to be rid of them."

Fortunately, the $50 from Uncle William came in just in time to more than offset that expense.

That afternoon, Bill fit in a visit to the widow of Archbishop Soderblom, a Nobel Peace Prize recipient, whom Bill described as "probably the outstanding leader of the Swedish church in the past couple centuries." He had died in 1931. Mrs. Soderblom was "75 or so now and just as lively and sharp-minded as a young woman. It was an honor to pay her a visit."

Indeed, Bill knew he could learn much from the wives of both parish ministers and archbishops. They could teach him more practical knowledge than most of the professors at Stockholm and Uppsala. Theology was important, but learning how to build a congregation, deal with diverse members, and handle disputes which might arise with tact and humility, was equally essential. He soaked up advice from anyone with that experience, especially pastors' longtime spouses. He hoped that Mary would be an important partner in his future ministry, just as Mrs. Soderblom had been for her husband at every level of his career.

That same day was Saint Lucia Day in Sweden. Early that morning, two girls from Bill's apartment marched into his room wearing white dresses with scarlet sashes. One, designated as the Lucia, had a crown of burning candles. Bill explained the custom to Mary,

> According to a Swedish legend, there was a daughter to a cruel king who sneaked out early one morning with a basket of food for the starving people in the countryside. Her basket never became empty and wherever she went, the people saw a halo around her head—that's the reason for burning candles. Now on the 13th of December, the prettiest blonde child is Lucia and serves coffee in bed. Of course, it has become commercialized now, so that every town has a contest to select Lucia.

That night Bill attended a Lucia fest. He was surprised to find out that he "had a place of honor just next to Lucia herself. She was nice— quite young and 'new studentish.'" Part of the fest was a dance. "I hadn't been at a modern dance in ages, so I thoroughly enjoyed it. Maybe it won't be too long until we can try it together. The South rather frowns on ministers dancing, but I guess we can go to Newberry or somewhere.... Now it is after 1 a.m. and time for me to lay me down to sleep. Love always, Bill."

Two days later, Bill wrote Mary from Stockholm. "Honeychile, I've kissed Uppsala goodbye—sad in one way, but no regrets from another. I have some nice memories and I made some good friends, but there is always something new waiting around the corner."

Once in Stockholm, Bill reunited with his friend Hal, who was down in the dumps. Hal's most recent girlfriend had just informed him that she was engaged to someone else. Bill was reminded of the letter he had received from Spin when she found her navy lieutenant in Norfolk during the war; he could commiserate with his former roommate. Thankfully, for almost a year, he had not gotten a similar "Dear John" letter from Mary.

On Monday, Bill quickly got his visa and permits for his trip to Belgium. "I was happily surprised at how easily it all went." However, his Hungarian friend Gyorgy had no luck. He had to have an official sealed letter from an American college to get his visa for the States. Without one, he had no option but to go back to Uppsala. Bill told Mary, "I guess the next time I see him will be when he comes to visit us—that will be the day when we are 'one' instead of 'two.'"

Bill also found time that day to visit Ulla Larsson, the archbishop's secretary who had invited him to her wedding back in October. She and her husband lived in a new apartment on the outskirts of town and invited Bill and Hal out for the midday meal. Bill enjoyed the visit, but as he wrote to Mary, "One thing that is hard about visiting newly married couples—you can't help but be envious of them."

Bill signed off on his letter that night after talking to Hal until 12:30 a.m. "God bless you, my love. My old heart will be beating out the minutes until I get to South Carolina once more. Yours, Bill."

Bill stayed one more day and night in Stockholm for the final graduation exercises. The graduation took place at a hall at the historical museum downtown.

It turned out to be quite pleasant. Mr. Larssen opened with a few words of welcome and then the new American

253

ambassador spoke for a few minutes. The rest of the program was in Swedish—Inspector Herlitz and short speeches by six of us students. Needless to say, most of the latter were not polished jobs (with one exception—one fellow had become a real Swede). But it was good to be together, and I think most of those present were amazed at how much Swedish we knew.

Later that evening, Bill and his friends "went out of town a little way to an inn for coffee and Christmas carols." But Bill had to leave that gathering early to catch his train out of town. He did not have a chance to write Mary that night but made up for it with a four-page letter just before arriving in Lund, including a description of his ride through the night.

The train was almost empty as I shared a compartment with a young girl with long blonde hair. She had just said goodbye to her fiancé and would be separated for a year while she studied art in Paris, so she was woebegone. This old man served as "father confessor." I think she felt better to have someone sympathize—at any rate it didn't disturb her sleep. I did alright myself since I could stretch out full length on the seat. And so to Lund!

Bill spent two days in Lund. On the first day, Bill walked around town, wandering through the familiar, narrow cobblestone streets and regretting that he did not have a chance to spend more time there. In his letter to Mary that night, he mentioned that "it seems queer to hear the local dialect again—as if people were talking with a mouthful of mush."

The next morning, at the post office, Bill found a batch of mail Georgy had forwarded, including a long-awaited letter from the North Carolina Synod. He excitedly wrote Mary, "They would be glad to have me in their synod and asked me to write when I get home. Indefinite but encouraging!"

That evening, Bill visited the docent who had been the chairman of the local committee for the LWF conference.

He is a prince of a fellow—as well as young and good-looking. He just got married last summer after the assembly, so I hadn't met his wife. She is a cute little thing—girlish, dark, and with dimples. They seem more like some married people than most of the newlyweds—an unusually pleasant pair. Without a doubt, they will come to the US sooner or later—perhaps next LWF—so maybe they can visit with us.

On Bill's last night in Sweden, he finished his letter to Mary with five lines. "It's time to quit this scratching and go to bed. I seem to be finally run down anyway. God bless you, Mary. My prayers are always for your happiness. I love you, Bill."

Chapter 49

Letters from Denmark and Belgium
(December 18–20, 1947)

Bill was in Copenhagen, Denmark, on December 18 for his next letter to Mary.

"Hi, little apple-dumpling. Now I've got my feet on Danish soil—or rather I've got my tired body stretched out on a Danish bed. I've really done nothing to be tired about but going through Swedish and Danish customs and lugging a couple heavy bags is a bit wearing."

There is no information on how Bill got from Lund to Copenhagen, but maybe he was too tired to elaborate. Presumably it involved a ferry across the Oresund strait between Sweden and Denmark. That night, he closed his letter to Mary, "So now to sleep. I find I love you just as much in Denmark as I did in Sweden—silly isn't it? Your Bill."

Bill was still in Copenhagen on Saturday night, December 20. He began his next letter to Mary with a confession. "Sweetheart, I forgot to fill my pen today so you, so you will have to put up with a pencil tonight. I always forget something or the other—last night I discovered that I had left my pajamas behind in Lund. I suppose I will sleep in my underwear until I get home since I didn't put an extra pair in."

Bill had "almost walked his feet off" wandering all around Copenhagen for two days. "Copenhagen is a beautiful city—especially the legions of interesting towers make it an unusual place. Then there are so many narrow little streets and old, old houses that look like they go back to the old 'guild' days. Everywhere you turn you run into water—canals, ponds, harbor, or something." The days were overcast, but one evening, the clouds broke, and "the towers were silhouetted against a pinkish sky."

As usual, Bill visited Copenhagen's Vor Frue Kirke cathedral, with its statues of Christ above the altar and the twelve apostles along the sides. However, "on the whole, and in a word," Bill thought the cathedral, with its Roman-like columned portico below several square block clock/bell towers, was "ugly." But he liked it more than a nearby modernistic church which was "the most hideous thing you can imagine."

When critiquing architecture and religious practices he felt were inappropriate, ineffective, or boring, Bill could be blunt, at least in private.

Because it was the last Saturday before Christmas, the downtown streets and stores in Copenhagen were full of people and decorations. Bill found the "Royal Copenhagen" china shop and bought several pieces—"one for Betty's wedding present if you don't take a fancy to it." That night in his penciled letter, Bill told Mary that if he had a way to ship them, he might have bought some more pieces. He closed, "Tomorrow morning, I'm off for Belgium."

Two days later, from the train station in Aachen on the border of Belgium and Germany, Bill completed the four-page letter he had started in Copenhagen. As it turned out, Bill had seen a familiar face at the Copenhagen train station. Pastor David Ostergren was the first LWF representative to the United Kingdom. He and his wife were on their way to England for a few weeks "to survey the Baltic refugee situation to see what the possibilities are for the Norwegian Lutheran Church to sponsor some Lutheran congregations" in the United Kingdom. So, Bill had pleasant company for much of the train trip and made yet another important contact.

In his letter to Mary, Bill described in detail the Denmark countryside, as seen from the passing train.

> It was really beautiful. The sun was shining, and the farms were either freshly plowed or touched with the new green of winter wheat. Every one of the Scandinavian countries has its own personality, all right. Denmark is flat and has hardly any woodland. There are old stone or white-washed farmhouses. Most of them are thatch-roofed, usually covered with bright green moss that really makes them picturesque. The churches I saw were all the same type. Generally, they were white with

bright red roofs. You notice that the towers are square with the roof quite unusual.

Bill drew a picture of the typical Danish church so that Mary did not have to imagine what they looked like merely from his written description.

Bill had no permit to step foot in Germany, but the locomotive to Belgium chugged right through post-war Germany. The view markedly contrasted with the Denmark countryside.

It isn't too pleasant scenery going through Germany these days. Not very much has been done in the way of repair. Individuals have fixed up one or two rooms in the best part of their bombed houses and are living there. The big buildings are still giant skeletons. We have been sitting here in the station at Aachen for an hour—or rather what is left of it. They fought from house to house here, so there is hardly a building undamaged.

As departure from Aachen to Brussels was announced, Bill quickly finished his letter and promised to get it in the mail as soon as he arrived. "God bless you always. I love you heaps and heaps. Bill."

Chapter 50

Letters from Marche, Belgium
(December 21–29, 1947)

The next night, Bill wrote Mary that he was "back in the bosom of the Bourguignon family" in Marche, Belgium, "a very pleasant place to be I assure you. They are certainly a swell bunch, full of life and all quite different personalities."

The Bourguignons and Bill had stayed in touch regularly after he was injured in the war, during his redeployment during the occupation, and after he returned to America in 1946. So, they welcomed him back into their home in December 1947.

Colette Bourguignon met him at the Brussels station. Bill told Mary that it was lucky Colette recognized him "because I doubt I would have remembered her. Three years make a lot of difference in the teens." They had about an hour to kill before another train ride to Marche, but, once there, the whole family was "waiting with open arms." Bill wrote,

> Little Therese threw her arms around me and gave me a couple of big kisses. She had sprung up and is now a cute little rascal of 12. "Mama" Bourguignon is exactly the same, but Monsieur's hair has turned a snow white from a dark gray. He is a very distinguished looking man. Jacque is the same, but Francine, who came home from school this morning, has become quite a young lady now. I would never have recognized her.

After "supe," they all caught up in French over coffee and a glass of cognac. "My French took a beating, of course. I find that I can understand fairly well when they speak slowly, but whenever I try to say anything, I can only think of Swedish words. It's disgusting! Fortunately, they are the easy-going kind of people who understand."

Luckily, the Bourguignon house had not suffered much serious damage in the war. The bombed-out windows had been replaced, and most of the structure was unharmed. As was his custom, Bill described the home to Mary in detail.

> You would love this house—if you didn't have to take care of it. It is 300 years old; has big, high-ceiling rooms; and is impossible to heat in these coal-scarce days. But it has charm— just like the Bourguignons. Most of the furnishings are well used—some common, over-stuffed chairs, some heavy oak antiques. In the big salon, there are a couple of Louis XIV and XVI secretaries and cupboards. And scattered around are odd and ends of china, brass, copper, wood, etc. that I'd love to have. Monsieur Max's office was the original kitchen, I think. At any rate, it has a huge fireplace with a mantel high enough to walk right under and all the old 'hanging irons' for cooking. The whole place seems to suit them—a mixture of aristocracy and easy-going friendliness.

Bill was excited to have several letters from Mary waiting for him at the Bourguignons. But he suddenly realized that he might not receive any more letters from her before he headed back to America. "I have no idea how you can write any more since I don't know where I'll be after Christmas or when I will be heading back for the States. Maybe you can stand the vacation. It won't be as pleasant for me though! There is nothing for me to do about it but cry myself to sleep every night, I suppose. Blow me a kiss to comfort me." At least he had a nice bed to cry in. "I have found a soft, comfortable bed to sleep in. It is a relief after that poor excuse I had in Uppsala."

Christmas Eve came and went without Bill writing again, but he wasted no time in doing so on Christmas morning. "I meant to write last night but Monsieur Max's brother's family came in and I didn't get to it. Then there was midnight mass and coffee afterwards—so it was 2:30 a.m. when I got to bed. I thought about you, you can be sure."

The day before, Bill and Therese had gone out of town a little way and cut a Christmas tree to bring back to the Bourguignon home, and then decorated it together. "It's a beauty—and of course you can hardly work with a Christmas tree without getting a bit excited with the Christmas spirit. The big salon was heated up for the occasion, so that added to the festivities."

The highlight of the evening, however, was the midnight mass.

> The church was packed to the walls. It was quite a beautiful service with three priests in the chancel with beautifully colored and embroidered vestments and a group of 20 altar boys in robes marching in and out with candles and things. In the middle of the service the lights were turned out and they had a candle procession through the church, carrying an image of the Christ child and put it in the manger which was in one of the transepts.

Bill contrasted it with the Christmas he had spent at the Bourguignon home during the war two years earlier. "All in all, it has been quite different from the other Christmas here when we celebrated down in the cellar. I dare say I won't forget either one of the days." He closed his lengthy letter with a few more thoughts. "Now it's a rainy Christmas Day. I can't help but be homesick for you. It's wonderful, though, to think that it will be the last Christmas we will be separated. I pray that God will bless us with many together. Love Bill."

Bill only wrote a six-line letter to Mary on Friday, December 26. "Hi Butch! I hope you had a happy Christmas at home. I certainly missed you and thought about you the whole day. In Marche, it was a good day to stay in the house and enjoy a family Christmas."

He made up for it with a letter almost four pages long on Sunday morning, December 28. He shared that he and the Bourguignons had exchanged gifts under the tree on Christmas. Bill had "brought along little souvenirs of Sweden for each of them," and they gave him "a couple little things as well." Bill lamented that Mary's package had not arrived, sarcastically suggesting that perhaps it will come back to the States in time for his birthday (August 11). Mary was also in the "doghouse" for another reason. In one of her letters sent several days before Christmas, Mary had thanked him for the gift sent through his sister

Clare. That did not sit well with Bill. "The idea that you would think of opening that package from Clare before Christmas; that's heresy in our family." He joked that she might need a spanking for prematurely unwrapping a Christmas gift.

On the Friday after Christmas, Colette took Bill back to Brussels for the day, meeting some friends from France. The French students gaped at the well-stocked stores. A year and a half after VE Day, retail supplies were still scarce in France. Belgium was in much better shape. "It was like another world for them to come to Belgium from France." The group enjoyed a midday meal at a fancy restaurant with a table set with "beautiful glass, china and silver." That evening, they had clams, French fried potatoes, and white wine at another restaurant, before going to see a play. But the show was so bad that they left at intermission and went across the street to see a movie—"*Father Vincent*, an excellent French film."

On Saturday evening, Bill went over to Janine Bourguignon's place, an apartment with "three big, old-fashioned, cheap rooms on the fifth floor of a house." They had "an uproarious time." Bill told Mary, "Perhaps they felt they could let themselves go when they were free from the pressure of parents and in a little more lively atmosphere." In that regard, Bill again offered a comparison. "There is a tremendous difference between the temperament of the Belgians and the Swedes. There is certainly nothing formal and cold about this bunch. They are full of life and spirit. Swedes would never be able to let themselves go like these kids do. It is an interesting contrast." However, Bill frowned on some of the Belgian habits. "One thing I don't care about is the way they always seem to have a cigarette or a glass in their hands. Every time you turn around someone is offering you something to smoke, something to drink, or something to eat. No dinner is complete without a couple wines or liqueurs."

As he closed his long letter, Bill turned his attention back to Mary.

All in all, in spite of my terrible French, it has been an interesting and happy couple of days. I'll be taking the next year to tell you all that has happened since we said "so long" way back in Greenville. It will be a wonderful feeling when I actually set my foot on a ship headed for the U.S. Every day makes me more impatient to give you a big bear hug. It's because I love you with all my heart! Your Bill.

On the Sunday after Christmas, Bill apologized for falling behind on his own letter writing, telling Mary, "I miss your letters so much that I ought to realize the need of writing."

Most of his letter that day dealt with the fact that the Bourguignons and all their friends were "very devout and loyal Catholics." For that reason, Bill generally did not discuss religion with them. But at Sunday breakfast, the family asked Bill quite a few questions about his Protestant beliefs. "I think I gave them a few things to think about. They are an unusually intelligent group and are serious about their faith. I don't think they are narrow-minded, but being from countries dominated by Catholics, they have a one-sided view."

That morning, Bill had separately attended service at a Church of Scotland church around the corner. It was the first English service he had been to since leaving the States. "So, I appreciated it. The pastor was not inspiring, but rather comforting and dignified." Bill was always evaluating and learning the pastoral traits he admired the most.

On December 29, finally under sunny skies, Bill took a trip to the city of Brugge, one of the most picturesque towns he had ever seen, with its canals, medieval buildings, and cobbled streets. "It is as near what it was in the Middle Ages as you can imagine. Even the new buildings have kept to the same style of architecture. I took a bunch of snapshots to show you. It would take too long to describe it on paper. That's a topic for one of those evenings we have together—happy day." After that thought, Bill told Mary, "This morning, I say farewell to the gang and go to Antwerp to try my luck. Wish me well! All my love, Bill."

Chapter 51

Letters from Antwerp and Marche
(December 31, 1947–January 14, 1948)

Bill made it to Antwerp on New Year's Eve and "spent three or four hours tracking down the two pieces of baggage sent by train and getting them out of the customs." Near the huge wharf, he found a seaman's mission and reading room, where he could stow his bags and sleep in a bunk bed until finding a ship on which to sail home.

The next day, January 1, 1948, he wrote his first letter of the new year to Mary. Despite being ready to jump aboard the first ship available, he had no good news. "Things don't look too promising for a quick trip home. I had hopefully imagined that it would only take a day or two to get a boat, but the man at the consulate said, 'a week or ten days,' if I am lucky."

So, with the pitter patter of rain on the roof, Bill slept in, dozing off in the reading room until noon. "There is really nothing to do, so I might as well be lazy," he wrote. Lazy or not, he was not thrilled at his predicament. "I can't say that I'm a patient waiter—not when it means sitting around twiddling my thumbs when I could be getting closer to you with every turn of a propeller. But there is nothing else to do right now."

Antwerp, as Bill described it to Mary, was "a big, busy town" with wide streets, plentiful traffic, and a significant diamond trading business. Practically every other door seemed to be a café or brasserie, but most of the buildings were "old style...and rather dilapidated." The local Belgians seemed to bustle through the days with a purpose, in contrast the Swedes, who were too afraid of an economic crisis to live with much optimism. "But the time will hang heavy on my hands until I'm on a boat heading across the Atlantic," he wrote. "Keep your fingers crossed for me until I walk up a gang plank. God bless you, sweet Mary. I love you. Your Bill."

Compared to Bill, Mary had not been lazy over the holidays. She had been investigating whether Bill could be "called" to establish the mission church in Greenville. And she had received a message from Dr. Karl W. Kinard of the South Carolina synod office expressing exactly that possibility. Mary quickly passed that message on in a letter, mailed to the Bourguignon address.

But Bill had already left for Antwerp when that letter arrived.

Perhaps God intervened, making Bill so bored in Antwerp that he decided to go back to Marche for a few more days. There, he read that message, his heart beating rapidly with excitement. He responded immediately on January 2.

> It is a good thing I came back to Marche. Your letter with the message from Dr. Kinard was waiting here. It sounds good to me! I will write him tonight and tell him that I am interested. Perhaps I can go to Columbia to see him before I go on to Mississippi. I don't know of any work that would be more of a challenge or one that I would rather be doing than that in Greenville. It would be wonderful with you there to top it off. There are a lot of things I would have to know about the situation before making up my mind. It is good to know that there is a possibility, at any rate.

Bill surmised that Mary was "probably having fits because there was no address to write to" after the first of the year. He suggested that until he got back to Greenville, she should write to Betty in New York, so he could read the letters on the train from New York to South Carolina.

"It won't be long now!! Bill."

By Saturday night, January 3, Bill was back in Antwerp at the seaman's mission. "My sweetheart," he wrote, "all alone on another Saturday night—tain't good! I've been sort of chomping at the bit the last couple days, but it doesn't do much good. I certainly hope something breaks the early part of next week."

Two days earlier, on his first visit to Antwerp, he had gone to a gathering at the mission to celebrate the new year, but he felt a bit out of place. The people seemed nice enough, but it was "just my luck to draw a table where a couple of girl sailors were sitting. Unfortunately, they had had a few too many before they came, so their company left something to be desired." Not wanting to repeat that experience, on the January 3, he stayed at the mission, feeling sorry for himself. He wrote Mary, "The days are particularly empty though when there is no hope of any letter from you. It will be a wonderful time when such things as letters are no longer necessary."

On Sunday, January 4, Bill filled his day with a visit to the Norwegian church for services in the morning and a trip to Antwerp's local opera to see Verdi's *La traviata* in the afternoon. "Europe has us beat ragged when it comes to art, music, and such cultural things." After describing these activities to Mary, he told her, "So, I can look back on a day that brings me one more day closer to the gal I love, Bill."

January 5 brought more bad news. Bill wrote,

> Mary my sweet, they have gotten me into a squeeze play here in Antwerp. This morning, I went to the legation to see if anything had developed over the weekend. It had! All bad! It seems that two American ships were sold to a Belgium company. They were delivered on Saturday and both crews are running loose now in Antwerp, waiting for jobs. They are paid plane passage back but most of them have decided to take the passage money and try to get ships from here. Being union sailors, they go to the top of the list. So, my chances of getting a job are practically nil.

Worse yet, when he went to the American Express office to see if passage was still available on the *Marine Juniper*, Bill discovered that the trooper ship's January sailing schedule had been canceled. Fortunately, he had not shelled out $135 for a ticket on that ship back in Stockholm.

There were only two possibilities left—"a cargo ship carrying a few passengers at $215 per head, sailing on the 13th, and a faint possibility of getting a little cheaper passenger ship from Rotterdam on the 20th." Bill ended up buying a ticket on the *Shooting Star*, the cargo ship sailing out of Antwerp for New York on January 13. "It's more money than I wanted to pay, but I'm glad to have something settled. The trip will take about nine days, so I figure I'll be pulling into Greenville about the 23rd or 24th—get the band out. I get thrilled just thinking about it. The long waiting will soon be over—God willing."

With a week to wait for the boat's departure, Bill called the Bourguignons and arranged to stay with them another five or six days. Bill told Mary, "It will be good to be a family member again—they don't put on any airs or do anything special, so I don't feel like I am imposing."

In all his excitement, Bill forgot to tell Mary that he loved her at the bottom of that letter!

Bill wrote Mary again on Friday night, January 9. "My sweet Mary, time is passing right along now. A couple more days and the *Shooting Star* will be puffing across the Atlantic and the miles between us will be growing fewer and fewer."

The days were quiet at the Bourguignon home that week. Bill helped around the house. He stacked wood on the porch, took the Christmas tree down, and did a few other chores to make himself useful. In the afternoons, he went for walks around the town with Therese, "wandering around the countryside after three years and recalling places and events of a less pleasant day." Bill's description of "less pleasant days" was an understatement. He walked by buildings he had seen shelled by artillery. They had been partially repaired, but the rebuilt sections were obvious. Although he had been about a thousand yards from the front lines during the Battle of the Bulge, he had seen the horrors of war up close. Now, he was seeing Marche in a new light of peacetime. No wounded warriors, no collapsing buildings, no sirens warning of incoming artillery, no bombers overhead. Yes, it was much more pleasant now. But the town and its citizens could never be completely restored.

On the morning of January 9, Bill accompanied Monsieur Max, Colette, and Francine to the town of LaRoche, about twenty miles away from Marche. LaRoche was almost completely destroyed in the war "when von Rundstedt came through the 'bulge.'" There, Bill saw the devastating effects of the destruction. He also saw wooden barracks built for the people to live in temporarily and the rebuilding process across the city. "The houses were going up in the same spots on the old foundations. A lot are about ten feet wide and three stories high, with all kinds of ridiculous angles. You can't help but notice how substantially they build though—solid stone and brick."

This time, Bill did not forget to express his love as he closed his next-to-last letter to Mary. "It's bedtime and I can blissfully pass another ten hours that will bring me just that much nearer the happy day that's waiting. I love you, my sweetheart. Your Bill."

Bill's last letter to Mary from Antwerp was written over January 12–13 and mailed the next morning. It was damaged in transit, or became frayed over the years, such that the last few lines on each page are partially disintegrated. But most of the letter is readable. "Sweet Mary, I'm back at the old stand, raring to get on that boat and push off for the States. The shorter the time gets, the more anxious I am to be on my way. Bad weather may hold us up until Wednesday I discovered when I finished up the papers for my ticket this afternoon. I'll know in the morning, so I'll not mail this until I know definitely."

While Bill was at the shipping office, he glanced at the *Shooting Star* passenger list. "There were eleven names, and I was the only American. It looked as if the majority were Belgian farmers in their forties and fifties. There were a couple younger passengers though— two Belgian nurses and an engineer, marked 'stateless.'" Though the next line is damaged, it looks like Bill told Mary that, with so few passengers, he imagined they would all be "tired of each other at the end of the trip."

After telling Mary how wonderful the Bourguignons were, "just accepting him as one of the family," Bill revealed that when packing that morning, he found Colette had snuck in "a little lace collar for me to give you," and Jacques had stuck a can of pipe tobacco in Bill's pocket so that he would not be short on the boat trip. Bill hoped that someday the Bourguignons would be able to come to America so that, for their kindness, "I can repay them, with your help."

As he finished that day's message, Bill wrote, "So long until tomorrow!"

Alas, the next morning, he added, "When I woke up this morning and heard the rain beating on the room, I was afraid it was bad news. It was! They couldn't finish loading the ship, so the sailing was postponed until tomorrow. Naturally, that didn't make me happy, but there is nothing I can do about it. I will send you a telegram when I get to New York to let you know when I will get to Greenville. I love you, Bill."

Since the skies were already dropping freezing rain in Antwerp, Bill wondered how bad the trip across the icy North Atlantic would be. Sleet, snow, and icebergs would be inevitable, along with nausea and sea sickness. But he had suffered rough voyages before, and he had been away from the love of his life far too long already. It was the only way home. He had no choice but to risk it.

Bill put his final letter in the mail on the morning of Wednesday, January 14, 1948, and then boarded the heavily laden cargo ship that afternoon, beaming with optimism about reuniting with his sweet, brown-haired apple dumpling, and anxious about his uncertain future as a minister. It was the last letter Mary received from her long-separated fiancé.

The *Shooting Star* never arrived in New York.

Epilogue

There are no letters to tell us about Bill's voyage on the *Shooting Star* across the frigid North Atlantic Ocean. Bill knew that no letters he could write on the ship would be mailed until he reached New York, and thus, none would reach Mary before he did.

We can only imagine the treacherous crossing of the Atlantic in the middle of January on a cargo ship not designed for passengers. Weather reports were not favorable, and it must have been a rough trip, especially given Bill's tendency to get seasick. But he would not have cared, because every stormy day at sea was one day closer to his sweet Mary. Mary probably received his final letter from Antwerp about halfway through his voyage and then fretted about his safety and his arrival for another week.

As it turned out, the *Shooting Star* survived the icy voyage and landed in Baltimore instead of New York. Surely you did not think God would let this love story end in tragedy!

So, Bill's train ride to Greenville was shorter than expected. Of course, that meant he bypassed a New York visit with Betty and Ted and missed any letters Mary may have sent to them in anticipation of Bill's arrival. When he finally arrived at the Greenville train station, we can only assume she greeted him with open arms and a huge hug and kiss.

There probably was not a band.

Most of Bill and Mary's dreams came true. Bill got the job of a "plain old pastor," developing St. Michael's, the mission church in Greenville, which he started on February 11, 1948, only a few weeks after he returned to America. After living separately until they married, Bill and Mary eventually moved into a duplex apartment owned by a married couple who had offered their basement as the site for the congregation's first services.

Mary and Bill were married in a double wedding ceremony with

Betty and Ted on May 22, 1948, at Grace Lutheran Church in downtown Hendersonville, North Carolina, only a few miles from Dogwood Dell. They honeymooned in Gatlinburg, Tennessee, after a wedding night at the Pisgah Inn on the Blue Ridge Parkway near Asheville. Betty and Ted went by train to the Catskills for their honeymoon, heading in a completely different direction.

Despite Bill's initial concerns about having a working wife, Mary kept her public health job after the honeymoon until shortly before their first child, Brent, was born in Greenville, exactly nine months and one day after their wedding. So much for not being in a hurry to have children like the Norwegians!

After getting St. Michael's church established and overseeing the building of its first sanctuary on Augusta Road in Greenville, Bill and Mary moved to North Augusta, South Carolina, for Bill to develop another budding mission, Holy Trinity Lutheran Church. There, Mary gave birth to three more boys, Michael in 1951; Eric in 1954; and me, David, in 1956. Four boys. Remember Bill's ideal family consisted of two boys and two girls!

But they were not finished yet. The birth of Bill and Mary Schaeffer's only daughter, named Ethelyn, came in 1960, two years after Bill left Holy Trinity to spread his international wings, becoming the Lutheran World Federation's senior representative in London, England. There, Bill helped develop and support Lutheran churches in the United Kingdom and ran the refugee assistance program first established by Pastor David Ostergren, with whom Bill had ridden on a train from Copenhagen on his way to Antwerp. In that position, on several occasions he helped preside over ecumenical services with the archbishop of Canterbury and other prominent British ministers.

Bill's contacts developed in his year in Sweden were instrumental in him getting that mostly administrative job with the LWF. His letter generally expressing interest in spending some time with the Lutheran World Federation, possibly in Sweden, landed on the desk of Carl Lundquist, for whom Bill had worked at the Lund and Oslo conferences in 1947, on the day that the position in London became available. Dr. Lundquist put Bill's "name in the hat," Bill traveled to New York for interviews, and a summer cablegram confirmed he got the job.

Ironically, Bill's predecessor in that London position, Pastor Vernon Frazier, left it to take over the senior pastor position at St. Matthews Lutheran Church in Charleston, South Carolina, where Bill had been a member as a child and his father had been pastor in the 1920s.

During spring and summer vacations during the family's seven-year stay in London, Bill and Mary took the five children all over Europe. The first trip included a visit to the Bourguignon family in Marche, Belgium. That trip also put an end to the notion of the family spending nights in hotels in Europe. It was just too expensive for a larger family. When funds ran out, the family slept in their small British Ford sedan. Subsequent trips involved camping almost every night in six-person, floorless Boy Scout tent. Many times, the tent was pitched on the side of the road or on nearby farms, including the infamous night in Greece when the family woke up and realized that the tent was pitched on a cow dung heap. Mary had a marginally more comfortable cot to sleep on than the rest of the family. According to all who knew her, Mary was a saint to travel under such conditions. Bill loved the rough camping accommodations, and Mary tolerated his adventurous spirit.

Two of those trips, including one with most of Clare and Johnny's family, were to Scandinavia. So, the whole family was able to see Stockholm, Oslo, Norway, and Lapland, with Bill as their guide. I still vividly remember suffering through a stormy passage across the North Sea from Bergen, Norway, back to England. And Mary finally got her colorful, finely knitted Norwegian sweater, which remained one of her favorites for decades. As predicted by Clare in 1947, Clare and Johnny's second child, Trudy, spent two years in London as Bill and Mary's au pair, taking care of the younger Schaeffer children, including me, a few years before that return trip to Scandinavia.

Betty and Ted had two children, Margaret Louise ("Peggy Lou") and Fred. Betty was killed in a car accident when her children were young. Ted remarried and settled in Albuquerque, New Mexico, where he taught Far Eastern Studies at the University of New Mexico for many years. Fred named his daughter, Lora, Bill's mother's first name. Without realizing the duplication, my wife Kim and I also named our daughter Lora in honor of Bill's mother, who died the year before I was born.

Marion ("Buck") and Sue were happily married for more than sixty years and had three children, Susan, Debbie, and Bill. Living in Tallahassee, Florida, they spent many summers at Dogwood Dell in yet another house built on the property. Susan and Debbie never knew their father's nickname was "Buck" until after Bill's letters from Sweden were discovered.

Newberry College continued to be an important hub for the extended family. Bill and Mary's oldest son, Brent, went to Newberry, and like his dad, became editor-in-chief of the *Newberry Indian*. He competed in tennis, sang in the Newberry Singers, and was valedictorian of his class. Marion and Sue's second daughter, Debbie, and Johnny and Clare's second son, Billy, went to Newberry at the same time, with Debbie introducing Billy to her roommate, "Hutch." Billy and Hutch are still married and have two children. Johnny and Clare retired in Newberry and hosted many Christmases there.

Dogwood Dell remained Mary and Bill's summer vacation site throughout their marriage. While in Greenville, Bill designed and built a small cabin at Dogwood Dell, which served as the crowded family home for the six months or so in 1965 after Bill and Mary left London and before Bill got his next parish assignment. Thereafter, many weeks in August each year were spent there, with adults and children of all ages enjoying watermelons chilled in the spring above their house. Everyone came running when Bill yelled "Watermelon!" at the top of his lungs, just like his dad a generation before. The cabin at Dogwood Dell also later served as Bill and Mary's retirement home and a gathering place for many Thanksgivings. The house recently has been renovated and expanded for the next generations of Schaeffers.

True to his convictions, Bill turned down two potential "calls" from Southern congregations when they balked at welcoming Africans or Black Americans as part of Bill's ministry. Bill refused to be affiliated with any church that hung on to segregation or discrimination. His churches would welcome believers of all ethnic backgrounds and skin colors, and his sermons reflected inclusiveness for all of God's children. Especially during his tenure in London, Bill made a difference, warmly welcoming families from Africa and India into the church and into his home until accommodations could be established.

Bill accepted a call from Emmanuel Lutheran Church in Bethesda, Maryland, in fall 1965. Over the next thirteen years, Bill preached to many government employees, State Department officials, a senior NASA representative, Senator Paul Simon, and United States Supreme Court Chief Justice William Rehnquist, among many other equally interesting members. He also was lucky enough to receive a complimentary membership for the whole family to the swanky Bethesda Country Club on Bradley Boulevard near the church, though he never played golf. My siblings and I certainly took advantage of the amenities.

While in the Washington, D.C., area, Bill held annual Christmas services for Swedes, at which he preached in Swedish and celebrated Saint Lucia Day, complete with white dresses and a crown of candles (with a fire extinguisher close at hand).

Mary and Chief Justice Rehnquist's wife, Nan, were active volunteers in the auxiliary at the National Lutheran Home in Washington, D.C. After years as a mother and housewife, Mary used her skills in public health education. She became a certified re-motivational specialist for senior citizens, and she trained others to do likewise. She continued to volunteer in her re-motivational activities for seniors well into her mid eighties. But, for most of her adult life, Mary was a mother, homemaker, and the best pastor's wife and partner Bill could ever have asked for in his thirty-five-year ministry.

In 1978, with all his children through high school, Bill felt he had spent enough time at Emmanuel. So, he gave up the nice house and country club membership in Bethesda to start yet another mission church in a former used car dealership showroom along the train tracks in Easley, South Carolina. When his sons questioned the wisdom of this move, Bill said, "I have one more church in me." And after four years, St. Matthias in Easley was well on its feet, in a new sanctuary with enough parishioners to fill two services every Sunday.

St. Michael's in Greenville, Holy Trinity in North Augusta, Emmanuel in Bethesda, and St. Matthias in Easley remain active churches to this day, an incredible legacy for that self-described "lazy" American seminary graduate learning the theological ropes in Sweden, Norway, and Finland.

After an eight-month stint as an interim pastor at a church on St. Thomas in the US Virgin Islands, in 1983, Bill and Mary moved back to his cabin at Dogwood Dell with Mary for their golden years. One of their first adventures was a three-month trip across the country in a rigged-up, blue VW bus, complete with a mini-fridge, a makeshift stove, and mattresses in the back. Bill's rudimentary travel habits and hobo spirit never really left his soul. Luckily, Bill had kept in touch with so many people he had met over the years who were living in the Midwest and West that Mary did not have to sleep in the car every night! But, with many nights in the back of the VW, she consolidated her sainthood reputation for the rest of her life.

After returning from their trip, Bill expanded his Dogwood Dell cabin to include an extra guest room, a workshop/garage, and a large utility room with sinks for processing vegetables from his enormous garden. Bill and Mary enjoyed living in their retirement cabin at Dogwood Dell for eighteen years, despite having only a woodstove for heat and no air conditioning for most of that time.

Bill and Mary were married for fifty-four years. In 1988 they celebrated their fiftieth anniversary at Grace Lutheran Church in Hendersonville, North Carolina, the same church (but different building and location) in which they were married. For that event, their children bought them central heating for the cabin at Dogwood Dell and sang an original song called "It Seems Like Yesterday" for them. Much to Bill's satisfaction, their marriage was much more than "serviceable." Indeed, it was passionate, intimate, and unswervingly unpredictable, adventurous, and fun.

Bill and Mary's kids have now renovated and expanded Bill's original cabin and replaced that central heating and added air-conditioning for future generations. Their eldest son, Brent, has also built his own home on the Dogwood Dell property, overlooking the pond there. So, Dogwood Dell, first established by Bill's father in the 1920s, will always be a special place for current and future Schaeffers. Clare and Johnny also built a cabin at Dogwood Dell, serving as a getaway for their six children; Brenta, Trudy, Henry, Dorothy, Billy, and Bobby.

Bill died in 2002 at age eighty-four from advanced dementia and natural causes, approximately six months after he and Mary moved to the RoseCrest Lutheran Continuing Community Center in Inman, South Carolina. Mary lived in an independent house at RoseCrest for fourteen years before moving into the assisted living wing there in 2015. She died at age ninety-five in April 2020, during the Covid-19 crisis, though it appears that her death was from natural causes, rather than the coronavirus. They are both buried at Oakdale Cemetery across the street from Grace Lutheran Church in Hendersonville, with Mary's ashes buried there fourteen months after her death due to the ongoing pandemic.

Mary's final Thanksgiving and ninety-fifth birthday party, with all five children and several grandchildren and great-grandchildren present, was celebrated at Dogwood Dell.

She loved and deeply missed Bill to the end. After another lengthy separation, this time for eighteen years without any letters, they are now together in heaven forever.

Mary in First Grade, 1930.

Bill's military photo, 1942.

Mary's college photo, 1943.

Bill's civilian photo, 1946.

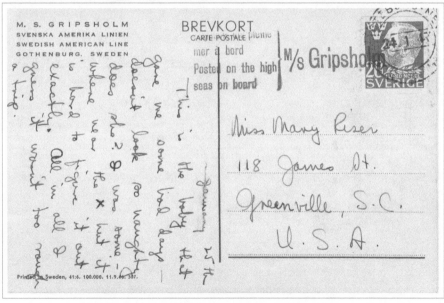

M. S. Gripsholm postcard, 1947.

Stockholms Högskolas Studentkår
Legitimationskort n:r 5131

Fil.stud.

William B. Schaeffer

Om ej avgång från Högskolan dessförinnan sker, är detta kort
giltigt till:

1 NOV 1947

William B. Schaeffer

Egenhändig namnteckning

Skattmästare

Vänd I

F 579

Uppsala Studentkårs Legitimationskort

SÖDERMANLANDS-NERIKES NATION

William René
Schaeffer, B.D.

Om ej utträde ur nationen dessförinnan sker,
gäller detta kort t. o. m.

William B. Schaeffer

Egenhändig namnteckning

Vänd!

Bill's Swedish student ID cards, 1947.

USA-studenter studerar religion och affärsliv

Två amerikanska studenter av de sextio som väntas hit har redan anlänt till Stockholm, från vänster Harold A. Nelson från Anaconda, Montana, och William B. Schaeffer från Jackson, Mississippi.

— Jag vill gärna studera svenska, för Sverige är en faktor att räkna med i amerikanskt affärsliv. Förbindelserna med Skandinavien utökas oupphörligt, därför har jag tänkt att ägna min framtid åt affärer med Sverige.

Dessa synpunkter framhåller en av de amerikanska studenter som kommit hit för att studera svenska språket under ett års tid. Två studenter anlände hit med "Gripsholm" förra veckan. Allt som allt väntas ett 60-tal studenter skriva in sig vid Stockholms högskola den 15 februari, och praktiskt taget alla är redan placerade i svenska familjer.

— Min mor är född i Värnamo, så jag har ju hört åtskilligt om Sverige, fortsätter hr Nelson, speciellt intresserar det mig att titta närmare på svensk kooperation, ekonomiska problem och skattesystemet. Svenskarna verkar mera konservativa än genomsnittsamerikanen.

Maten är rikligare här än hos oss. Flickorna är inte så makeupade, vilket är mera en kritik från vår sida, men i stället är de betydligt naturligare.

Som många andra amerikaner gillar jag mest Ingrid Bergman.

Studenten William Schaeffer från Jackson, Mississippi, är teolog och framhåller att en lutheran har ofantligt mycket att lära här i Sverige. I synnerhet nu sedan Tyskland är ur räkningen vill man helst komma hit för att studera i detta ämne.

— De kyrkliga förbindelserna mellan USA och Sverige har ju betydligt vidgats på senare tid. Hos oss har också intresset för religion stigit, många känner att det är den enda starka grunden i deras liv. Kriget och dess upplevelser har väl också bidragit att stimulera intresset för religion bland ungdomen.

— Vi beräknar att lära oss svenska under en fyra månaders koncentrerad språkkurs på högskolan, och därefter komma in bland de svenska studenterna, antingen här, i Lund eller Uppsala.

— Vi har ett par månaders ferier i sommar, och då tänker jag för min del cykla runt i Sverige för att komma i kontakt med folket, både i stan och på landsbygden. Men i Lappland blir det knappast, ty där är avstånden för stora mellan gårdarna.

Stockholm newspaper article, 1947.

Bergen, Norway
August 11, 1947

This is for from a fancy way in which to make a formal proposal to the girl you love; but since our courtship has been a bit unusual, perhaps this is in keeping. At any rate the young fellow on the opposite side is no more earnest and ardent than I am — and Norway seems to have no suitable card to fit the situation.

You can be certain, Mary, that when the ring goes on your finger, it only seals the love that I have had for you for a long time. May God bless our engagement and marriage to come.

Bill

Bill's "formal" proposal card, 1947.

Bill and Mary's wedding day, May 22, 1948.

Bill and Mary's fiftieth anniversary, May 22, 1998.

Author's Note

As the author of this book, and through these letters and other research, I have learned more about my parents and their love story than I ever did in my first sixty-four years. When I asked my mother about love and marriage, she always told me, "When you meet the right one, you will know it."

What I did not know was that she knew this from her own first-hand experience. Despite essentially still being strangers, my parents were crazy enough to fall in love and get engaged after a short courtship. The letters from Sweden not only vividly depict the sudden love and commitment my parents experienced, but also reveal all the things they did not know about each other when they made that commitment. But their love continued to grow as they learned more about each other even through the long separation.

Well, I know now that my mother was right. "When you meet the right one, you will know it." In what can only be attributed to the impulsive genes from my father, I asked my wife, Kim, to marry me just eight days after our first date and a few months after we met at our church in Atlanta. Incredibly, Kim said, "Yes," hoping I was not an axe-murderer. The parallels between my parents' love affair and my own are eerie. We knew little about each other, beside the fact that we were both Lutheran churchgoers. Like my dad, I had not yet met my wife's parents. And Kim had not met mine. Like my dad, I did not give Kim a ring when we got engaged; I did not have time to buy one. Plus, like my father, I wanted my fiancée to pick out her own ring since she would be wearing it for the rest of her life. Unlike my father, however, I was there to give it to her once the jeweler completed the setting.

Like my parents, Kim and I look back and realize that we were essentially strangers when we committed to spend our whole lives as husband and wife. To this day, we cannot adequately explain how we knew we were meant to be together. But we certainly were not separated for any time at all, let alone for more than a year and across an ocean. A few days into our short courtship, I told my wife that we did not have to see each other every day, so we missed getting together one day. The next day, I told her, "Let's not ever do that again."

Whatever brought us together so quickly, we have now been happily married for almost forty years, and we look forward to many, many more happy years together—perhaps as many as fifty-four years or more to match or exceed the length of my parents' marriage!

Their example of love and commitment will always be a beacon to our family.

Almost as eerie for me in reading these letters are the personality traits I share with my father. Loving peanut butter, watermelon, "pigging out" when starving, going on crazy adventures, and slow dancing are just a few examples. More importantly, like me, my dad was a person who enjoyed meeting and socializing with people of varied backgrounds. As an adventurer, he struggled to climb mountains on his bike and skis and wrote about encountering and conquering a series of false summits. He never shied away from a challenge or adventure. I have struggled to climb high-altitude mountains and have been fooled by many false summits all over the world—not on skis or bikes, but on my own two feet—and I have written two books about those experiences.

As he mentioned in one of his letters, my father also considered himself a "lone wolf," being very content to explore on his own, with no one to tell him what to do or how to act. That sort of independence and quiet solitude away from the busy and complicated world also appeals to me. Standing atop a mountain alone, viewing God's magnificent creation below, can be a very spiritual, personal experience. I always feel closer to God at the apex of those climbs. I believe my dad felt the same way as he struggled to reach the top of many Norwegian mountains and enjoyed God's incredible creation on his bike and skis back in 1947.

Although not a great athlete, my father loved to push the limits of his physical abilities, and through persistent effort, he learned to be good at almost everything he tried. I can certainly relate to that, being good at a lot of things, and great at very few.

My dad never considered himself an academic, or even a diligent student, though he probably was a bit more diligent than he let on. He still did well on tests and exams. However, he did not let his studies interfere with meeting people, having fun, or going on just about every adventure or to every interesting event that presented itself. I managed to do well at Duke University, graduating magna cum laude, despite playing varsity soccer, singing in the Duke Chorale and in a barbershop quartet (another trait of my father's), performing in musical theater productions, working the dining halls, and rarely being seen in any library.

Like my dad, there were always a few cute girls or interesting events to distract me from studying!

My father was creative in multiple ways, always having projects to work on or plans to complete. If he felt he could do the projects himself, he did them without professional help, rolling up his sleeves and constantly saving money and living thriftily. He built a house and did almost all the construction himself. I never did anything at that scale. But I built fences, a pergola, and a woodshed at my house in Atlanta and have helped my brother Mike do a lot of interior wood trimming, painting, and window treatments at the Dogwood Dell cabin my father built—hardly comparable, but we saved a lot of money doing it. Mike shares my father's thrifty construction skills, currently renovating a barn and turning it into an apartment for his son, using recycled wood and other materials. Early on as kids, we learned from our dad that if the job can be done by our own hands, we should do it and enjoy the fruits of our own labors. We also learned thriftiness from our mother, who was a master at stretching her household budget.

As repeatedly mentioned in his letters from Sweden, my father felt that he could never be part of high society, and he never felt completely comfortable socializing with the elite. He was always satisfied with being a regular guy, a common man, with strong ideas of right and wrong. Still, he certainly held his own with the affluent and influential members of his congregation in Bethesda, Maryland, and became a lifelong friend of Chief Justice Rehnquist. Likewise, despite being able to mingle with high society at charitable balls or ritzy events for organizations I served in Atlanta, I always preferred to drink beer with my soccer buddies or hang out with friends at backyard barbeques. I specifically designed my books on climbing as "a regular guy's guide" to various mountains and treks. Regardless of my financial status or professional accomplishments, I will never consider myself part of the "upper crust." Like my dad, I prefer being a regular guy who occasionally does some extraordinary things.

Incidentally, despite the tobacco references in my dad's letters, I do not ever remember my father smoking a pipe or lighting a cigarette. I suspect my mother, the public health advocate, not so subtly disabused him of that unhealthy habit. Neither I nor any of my siblings ever smoked cigarettes. My parents would not have tolerated it.

Finally, my father recognized the blessings of God in his life, including the gift of his wife, who was an equal partner in his ministry. He was always humble about his position as an ordained minister. He shied away from unnecessarily ritualistic symbols in the church in favor of simple and flexible vestments and chancels. He liked traditional church architecture. His sermons were less soaring and more practical, understandable, educational, compassionate, and adapted to address the challenges facing his parishioners on an everyday basis. They were always strictly scripturally based and well-delivered with strong faith and conviction. He cringed at televangelists' materialistic themes. My father walked humbly with his God, and he kept his faith and service simple, straightforward, and honest.

Likewise, my wife is an equal partner in our marriage and a blessing from God. After all, we met at our church and fell in love on a church youth retreat at which we were supposed to be chaperones. Whoops! As for ecclesiastical grandeur, one of my favorite musical pieces is "A Simple Song" from Leonard Bernstein's *Mass*, in which I performed at Duke. In *Mass*, the lead character, a young priest, sheds all the gaudy vestments and glitzy religious symbols to sing a simple song to God, devoid of the trappings of the high church. My one attempt to sing "A Simple Song" as a solo at our church was quite a challenge due to the vocal range it entails, but my heart was in it!

None of my generation followed our father into the ministry. I was his last hope and nearly went in that direction with a double major in economics and religion in college. However, when it came time to make that decision when I was a junior, my faculty adviser, who was also my favorite religion professor at Duke, asked me some questions about my faith that I could not confidently answer at that time. So, I made the difficult decision to go to law school instead of seminary.[8]

Still, it has been one of my greatest spiritual pleasures to serve as a lay assistant and assisting minister at St. Luke Lutheran Church in Atlanta for over thirty years. It was my honor to serve as assisting minister for my father and serve communion with him when he filled in and preached one Sunday at St. Luke. That was a particularly special day I will never forget.

By the way, my mother never had to "just sit and take it" when my father was preaching, as he had worried immediately after their engagement. Rather, she listened as attentively as she could, while keeping five children under control. She frequently commented on his message over Sunday dinners.

Everyone who knew my mother, loved her. Indeed, my dad made the best decision of his life when he traveled to Greenville in January 1947, proposed, and then shared his love for her through his letters from Sweden.

And, quite coincidentally, my wife and I are now members at St. Matthews Lutheran Church in Charleston, South Carolina, the same church in which my grandfather served as pastor and my father attended in the 1920s. When I read his July 13, 1947, letter to my mother from Sweden, the one in which he mentioned, out of the blue, that he "always liked Charleston, particularly St. Matthews Church," I was astonished to realize my father was also a member of that church as a child. The raised "Goblet-styled" pulpit he used to climb and the marble altar and baptistry installed during his father's tenure as pastor are

---

[8] While at law school, I obtained a summer internship with a small law firm in Bethesda, Maryland. Like my father, I spent those intern months at the home of Pauline Bresnahan, who was just as spunky, sassy, and interested in my social life as she was for my father. We called her "Auntie Pauline," and I thoroughly enjoyed verbally jousting with her throughout that summer. My whole family celebrated my parents' thirty-fifth wedding anniversary at her home in 1983, shortly after my wife and I got engaged. Auntie Pauline never told me about the letters my father had sent her when he was in the army, but she must have given them to my mother at some point.

still there, and the carillon in the high steeple still peels out across the city before Sunday morning services.

It is a small world, a world my father and mother made smaller and much better, despite their initial separation of three thousand miles. After that challenge, they were inseparable partners in marriage and in their ministry to others.

And one more thing. While I remember my father calling my mother a "rascal" a few times when she surprised him with a gift or other favor, I never heard him call her "Butch" or "Apple Dumpling" or "Sugar Plum" or "Honeychile." Perhaps those nicknames became less popular in the 1950s before I became cognizant of such things!

Until the day he died, my father called his wife *Mary*, but with a long "a" such that it sounded more like "Mayree." It wasn't a nickname, just a Southern variation of a tradition biblical name from a worldly, but humble Southern gentleman and devoted minister who loved her to the very end.

As he said in his very first letter from New York the day after his proposal, Mary was "a gift from God." Now that they are back together in heaven, she still is, and he is for her too.

Acknowledgments

First and foremost, I want to thank my dad, William B. Schaeffer, for being an incredible letter writer, and for my mother, Mary Riser Schaeffer, for keeping his letters for almost seventy-five years. Their love and devotion to each other throughout their marriage long outlasted these letters, but the letters formed the foundation for the growth of their love that ultimately made my very existence as a fourth child possible.

Second, I thank Ms. Pauline Bresnahan for her lifelong friendship with my father and our family and for keeping all the letters my father sent her and her mother during his military service. That separate batch of letters shed light not only on my father's war experience and injury following the Battle of the Bulge but also on his search for a wife before courting my mother.

Without these letters, there would be no book and no story to tell. I only wish that I had possession of the letters years before when my parents, Auntie Pauline, and others were still alive to answer the many questions left to be resolved when I read the letters.

Third, I want to thank my siblings for allowing me to write this book and have it published despite the possibility that some of my father's adventures may surprise those who knew him only as a highly successful, but mild-mannered mission developer and pastor. Indeed, much of his journey to find a wife surprised us all. Perhaps that is why my mother insisted that they not be read until after she died.

A special thanks to my brother, Brent, for his comments and copyediting during the writing process and his collection of photos of my parents' early days. And to my brother, Mike, who discovered and saved several informal autobiographies of my parents and my grandfather, H. Brent Schaeffer, which were helpful in providing details related to my parents' early histories.

Great appreciation is due to my daughter, Lora, for her

immeasurable insights and compelling advice on the format, themes, research, and writing techniques for this nonfiction historical romance. It was a close call on whether this book would be strictly a biography, or a creative novel merely based on the letters. I used more of her advice than she knows.

I thank Pastor Eric Childers, Pastor Rebecca Wicker, and archivist Melinda Summer of St. Matthews Lutheran Church in Charleston, South Carolina, for their help in researching my grandfather's tenure at that church, which helped confirmed some of my father's first memories of church life as a child and which started his journey into the ministry.

I thank "Doc" Schneider, Marc Jolley, and the wonderful staff of Mercer University Press who have supported my various book writing adventures about mountaineering and now have graciously and ecumenically taken the chance to publish a book about love and religion for a Lutheran minister in the World War II era. The Civil War and Baptist history are key focuses for the Mercer University Press, so I am grateful for this opportunity to marginally expand its literature horizon.

Finally, I could not have written this book without the support and encouragement of my wife, Kim Schaeffer, who grew tired of me constantly yelling downstairs about yet another thing I never knew about my father as I read these letters. She knew I just had to write a book about this love story, and she has endured my many writing sessions, my occasional frustrations, and my ongoing enthusiasm about the entire process!

Index

Index